THE DIGESTED
21ST CENTURY

Also by John Crace

Vertigo: One Football Fan's Fear of Success

Brideshead Abbreviated:
The Digested Read of the Twentieth Century

Baby Alarm: Thoughts from a Neurotic Father

Harry's Games: Inside the Mind of Harry Redknapp

THE DIGESTED 21ST CENTURY

John Crace

CONSTABLE • LONDON

Constable & Robinson Ltd
55–56 Russell Square
London WC1B 4HP
www.constablerobinson.com

First published in the UK by Constable
an imprint of Constable & Robinson, 2014

A copy of the British Library Cataloguing in Publication Data
is available from the British Library

ISBN: 978-1-78033-858-3 (hardback)
ISBN: 978-1-78033-908-5 (ebook)

1 3 5 7 9 10 8 6 4 2

Printed and bound in the EU

For John Sutherland, superprof

Contents

Contents

CONTENTS

Chick Lit

CONTENTS

Contents

CONTENTS

Contents

CONTENTS

CONTENTS

Phenomenon

Introduction

Between the start of the twentieth century and the beginning of the First World War, L Frank Baum wrote *The Wonderful Wizard of Oz*, Colette wrote *Claudine in Paris*, Joseph Conrad wrote *Heart of Darkness*, Baronness Orczy wrote *The Scarlet Pimpernel*, EM Forster wrote *Howards End*, Thomas Mann wrote *Death in Venice* and Marcel Proust wrote *Swann's Way*. All these books have entered the literary canon and are still read today.

The Digested Read started life in early 2000 and has been running continuously in the *Guardian* ever since. Its premise is quite simple: to take the book that has been receiving the most media attention in any given week and rewrite it in about 700 words, retelling the story in the style of the author. However the emphasis is often on those aspects of the book that the author might prefer to have gone unnoticed: the clunky plot devices, fairytale psychology, poor dialogue, stylistic tics, unedited longueurs and the emperor's new clothes.

Is the Digested Read parody, pastiche or satire? The distinctions frequently are blurred. It can be all three, depending on the book in question; but it is always meant to be entertaining, funny and informative. Literary reviewing has become more critically objective since I began writing the Digested Read, thanks mainly to the growth of literary blogs and below-the-line conversations on newspaper websites. But it is still relatively cosy compared to theatre, film and music reviewing.

The literary world is quite small: many reviewers are also authors. That can blur the critical boundaries; sometimes towards a hatchet job as old enemies settle scores, but mostly towards reviews that are rather more anodyne and favourable than they might otherwise have been. Who wants to make too many waves, when it might be your book being reviewed next? Some writers also seem to be given an inexplicably easier ride than others; almost as if the literary world has collectively decided that some authors are beyond adverse criticism.

For many authors, writing is a lifetime's career. And like most careers, it has its ups and downs. An author might well follow one great book with a couple of duds before finding their touch again; not least because when a writer becomes a bestseller, their publisher often finds it trickier to suggest useful edits. Publishing is a business; no one would dream of marketing a book with the catchline: 'Not as good as her last book, but bear with her because she will come good again in a few years time'. Every book by an established author is sold as if the career progression were on a relentless upward curve.

While the Digested Read does have fun – fairly, and yes, sometimes unfairly – at the author's expense, it is also intended as a corrective to the publishing industry itself: the disparity between the hype with which the publisher is promoting the book and the reality to which it can seldom live up. Which brings me back to where I started. This collection of the best – or worst, depending on your point of view – Digested Reads from the last 14 years are all books that publishers believed were important. They are the books that came with the big marketing budgets and promotional tours. They are the ones publishers expected to reach the bestseller lists. In some cases they are the books publishers hoped might still be read in a hundred years' time. So, which of these books will be the *Howards End* or *Swann's Way* of 2114? You tell me.

SERIOUS FICTION

The Laying on of Hands
by Alan Bennett (2001)

Anyone looking around the congregation and its celebrity assortment might have imagined that Clive had been a sociable creature. But the gathering owed more to Clive's discretion than his friendships, and many household names had been mildly irked on entering the church to discover they were not the sole centre of attention.

Clive had died in Peru and, when a young man dies in unknown circumstances of an unknown disease, the question, 'What did he die of?' often assumes a personal dimension for those who remain. Father Geoffrey Joliffe, who was about to take the service, was no exception.

By profession, Clive had been a masseur, but he had interpreted the word generously, and although Geoffrey had little reason for anxiety – his guilt had kept their encounters to minimal bodily contact – his confusion of God with Joan Crawford often was enough to inspire alarm.

As the service neared its conclusion, Father Joliffe had some regrets. Much had been spoken of Clive's charms, but nothing that he felt truly captured the essence of the Clive he had known.

'If anyone has any further reminiscences they would like to share, they are invited to do so now,' he improvised. Various people stood up to extend their thoughts, before Carl stepped forward. 'I would like to tell you what Clive was like in bed,' he began.

'I didn't know he was gay,' chorused several women.

'And when someone that young dies of Aids, it's time for anger as well as grief,' Carl continued. The mention of the word that mustn't be mentioned caused a frisson.

'He didn't die of Aids,' said a young man, named Hopkins. 'I was with him in Peru. He was bitten by an insect.'

'They all say that,' snarled Carl.

'I'm his doctor,' ventured a smartly-dressed man. 'His latest blood test was negative.'

As the congregation peeled away, their hearts were considerably lighter than when they entered. Hopkins approached Geoffrey. 'I have Clive's diary,' he said. Seeing his initials against several dates, Geoffrey laid his hands on Hopkins' knees. 'I'll take care of that,' he whispered as Hopkins bolted for the door.

Some weeks later there was a knock on the vestry door.

'I thought, why not?' said Hopkins.

Digested read, digested: The Little Book of Revelations.

Life of Pi
by Yann Martel (2001)

My name came from a swimming pool. Piscine Molitor Patel. At my first school, the other boys called me Pissing, so when I moved I changed my name to Pi. I've spent a lot of my life looking for God. That's why I'm a Hindu, Muslim and a Christian. I'm not sure why I've never converted to Judaism or Shinto. My father ran the zoo in Pondicherry. He really loved his animals, so when the zoo had to close he decided to bring them with us to Canada.

The Tsimstum sank several days out of harbour. My father, mother and brother all drowned. I had been taking a walk on the deck when the ship went down and was thrown into the lifeboat by a couple of sailors. I came to and found myself sharing a boat with a zebra with a broken leg and a hyena. Shortly afterwards, I made the mistake of helping Richard Parker aboard. Richard Parker was a Bengal tiger.

The hyena started eating the zebra alive. The zebra howled piteously. Richard Parker just looked on. An orang-utan floated by on a huge mound of bananas. The hyena had him as well.

As we all got hungrier I became more anxious. Before long the hyena and Richard Parker were locked in battle. Richard Parker won, and the pair of us began our strange life aboard.

I learned how to provide him with fresh drinking water, and shared the flying fish I caught. I had to work hard to make him accept I was the alpha male. As the weeks turned into months, our food began to run out and we went blind. 'How are you?' said Richard Parker. Fancy Richard Parker being able to speak, I thought. But it wasn't Richard Parker. It was a blind Frenchman in the middle of the Pacific. Richard Parker ate him, too.

Later we made landfall. It was no ordinary landfall, as it was just a floating mass of algae and trees. Richard Parker ate the meerkats. We left when we discovered the island was carnivorous.

After 277 days at sea, we reached Mexico. Richard Parker made a dash for the jungle. I was picked up and looked after by the locals. Two Japanese officials from the shipping company came to find out what happened. I told them, but they didn't believe me.

'Would you prefer if I said my family escaped with me, but died on the way?'

'That's much better,' they said.

Digested read, digested: Johnny Morris goes to sea and returns with the Booker. Or did I dream that last bit?

The Little Friend
by Donna Tartt (2002)

For the rest of her life, Charlotte Cleve would blame herself for her son's death because she had decided to have the Mother's Day dinner at six in the evening instead of noon, after church, which is when the Cleves usually had it.

'Do I have to be in a book with such a clumsy opening sentence?' asked Harriett, Charlotte's petite precocious 10-year-old daughter with the brown bob who bore absolutely no resemblance to the author.

'I'm afraid you do,' replied her mother. 'It's meant to convey the stultifying claustrophobia of a deeply dysfunctional family from Mississippi. Ever since your brother Robin was found hanged 10 years ago, your elder sister Allison and I have been in a catatonic state, and we're surrounded by a variety of misfits and inbreds.'

'Hmm,' said Harriett. 'I'd better try to solve Robin's murder.'

'Good idea,' her friend Hely added. 'I bet it was a Ratcliff. They're a bad lot and some of them have been in prison.'

'You're right. I bet it was Danny. He was about the same age as Robin.'

'There's a cage of poisonous snakes at Eugene Ratcliff's. Let's steal a cobra.'

Harriett and Hely stood on the bridge. As Danny's car passed beneath, they tipped the cobra over the parapet.

'We almost killed Danny's granny,' cried Harriett.

'Never mind,' said Hely. 'We didn't know she was driving the car.'

'I shure doan trust those kids,' yelled Farish Ratcliff, 'an I shure doan trust you. Show me you've still got the drugs, or I'll kill you.'

'The drugs have turned him crazy,' thought Danny, as he shot Farish in the head. Danny drove out to the water tower. 'Just get them drugs and get away,' he told himself. 'Gosh, I miss Robin. I sure do wonder who killed him.'

Harriett pulled open some of the packages. She didn't know what was in them but she knew Danny wouldn't like it.

'You brat, I'm going to kill you,' Danny shouted, moments before he drowned.

'Get rid of all the evidence,' Harriet begged Hely from her hospital bed.

'Poor old Harriett. Fancy having epilepsy,' murmured her mother.

'You know Harriett had Farish shot and drowned Danny for killing Robin,' Hely told his brother.

'You've been drinking too much coke.'

Digested read, digested: Small girl with big ambitions gets hopelessly confused in a laboured adventure. Still, she was well paid.

Cosmopolis by Don DeLillo (2003)

He paced through his 48-room apartment, past the Borzoi cage, past the shark tank. The yen had risen overnight. Eric Packer didn't know what he wanted. Then he knew. He wanted a haircut.

'There's gridlock because the president's in town,' said Torval, as the stretch limo pulled into the traffic. 'You'd be better off not using the car.'

'How do you know we're in the car and not in the office?' Eric snarled, staring at his bank of screens.

He glanced out the window. Was that his wife, Elise, the heiress? 'I didn't know you had blue eyes,' she said.

'When are we going to make love?' he replied.

Michael Chin got in the car. 'I know where there's a Rothko for sale.'

'I'll buy the whole gallery.'

The car stopped to pick up his finance director, Jane Melman. 'Your position on the yen is critical,' she said.

'It can't go any higher,' he answered, passing her a bottle to masturbate herself.

They stopped by Dr Ingram's surgery for his daily check-up. 'Your prostate is asymmetrical.'

Back en route, they passed a bookstore. Eric spied his wife again. 'You smell of sex,' she whispered.

'Have lunch with me.'

'Is this what I wanted,' she said, looking at her plate.

'I need a haircut.'

Eric got back in the limo. The yen had to chart. He was the most powerful man in New York. He made the markets. He was like the famous novelist who could write utter crap and know that neither his editor nor the critics would notice – or dare say a word against him.

They stopped by the apartment of Kendra Hays, his bodyguard. She kept on her Zyloflex body armour while they had sex. 'Shoot me with your stun gun,' he said. 'I want to know how it feels.'

He showed no curiosity when he bumped into Elise again. 'My portfolio is valueless and someone is mounting a credible threat on my life.'

'You still smell of sex.'

He hacked into her account and stole $735m. Losing it was the best way of resisting it.' Why am I not interested in he who wants to kill me?'

'Because no one else is,' yawned Torval.

Anti-globalisation protesters sprayed paint on the car and a man set himself on fire.

'That's just not original,' Eric said, while urinating.

The barbershop was closed, but Anthony came to him.

'Your hair is ratty.'

'I knew it was time.'

Elise walked through the door. 'I've lost all your money,' he said, as he straddled her.

'What do poets know of money? Our marriage is over.'

Eric heard gunshots. He fired back.

'My name is Richard Sheets,' said his assailant. 'I hate you because you made me hate the baht.'

Eric shot himself in the hand. 'I've got an asymmetric prostate.'

'So have I. But I've still got to shoot you.'

Digested read, digested: A Manhattan journey that is as deadly for us as it is for Eric.

Notes on a Scandal
by Zoë Heller (2003)

This is not a story about me. But since the task of telling it has fallen to me, it is right I should tell you a bit about myself. My name is Barbara Covett. It won't mean much to you, I'm sure, but you'll soon recognise my type. I am the unreliable narrator, the first resort for any hack who wants to be taken seriously as a novelist.

Sheba is upstairs sleeping, so now is a good time to continue. She doesn't know I am writing an account of last summer's events.

But I think it will be valuable to document the hysterical prurience her actions unleashed.

I first met Sheba when she came to teach pottery at St George's. I recognised immediately that she was different to the rest of us – posher, more confident. I kept myself to myself at first. I'd taught at the school for umpteen years and seen many teachers come and go, and I must confess I had my doubts about her.

She later told me of her first meeting with the Year 11 boy, Connolly. 'He tried to kiss me,' she said. 'You must tell the head,' I cautioned. 'Oh, no. It was just an innocent advance. It's over.'

This turned out to be far from the truth, but it was not until some months later that Sheba confided in me that she and Connolly were having an affair. 'It's so exciting,' she said, 'We're in love.'

It struck me at the time that it was almost unbelievable for a 40-year-old woman to be so head-over-heels in love with a 15-year-old boy. But then it also struck me as unbelievable that she would have become such good friends with me, a dowdy working-class spinster. Still, it's only fiction after all.

'You must stop the affair,' I urged. 'You'll damage your family and your career. Think of your poor son with Down's syndrome whose purpose in life is to create moral dilemmas and engage the reader's sympathy.'

Sheba promised she would end it, but her repeated absences suggested otherwise. I must own up here to some envy that she made so little time available for me, and when Brian Bangs, the staff-room Lothario, told me he had a crush on her, I couldn't resist intimating my knowledge of the affair.

'I think Bangs knows,' I later warned her, but by then events were out of control. Connolly, I gather, had tired of the affair, but his withdrawal only spurred Sheba to greater follies. She began taking risks and before long Connolly's mother found out and accused her of sexually abusing her child.

Sheba had to leave the school, of course, as did I. Her marriage ended and we now share a house. She is coming downstairs.

'I've found your notes,' she yells. 'It didn't happen like that at all. I'm leaving.'

But she can't. There's no place else for her to go.

Digested read, digested: Unbelievable love triangle between the posh, the old and the spotty.

Crossing the Lines
by Melvyn Bragg (2003)

The tinker drove his horse and cart through the streets of Wigton as cars hummed past. He shook his head sadly. 'I'm just a cliché to illustrate how the Cumbria of the mid-50s had one foot in the past and one in the future,' he thought to himself.

Sam and Ellen dwelt on the portentousness of the novel in which they were appearing. Ellen's mind turned to Mr Hawesley – she could never call him William. She knew he was attracted to her, but she could never leave Sam. These were deep, northern thoughts – the kind that were best left unarticulated.

'Our Joe's a good kid,' Sam said eventually.

'Aye,' Ellen replied.

Joe felt himself to be on the cusp of adulthood. He felt a longing to remain part of Wigton, yet at the same time he yearned to break free of its parochial boundaries. He sensed he had a greatness – a knighthood even – within him, but somehow it still felt an inch or two out of reach.

He stroked his thick, luxuriant hair, his enduring symbol of potency. He watched Richard swagger around the school, and felt a twinge of adolescent insecurity. Would Rachel fall for Richard's athletic charm or would his hair win the day?

'Would you like to see *On the Waterfront*?' he asked.

'Aye,' Rachel answered.

'We could go dancing afterwards.'

'Aye.'

'So we're going out together, then?'

'Aye.'

As the music changed from the foxtrot to skiffle, Joe reflected on how Wigton had one foot in the past and the other in the future.

'I'm worried about Suez,' he said, a year later.

'Why are we talking about this?' Rachel asked.

'To show that this book isn't just a saga, but an important literary event that refracts global events through the prism of small-town northern life.'

'I've won a scholarship to Oxford,' smiled Joe. 'But first I must go to Paris to be intellectual. And to show the French my hair.'

Rachel lowered her eyes. She knew she was just an ordinary northern girl, and that she was losing Joe.

'Dear Joe, It's over. I've met a man called Garry,' she wrote. Joe had never known such pain. 'I love you,' he cried. 'Say we'll never be apart again.'

'We'll be together for ever.'

Joe tugged on his pipe and discussed Beckett with James and his fellow undergraduates. How they admired his intellect and hair. How he admired their class. He hoped Rachel would like them.

'It's over,' she said. 'I can hold you back no longer. Go, conquer the wider world of media and academe.'

Joe knew she was right. He was too good for her. It was time to move on. But when would fame be his?

'All in good time,' James muttered.

'In our time,' replied Joe.

Digested read, digested: The secret diary of Melvyn Bragg, aged 16 3/4.

Never Let Me Go
by Kazuo Ishiguro (2005)

My name is Kathy H. I am a carer. As I drive around the country looking after my donors, I like to reflect, in my elegant and refined way, on my childhood at Hailsham.

I realise now how lucky Tommy, Ruth and I were to be brought up in such surroundings. We even had a sports pavilion where we would go to chatter amongst ourselves. You may wonder why I mention these details, but such empty observations are the hallmark of the consummate prose stylist.

From time to time, we would talk about donations and the world outside, and then we would shrink back into our sheltered lives. It may strike you that I like to hint at truths. This is because I fear you might stop reading were you to guess that the story really was as predictable as it first seemed.

Our guardians, particularly Miss Emily, took good care of us. Most of us, apart from poor Tommy, became competent artists and we were, in our way, quite happy, though a sense of dread would run through the school when Madame came by to take the pick of our artwork.

We had very few personal possessions but that never bothered us. My treasured item was a Julie Bridgewater tape. How I loved to dance to it! Sadly, it got lost one day.

I can see you are becoming deeply affected by the poignancy of our situation. I should have loved to have told you at this point of how we felt about having no parents, of how we tried to escape into the outside world. But I can't. Emotion and interest have no part in this story.

As we grew older we started to have sex with one another, though the enjoyment was tempered by the fact that none of us could have children. Tommy and Ruth even became a couple when the three of us left Hailsham and went to live at The Cottages.

Improbable as it may seem, I used to enjoy looking at porn mags, though this was partly because I hoped to spot my possible. We were all obsessed with meeting our possible – our real-world entitie – and Ruth once thought she had seen hers in Norwich. But it turned out to look nothing like her, which left her depressed for days. I suspect you're beginning to know how she felt.

Ruth and Tommy split up before Ruth made her first donation and she completed while making her second. I became Tommy's carer and we started to have sex after his third donation. We hoped to defer his fourth donation for a few years, but a chance meeting with Madame and Miss Emily stopped that.

'Deferrals are not possible,' Miss Emily said. 'You are mere clones – organ donors – and we've tried to make you as happy as possible.'

This came as quite a shock, though I dare say not to you. Tommy completed during his fourth donation so I'm left alone, to drone on.

Digested read, digested: The triumph of style over substance.

Extremely Loud and Incredibly Close
by Jonathan Safran Foer (2005)

What about a teakettle? What about little microphones? What about writing the same book again and seeing if anyone notices?

I'm nine years old and I'm an inventor, computer consultant, astronomer, historian, lepidopterist, and I write to Stephen Hawking. I'm no ordinary boy, but the creation of a writer who's trying too hard. That's why you'll find doodles, photographs, pages with just a few words on them, blank pages and very small print littered throughout the text.

Dad got killed on 9/11. We used to look for mistakes in the *New York Times* together. I picked up the messages he sent from the World Trade Center before he died, but I never told Mum. She spends most of her time with Ron.

Why I'm not where you are – 5/21/63. I've lost the power of speech, I can only communicate in writing. Then you came along, you whose eyesight was failing and asked me to marry you.

I can feel my prose dazzling from within. I find a key on the bottom of my dad's vase. This is the key to his life. I see the word 'black' printed beside it and decide to visit every person called Black in the telephone directory. I will travel the five boroughs on foot and find the entrance to the mystical sixth.

My feelings – Dear Oskar, This is hard to write. Your grandfather could not speak and I could barely see, but we joined our lives in a place of Nothing and Something. He left when I was pregnant with your father. Love, Grandma.

In the evenings, I've been playing Yorick in Hamlet, but Mum only came once because she was out with Ron. In the day I've been walking the streets with a 103-year-old man.

Why I'm not where you are – I lost my love and punctuation in the firestorm of Dresden your grandma was her sister when she got pregnant I had to leave rather than love I wrote to my son everyday but never sent the letters I came back! to New York when I discovered he had died and went to live with your grandma again but you only know me as the Renter what is the sum of my life 46638902836485969070 464532537

The key belongs to someone else. It has no catharsis; in its place there is only sentimentality. My mum loves me after all. My grandpa and I dig up my dad's empty coffin and we place his letters inside. I rewind the pictures of 9/11 and my dad returns to me.

Digested read, digested: Extremely annoying and incredibly pretentious.

Memories of My Melancholy Whores
by Gabriel García Márquez (2005)

The year I turned 90, I wanted to give myself the gift of wild love with an adolescent virgin. I thought of Rosa Cabarcas, the brothel owner.

'You ask the impossible, my mad scholar,' she said. But I implored her and she promised to ring back within the hour.

I'm ugly, shy and anachronistic, and I live alone in the house where my parents lived, scraping by on a meagre pension from my mediocre career as a journalist. And I have never been to bed with a woman without paying. In short, I am without merit or brilliance.

JOHN CRACE

On the morning of my 90th birthday, I awoke, as always, at five in the morning. My only obligation was to write my signed column for Sunday's paper, for which, as usual, I would not be paid. I had my usual aches and pains – my asshole burned – but my heart lifted when Rosa rang to say I was in luck.

I gazed at the phosphorescent sweat on the naked body of the 14-year-old virgin asleep on the bed, and admired the brilliance of my language. 'She was nervous,' Rosa informed me, 'so I gave her some Valerian.'

She did not stir. 'Let me call you Delgadina,' I whispered, for like most solipsists I preferred to invent my own names. I may have slept myself and a tiger may have written on the bathroom mirror – we magical realists can never be too sure of anything – and when I left her snoring in the morning she was still as pure as the night before.

'You fool,' spat Rosa. 'She will be insulted you did not care enough about her to abuse her.' But I did not care: I had detected the fragrance of Delgadina's soul and had realised that sex was the consolation we receive for the absence of love.

I had planned to tender my resignation at the paper, but I was so moved at being given a voucher to adopt a stray cat that shat and pissed at will, that I resolved to continue.

And my fame grew. Every evening I would go to Rosa's house and spend the night admiring the sleeping Delgadina – whose body was filling out agreeably – while reading out loud the great works of literature; and by day people would read out loud the tacky sentimentality of my columns.

Late into the year, Rosa interrupted my reveries. 'A client has been murdered,' she shouted. 'Help me move him.'

I returned night after night, but Rosa's house was locked up. I pined for Delgadina. I sensed my cat might lead me to her, but like my own writing, he led me up a cul-de-sac.

17

At last, Rosa returned. 'Whore,' I said. 'You have sold Delgadina to secure your freedom.'

'How wrong you are,' she cried. 'Others may consider you a sordid, delusional old man, but Delgadina loves you. She kept her distance because she wanted to save herself for you.'

My heart soared. I was not a perv. I was a 91-year-old man with so much love to give and so much life to live. I will survive.

Digested read, digested: 100 pages of turpitude.

The Possibility of an Island
by Michel Houellebecq (2005)

Daniel 1,1: I get so tired writing comic sketches about gays, blacks, Jews and Muslims these days. But being thought to be avant garde has its advantages; people take you seriously and pay you shed loads of cash for any old tosh. And you get lots of pussy, too.

Daniel 24,1: Look at those savages in the distance. They are humans. I sit alone in my fenced-off compound sending the odd email to Marie 22.

I am not happy, I am not sad.

I never cry and I'm never bad.

Daniel 1,2: I don't know why I married my first wife and I didn't care when my son committed suicide. That's how shocking I am. I met Isabelle when she came to interview me after the success of We Prefer the Palestinian Orgy Sluts. She was OK; her tits didn't sag and I felt almost affectionate towards her. We stayed together for a while in a house I had bought in Spain with my many million euros.

Daniel 24,2: I am neo-human. I sit here with Fox, reflecting aimlessly on our previous incarnations.

I'm even deep.

When I'm asleep.

Daniel 1,3: Isabelle aged badly and I grew tired of her. I acquired a dog I called Fox, who was much better company. One morning some neighbours invited me to join the Elohim sect. Weighed down by my professional ennui I was naturally sceptical, but the prospect of free love and everlasting life was undeniably attractive.

Daniel 24,3: Marie 22 sent me an email.

My breasts are low.

It's time to go.

She is about to become Marie 23.

Daniel 1,4: With Esther I thought I had discovered happiness. Just looking at her 22-year-old body gave me a hard-on and she willingly let me fuck her in every orifice.

Daniel 25,1: Daniel 24 has had enough. The Supreme Sister has called him.

Daniel 1,5: Esther left me as I knew she would, but my Fourierist principles had drawn me ever closer to the Elohim. I had even taken to writing doggerel.

Just one push.

On a friendly bush.

Vincent had replaced the Prophet and he was convinced the time of human cloning was drawing ever nearer.

Daniel 25,2: It was around this time that the early leaders pioneered a genetic mutation of autotrophism, allowing the new species to survive on minerals and water.

Daniel 1,6: Sometimes I think I overstated my despair; though not that of my readers. I chose to visit Isabelle. 'I still love you,' she said, before committing suicide.

Daniel 25,3: Marie 23 has escaped to live with the savages. I read Spinoza.

Daniel 1,7: Occasionally my cock showed signs of life, but I had come to realise that happiness was the preserve of the young. Vincent suggested that Fox and I should have our DNA copied. 'It is time for you to commit suicide,' he said. 'You will be an example for millions of others.' I sent a last poem to Esther.

You are in clover.

But my life is over.

Daniel 25,4: I'm tired of feeling nothing. I break out. I smell the pestilential ordure between a savage's legs and make for the hills. I will die. I am finally alive.

Digested read, digested: 25 Daniels don't give a damn. And neither will you.

No Country for Old Men
by Cormac McCarthy (2005)

Moss fingered the heavybarreled .270 on a '98 Mauser action with a laminated walnut and maple stock. He glassed the Texan desert with a pair of 12 power german binoculars. There were men lying on the ground beside two four wheel drive trucks.

Agua, said the one man still alive. An H & K on his lap and an exit wound in his throat.

Aint got no water.

Moss checked the back of the truck. Packets of a brown powder and a valise. He flipped the catch. $2.4m. He left the powder, took the valise and headed home. This kind of changed everything.

Where you been?

You dont need to know, Carla Jean.

He woke at 1.06. Theres something I gotta do.

What is it?

You dont need to know.

Moss headed back to the trucks. The Mexican was dead. Shots from a sawn-off shotgun rang out and Moss headed for the road, blood streaming from his back.

I dont know when things started getting nasty roun here. Folks say it was after Vietnam but I reckon it started before that.

Sheriff Bell surveyed the eight bodies bloating in the sun. Things are gonna get tough for Moss and Carla Jean, he reckoned.

Moss checked the curtains at the motel. He had company. He lifted the air vent. Two Mexicans pooling blood and the money in the corner. He retrieved the money, removed the transponder and a blast took him in the back. He fired the sawn-off and limped down town. He was a dead man. Shots from a machine-pistol rang out and four Mexicans lay dying. A reprieve.

Chigurh was a patient man. He stitched his wounds. He hadn't got the money yet. But he would. Too bad those Mexicans got in the way. But four less to deal with later.

The man called Wells.

Find me the money and get Chigurh.

Wells tracked Moss to the hospital.

Wheres the money?

Safe.

You wont be. Call me.

Chigurh cornered Wells.

How does a man decide in what order to abandon his life?

Wells shrugged and the bullet blew away his forehead.

Chigurh went to the man.

You sent Wells to kill me. Now you gonna die.

He fired into the carotid as his phone rang.

It's too late, Moss. But you can save your wife.

Not if I get you first.

Chigurh crept up on Moss. Time to die.

Bell shrugged as he saw the putrefying corpse. What could he tell Carla Jean?

You know who I am?

Carla Jean nodded.

I promised your husband I'd kill you and I keep my promises. You stay settin there. He aimed carefully and fired.

My granddaddy was a sheriff and I was proud to be a sheriff. But I reckon I've had enough.

There was no sign of Chigurh. This country could kill you in a heartbeat.

Digested read, digested: Once Upon a Time in the West.

Everyman by Philip Roth (2006)

Around the grave in the rundown cemetery were a few of his former advertising colleagues, some people who had driven up from the Starfish Beach retirement village, his elder brother, Howie, his second wife Phoebe, his two sons, Lonny and Randy and his daughter, Nancy.

'This is how it turns out. There's nothing more we can do, Dad,' said Nancy, throwing some dirt on to the top of the coffin. The day before the surgery, he had remembered going into hospital as a boy for a hernia operation and how the boy in the next bed had died. But this was not the first death he had known; the year before he had found a German submariner washed up on the shore. 'It happens,' his father had said.

He had got married and divorced – he couldn't blame Lonny and Randy for hating him – and he had remarried. He had been happy with Phoebe and Nancy was adorable, but really the next most interesting event in his life had been when he had had life-threatening surgery at the age of 31 on a burst appendix.

Twenty-two years of excellent health passed and then the EKG showed radical changes in his heart that indicated severe occlusion of his major coronary arteries. It was touch and go whether he would make it. By now he had moved on to his third wife, but she had no taste for a crisis so by the time he recovered he went home alone.

He fell in love with his nurse – a not uncommon experience – and she moved in with him after his father died. The night of the funeral he could almost taste the dirt finding its way into his father's mouth and choking him.

For the next nine years his health remained disappointingly stable, but then in 1998 his blood pressure began to mount and the doctors diagnosed an obstruction of the renal artery and he was admitted to hospital for angioplasty. Again his luck held, and he returned home to his one real pleasure – revising his will.

After 9/11 he moved out to Starfish Beach where he might have enjoyed himself teaching painting classes. But fortunately enough of his elderly students were dying of cancer and his star pupil overdosed on sleeping tablets to save him from any feelings of positivity.

From time to time, he cast his mind back to his wives, his mistresses and his former job. He had had some good sex and some bad sex and his career had been better than average, but all it really amounted to was a diversion between hospital visits. And in the last seven years of his life, he was pleased to note that he had needed major surgery at least once every twelve months. A stent here, a stent there: what more could one ask? How could he have ever envied Howie his good health?

He had been going to ask Nancy if he could move in with her, but just as he was about to call, she had phoned to say that her mother had had a stroke and would be moving in instead. 'I'm sorry to hear that,' he had said before phoning the widow of his former boss and an old friend who had terminal cancer to offer his condolences. He had then befriended a grave digger, before entering hospital for surgery on his right carotid artery. This time there was no coming back.

Digested read, digested: Life's a bitch and then you diet.

Travels in the Scriptorium
by Paul Auster (2007)

The old man sits on the edge of the narrow bed. His mind is elsewhere, stranded in the figments of his head. Who is he? What is he doing here? Who cares?

There are a number of objects in the room, each affixed with a strip of white tape bearing a single word. On the table, for example, is TABLE. On the lamp is the word, LAMP. And on this book, BOLLOCKS.

Is this a prison? Is it a house? The old man has no memory. But perhaps he isn't even old? So let's drop the epithet old and refer to the person as Mr Blank. For this should tell both you and him everything you need to know; that you are trapped inside some meaningless pretentious crap that is passing itself off as cutting-edge post-modern metaphysicality.

Mr Blank remembers his old rocking-horse, Whitey. He doesn't know why. But you do. Because it is obviously going to crop up again later. A phone rings.

Who am I talking to?

I'm James P Flood.

Refresh my mind.

The ex-policeman who visited you yesterday. Save me from your dream. My life depends on it.

Mr Blank has no memory of yesterday. You wish you had no memory of today. But never mind about James P Flood, because he's as pointless as every other character in the book. Which, as you have probably guessed, is the whole point.

Mr Blank looks at a picture of a woman. He thinks it might be Anna. But isn't Anna dead? A woman walks in.

I'm Anna.

Are you a different Anna?

Who knows? I forgive you for killing me, anyway.

Mr Blank starts reading a manuscript about a man called Graf locked in a Confederation prison in Ultima.

I don't get it, he says.

That's the idea.

Who are you?

Another character.

Mr Blank misjudges the distance to the toilet and urine squirts down his pyjamas. Why did this happen? Why does anything happen? He picks up the manuscript and continues reading about Graf and his dreary adventures in the Confederation. He throws the papers down angrily. The story has finished in the middle. If only.

A character called Sophie lets him touch her breasts.

Now make up the rest of the story.

Graf is riding Whitey. He thinks about three possible endings for his wife but none is satisfactory. So let's ignore her. Let's tell the story of Ernesto Land instead.

Mr Blank picks up a book. It's called *Travels in the Scriptorium*. It starts, 'The old man sits on the edge of the narrow bed.' Gosh, he thinks. The characters have taken over the novelist. How predictable.

The satirist puts down a book. He knows why he's read it. He's been paid. But he can't see why anyone else would bother.

Digested read, digested: Blankety Blank.

The Cleft
by Doris Lessing (2007)

This evening I was watching my slave, Marcus, try to avoid the attentions of Lolla. I knew he would rather be playing with the other boys but would end up spending the night with her. This banal observation about the nature of relations between men and women impelled me to retell the story of the beginnings of the world that has been gathering dust on ancient parchments in my cellar.

You want to know about me? My name is Maire. There is always someone called Maire. I was born into the family of Cleft Watchers, like my mother, her mother and all the Old Shes before them. We women lie in the swirling jellied waters of the pools and every month when the moon is at its highest, we climb to the indentation we call The Cleft where the red flowers grow and we have our blood flow. That is, all who are not going to give birth.

I cannot say how it started. Only that it was ages ago. How long ago is ages? Who can say? The Old Shes must have known something because before the first Monsters were born, there were only Shes, only Clefts. When these first deformed babies with Tubes between their legs were born, we would take the Monsters – these Squirts – to the Cleft where we would dash them on the rocks. But then the Eagles, with their meaningless capital letters, began to snatch some of the baby Squirts from our clutches and drop them in the forest.

As a descendant of one of these Monsters, I feel the need to intervene – if only to break up the plodding predictability of the story. For future reference, my amazing Roman aperçus are the passages printed in italics – so it's quite simple to skip them if you feel like you're dozing off.

How did the first Squirts survive? No one really knows, but we must presume they were suckled by deer. All the documents relate is that eventually the Squirts and the Clefts were united – the Squirts through an aching need in their Tubes that they never fully understood and was only relieved by mating – and the Clefts through a primal maternal bond.

And how long ago did this take place? No one knows. Only that it must have been ages after the first ages.

I was talking to my wife, Julia, the other day and it occurred to me that men and women are quite different. Women are much more intuitive, while men tend to be much more unthinking. But I expect all you women already know that!

Some of the Old Shes weren't happy about the arrival of the Squirts and planned to kill them. But the younger Clefts, led by another Maire, were prepared to forgive the occasional gang rape and stepped in to save all the Squirts whose Tubes made them too stupid to save themselves. How did everyone feel about this new prelapsarian state? We don't know because everyone was stuck in a 1960s feminist timewarp and had no inner world or emotions worth mentioning.

Ages later – how long we don't know, only that it was ages after the last bit and ages and ages after the first bit, the Squirts were led by Horsa and the Clefts by Maronna. At this time the Squirts used to run around doing dangerous things and didn't bring up their babies properly, and the Clefts were cross about this and used to scold the Squirts. One day Horsa took a group of people off to explore the island. The Clefts were very worried, but after a bit of a tiff everyone made up in the end when the rock Cleft exploded.

I was thinking about how similar this was to Vesuvius. If only I had lived in Pompeii I could have saved us all a lot of bother.

Digested read, digested: Men are from Mars, women are from Venus.

On Chesil Beach
by Ian McEwan (2007)

They were young, educated, and both virgins on this, their wedding night. As they sat down to dinner in the honeymoon suite of the Dorset hotel, Edward was mesmerised by the prospect of inserting his member inside the moist cavity of this formidably intelligent woman. All that troubled him was the worry of over-excitement.

Florence's anxieties were more serious. She loved Edward with a passion but had no desire to be penetrated. She had read the references to glans, mucous membrane and engorged penis in the modern bride's handbook and felt nothing but a visceral dread.

'I love you,' they said to one another for the hundredth time that day. And they truly meant it. Edward had a first-class degree in history but, on this July day in 1962, he doubted if any other man had ever been as happy. He looked at her long pizzicato fingers and felt a constriction around his crotch as if his trousers had shrunk. Would she take the lead, as first violinists often will? He remembered too well her revulsion at his stiffening manhood when he had placed her hands on his trousers at the cinema, and how it had set their physical congress back by many months.

Edward had prepared for this day by refraining from self-pleasuring for a week and when she suggested lying on the bed he felt all those unimportant details, such as Harold Macmillan and H-bombs that had only been included to provide a veneer of context, race from his mind. Florence reminded herself how much she loved him, as Edward's tongue parted her lips and greedily explored her larynx.

They had known each other all their lives – he from the squalor of his family hovel and she from the palatial splendour of her mansion – but they had only got together by chance at a CND meeting. He had marvelled at her musicianship and longed to savour the tautness of her nipples. She had thought him a good egg and the ideal husband.

He tugged clumsily at her zip and she froze as his hands inched up her leg to caress a hair that had escaped from the lace of her knickers. She broke away. 'I'm a little scared,' she said. Edward restrained his annoyance and comforted her before resuming his manual ministrations. To her surprise, she began to feel a sense of pleasure as his fingers circumnavigated her pubis. How she wished they could stay like this! But she remembered the manual and tried to guide him in. His back arched in muscular spasms as he emptied himself in gouts, coating her belly, chin and knee in tepid, viscous fluid. She knew she had done something wrong, yet she could not conceal her disgust and she ran out the room, heading outdoors to the Chesil beach.

He found her two miles along the deserted shingle.

'You are disgusting,' she said.

'You are frigid,' he replied icily.

They both knew there was something they should say to make matters better but neither could find the words.

'Maybe we could remain in a sexless marriage,' she mouthed in a gesture of conciliation, 'and you could occasionally get your needs met by other women.'

'It's over,' he gasped.

'Don't you think we're being rather melodramatic and that even in 1962 a couple might get over a crap shag on their wedding night?' she cried.

'Of course, but if we don't split up, the whole book's pointless.'

She ran off down the beach and into a waiting taxi.

Edward returned the wedding presents and moved on to a life of inconsequential journalism, punctuated by inconsequential affairs. Yet he never loved any woman as much as Florence again. She gave herself to her music and wondered if Edward would ever know that if he had but called her back that day, she would have melted into his arms forever.

Digested read, digested: One messy outburst and it's all over.

Engleby by Sebastian Faulks (2007)

My name is Mike Engleby and I'm in my second year at an ancient university. I'm not going to name it, but you can safely assume it's Cambridge. There's someone I've met called Jennifer Arkland. She's standing for election to a Society committee. I think I'll join Jen Soc.

I won a prize to come to my college, but I have no memory of it. My memory's odd like that. I'm big on detail, but there are holes in the fabric. You know what that means? Of course you do. It's only page two and already I'm signalling that I'm using one of the laziest and most devalued devices of modern literature: the unreliable narrator.

From now on you won't really care about a single word I write, but as I don't either I may as well carry on. I drink quite heavily, smoke a lot of dope, take loads of downers and don't really have many friends. I expect I will have even fewer by the end of the book. Especially among the readers.

Anyway, let me tell you some more about myself. As it's the mid-70s, I like to listen to Procol Harum and Focus and have many dull opinions about pop music. You're supposed to take this as yet another intriguing sign of the personality disorder there's meant to be some doubt about whether I have, but I suspect you'll probably reckon it's just what Seb thought back then.

I'm quite clever, really. I can play with time and narrative in the way that all great writers can. One moment I can be talking about how well I am getting on with Jen on a film shoot in Ireland – even though I'm obviously not – and then I can flit around between my childhood beatings from my father and how I was bullied by Baynes at my boarding school.

Sometimes I get quite angry. Not that I'm necessarily aware I'm angry because my memory isn't that good. But when I do – supposing I do – I take some Valium and waste more time on trivia. I've often felt that the best artists frequently produce complete rubbish towards the end of their careers. Just look at Monet. And this book proves the same thing applies to writers.

Jen has gone missing. I wonder if something bad may have happened. By the way, did I mention that I was once admitted to a mental hospital? No, thought not. But you probably guessed that anyway and were just as bored by the thought as I was. The police think Jen is dead. Despite searching my room for three days they didn't find my stash of dope up the chimney, or Jennifer's diary that I'd hidden in the cistern.

But never mind. I like reading Jen's diary. It's very dull and uninformative – she refers to me as Mike (!) – but I've memorised it anyway and can waste pages repeating it, just to show that I can adapt to the style and tone of a 21-year-old woman.

There was a suggestion I might become a spy after leaving university but I became a journalist instead. How I enjoyed the irony of a compulsive liar becoming a hack. Imagine if I was to interview Jeffrey Archer. Oh, I just did.

At times I have flashbacks to a woman I might have killed after a Graham Parker gig and I sometimes also think I might have murdered Baynes. But as I have created a new genre in which no one gives a stuff whether any of this really happened or not, I won't lose too much sleep over it.

Oh dear, it's all coming to an end. Jennifer's body has been found and I do seem to have killed her after all. The psychiatric reports say I'm mentally ill, though the critics insist I'm no American Psycho. Perhaps I'm just a bit of a loser instead.

Here I am then, still in a secure hospital 30 years later.

Sometimes I can rewrite Jen's diaries so we are together. Sweet. Don't feel sorry for me. It's I who should feel sorry for you.

Digested read, digested: Mike doesn't care much one way or the other and neither will you.

Michael Tolliver Lives
by Armistead Maupin (2007)

'Hey,' a man called out as I was walking down Castro Street, 'You're supposed to be dead.'

Who was this guy?

'You are Michael Tolliver?' he continued hesitantly. And then I remembered. Not his name, but his dick. How its less-than-average length was made irrelevant by its girth.

That's the problem these days. Thirty years after writing about gay sex and Aids, no one is really interested any more. Everyone is writing about sex and, thanks to the drug cocktails, a lot of us didn't die. So what's the story?

Well there isn't one really, but my publisher thought you might like a follow-up and I could kind of use the money, so here we go.

We might as well start with Ben. I met him via the internet – CLEANCUTLAD4U – and he's 21 years younger than me. But we fell in love and got married. Perhaps I shouldn't have started with Ben, after all. Because what's there to say, other than we're blissful? So maybe I mention the phone call I got from my brother, Irwin. Neither he, nor his nutty religious wife, Lenore, have ever been able to stand gays, so a phone call was unusual.

'Mum's dying,' he said. 'You may want to come out to Florida to say goodbye.' It's weird, this. I always expected to die first. So now I find myself having to prepare for other people's deaths and worrying about dying of something other than Aids. This might be an interesting subject, so I'd better trivialise it.

I'm lying on my front, pushing my ass up towards Ben. 'You will be careful about how you stick it in, won't you?' I said teasingly.

Ooh, what a dirty mind you've got! Ben was only giving me my weekly testosterone injection. Sweet. A man needs all the help he can get at my age.

I suppose you also want to hear about all the old characters who used to hang out at Barbary Lane. My LOGICAL family, rather than my BIOLOGICAL family. Geddit? Well, Brian's still around and he's bought a Winnebago. Ben thinks he's hot, but Brian's always been dead straight, so no chance there.

Anyway, ever since Mary Ann left, Brian's been worried about bringing up their daughter, Shawna. But he shouldn't be. He's done a great job. She's working in a strip club – a mastaburtorium she calls it – and she's about to move to New York to publish her sex memoirs. She's worried how her dad will feel about her leaving San Fran, but I told her he'll get over it. Hmm, maybe that's not so fascinating.

Well then, there's dear old Anna Madrigal. At 85 – having spent half her life as a man and the other half as a woman – she's still our mummy. But she's taken to talking enigmatically so she'll probably die at some point.

What else? There's a friend of mine called Jake who's a transsexual. 'I haven't had the addadictomy,' he purred. 'I said, I haven't had the addadictomy'

'I heard you the first time,' I said.

'Well, it's my only gag and I didn't want you to miss it.'

So we fly to Florida to see Mum, and it's all kind of bittersweet. She doesn't like gays that much, but she loves me and Ben and gives us power of attorney to stop Irwin and Lenore prolonging her life.

We also get to hear some great gossip on how Mum twice nearly left Dad, and how Dad once got it on with Lenore. Imagine! I couldn't, but people are supposed to reveal family secrets on their deathbed and this was all I could come up with.

Mum is taking her time to die, so we fly back to San Fran to do a bit more gardening and the bathhouses, when my arthritis allows, and then Irwin calls again to say she really is on her way out. But then I hear that Anna is dying so I stay with my LOGICALs and even Mary Ann turns up from New York to say goodbye. And that's all there is to it, really.

Digested read, digested: Michael lives and Tales of the City die.

Bright Shiny Morning
by James Frey (2008)

Two teens. Two teens stuck in an eastern town. Two teens stuck in sentences of arbitrary punctuation and repetition arbitrary punctuation and repetition that is meant to suggest something hip, something beat but just feels a bit tired and mannered. 'I can feel the glow of the west,' Dylan says. 'I'm gonna jack me a car, drive us west to California.' They reach the ocean they carry on driving. The car starts sinking. 'I think we've gone too far,' says Maddie. They swim back to shore and this is where they stay. Los Angeles.

Her parents call her Esperanza they can't speak English but they live in LA and they got hope. She's pretty but she's ashamed of her thighs she flunks school because of her thighs she takes a job cleaning for Mrs Campbell she pretends not to speak English as it's the only way she can get a job with her thighs.

There are lots of facts about Los Angeles in Wikipedia, facts that if you jot them down one at a time might somehow seem quite deep. All the Los Angeles banks were robbed at least once in 1895. See what I mean?

Old Man Joe's hair turned white when he was 29 he aged 40 years in one night. He's now 274, drinks chablis out of toilet cisterns on Venice Beach that's about as interesting as he gets. You're gonna age 40 years reading about him.

Amberton Parker. Amberton Parker the most unconvincing Hollywood film star you'll ever meet. He kisses his wife Casey in bed with her lesbian lover leaves the kids with the nanny leaves the house. He meets Kevin a black ex-footballer at his agency knows he's got to have him sends him cars private jets knows that Kevin can't say no or Amberton will leave the agency. He fucks Kevin he's in love.

James has a dream. He's gonna be a somebody. He smokes a bit of weed nicks candy bars from the 7-Eleven writes this book about how he's one nasty smackhead goes on Oprah becomes a celebrity. Then everyone finds out it's just a million little lies and he's a nobody.

Los Angeles gets a lot bigger in the 20th century.

Dylan gets a job in Tiny's Hell's Angel motorcycle repair shop keeps his head down buys donuts for Maddie. They are in love. They have a dream. Some tattooed guys beat up Tiny over a drug deal. Dylan says nothing knows he shouldn't do nothing but takes $20,000 and walks out. What a berk.

Mrs Campbell treats Esperanza like shit but Esperanza takes it 'cause she needs the money one day Mrs Campbell goes to Palm Beach and leaves Esperanza alone in the house with her son Doug. 'I'm a neek,' he says, 'but I've fallen in love with your fat thighs.' 'You ain't nuthin but a pervert,' Mrs Campbell yells on her return. 'You're sacked.' She gets another job he finds her there's a happy ending.

He wants to help her this girl Beatrice. He wants to redeem her redeem himself. He tries to get her away from the men but they kill his mate. Old Man Joe cries into his chablis. He's fucked up again.

Los Angeles is home of Hollywood, home of the porn business, home of the rich, home of the poor, home of homeys. No kidding.

'Kevin is suing you for $20m,' says Amberton's agent. 'Give him the money I'm heartbroken and sign me up for another $100m movie,' Amberton sobs. Casey smiles in appreciation as she goes down on her girl.

Dylan gets a job as a caddy on the golf course they're making something of their lives they have friends they get married they are gonna have a baby. Then Tiny's mates come along and kill him he never saw that coming but you did.

James still has a dream he's gonna be a somebody. He starts writing a novel about all these characters in LA makes it random makes it beat thinks the critics have gotta take him seriously this time. He starts writing he doesn't care much what he can't stop writing. He knows it's all a bit contrived a bit obvious but he can't stop. He's written 500 pages and he can't stop. James has a dream a dream. It's a nightmare.

Digested read, digested: James gets lost in La La Land.

The Little Stranger
by Sarah Waters (2009)

I first saw Hundreds Hall after the war when I was 10 years old, on the occasion of the Empire fete. The Ayres were big people in the village but after that summer they lived more privately: their daughter Susan died of diphtheria and their later children, Roderick and Caroline, kept themselves to themselves. So when I saw the Georgian mansion again 30 years later, I was appalled by the decay. A telephone call from Roderick renewed my acquaintance. I had bettered myself considerably in the intervening years and had returned to Warwickshire to pursue my career as a doctor. 'You'd better come over, Dr Faraday,' he said. 'Betty has a stomach ache and you can't let a servant die these days.'

I replied that I understood how difficult it was to cope now Britain was entering a new social order, for I myself was quite concerned that the new National Health Service would reduce my earnings.

Betty was an utterly unmemorable member of the lower orders. 'Do you think you might be a lesbian?' I asked. 'Nay, sir,' she replied. 'Well that's unusual for a Sarah Waters book,' I said.

It turned out that Betty was terrified by a ghostly presence within the Hall, and I passed on her concerns to Caroline, a plain, natural spinster with thickish legs. 'There's nothing queer going on here,' she said tartly. I resolved to keep a close eye on the family by offering to treat Roderick's war wounds that still distressed him greatly.

A few months later, Mrs Ayres decided to have a party and the octagonal chinoiserie room was opened for the occasion. I was talking to the Baker-Hughes when Caroline whispered to me that Roddie was refusing to come down. I found him in a complete funk and concluded he was already inebriated, so I returned to the party to discover that the Ayres's dog, Gyp, had bitten off the cheek of a young girl.

'What makes it so bad is that the girl is upper-class,' Caroline said. 'A prole could cope with disfigurement so much better.' We obliquely debated the decline of the old social values for several pages, before I persuaded her to let me put Gyp down.

Roddie continued to be delusional, claiming the house was possessed by a poltergeist, and Caroline did alert me to several scorch marks and strange happenings, yet I rather closed off any curiosity about the supernatural that the reader might have had with my dogged rationalism. 'He is haunted by his wartime experiences and his inability to cope with a Labour government,' I ventured, as his room erupted in a mysterious fire. 'I shall send him to a posh mental asylum.'

I began to notice that Caroline was not altogether plain and entertained hopes that she might favour me. We went to a ball one night and on the way home, I pressed my hand against her breast. 'Not now,' she cried, kicking me in the chest.

'Perhaps, then, you will agree to be my wife?' 'OK.'

'I had hoped Caroline would do rather better than you, you ghastly little arriviste,' Mrs Ayres said, 'but we all have to compromise these days. In truth, I have never really got over my darling Susan's death. Her name keeps appearing on the walls as if by magic.'

Two weeks later, Mrs Ayres hanged herself in her room. 'The poltergeist has won again,' Caroline said. 'Don't be silly,' I replied. 'She was haunted by her inability ... blah, blah. And look, now the old bat's dead, why don't we get married in six weeks' time?' 'OK,' she nodded absently.

The wedding preparations were proceeding, with me doing everything, including buying the dress, and Caroline doing absolutely nothing. 'I can't go through with it,' she declared one night. 'I do not love you.' My embarrassment was excruciating but luckily the poltergeist pushed her over the banisters and killed her.

'The ghost has won,' Betty gasped. 'Don't be silly,' I said. 'She was just haunted by her inability to ... blah, blah.' Though I couldn't also help wondering if she hadn't been a lesbian all along.

Digested read, digested: Everyone gives up the ghost.

The Original of Laura: A Novel in Fragments
by Vladimir Nabokov (2009)

One: Fat men beat their wives, it is said, and he certainly looked fierce when he caught her riffling though his papers. Actually she was searching for a silly business letter – and not trying to decipher his mysterious manuscript. Oh no, it was not a work of fiction, it was a mad neurologist's testament, but the thing was, of course, an absolute secret. If she mentioned it at all, she added, it was because she was drunk. And because the Nabokov estate was too greedy not to pass off the barely intelligible marginalia of a dying writer, long past his best, as an unpublished masterpiece.

Unsure of to which particular he the opening referred, Flora demanded to lie down, as this enabled her to surrender to one of her many lovers and for her nymphean form – her cup-sized breasts and pale squinty nipples seemed a dozen years younger than this impatient beauty's – to be described with erotic longing, while Paul de G ogled some boys. 'Have you finished?' she inquired. He nodded in flaccidity. 'Not even a quickie? Tant pis! Then I must go home to my morbidly obese husband and our mulatto charwoman.'

Two: Her grandfather had emigrated from Moscow with his son Adam in 1920. Adam had married the ballerina Lanskaya, who took lovers mostly of Polish extraction. Three years after their daughter Flora was born, Adam filmed himself committing suicide while pining for a boy who had strangled another boy. Lanskaya was confused: what had been meant to be sensational was just tired and desperate. But having no other options now that she was past 16, she found a new lover, Hubert L Hubert, who had dropped the m's from his name in a sad 20-year migration from Lolita while maintaining his penchant for pre-pubescent girls. Flora took exception to his caresses and kicked him in the testicles. 'You naughty girl,' her mother said. 'Mr Nabokov – I mean, Mr Hubert – is a very nice man'. There is little to add.

Three: Flora lost her virginity at 14 to a ball boy with an enormous member. She and her friends like to compare the dimensions of their lovers while bycycling. This, then, is Flora, the artistic enigma, the DELTA and the SLIT. At 11 she had read Freud and wondered how people could get away with writing so badly. But then, she had never read this. Perhaps we should mention the sweet Japanese girls and French writers beginning with M. Perhaps not.

Four: Mrs Lanskaya died on the day her daughter graduated – a passage that for no earthly reason resembles the rythym of another novel, *My Laura*, and a hideously fat man stared at Flora's white legs.

Five: For no good reason, Flora determined to marry this immensely fat man, the eminent neuroscientist Dr Philip Wild, though she regretted her decision when she discovered he was a miser.

Five – or should it be six?: The novel *My Laura* was begun soon after the end of the love affair it depicts. And, like this, was torn apart by every reviewer. The I of the book is a neurotic who set out to destroy his lover while annotating her. Philip Wild quite liked the descriptions of himself.

Six: Suicide made a pleasure. It would be after this.

D1, D2, Aurora, Wild 1, Wild 2: Philip Wild could no longer maintain any pretence of coherence. He could manage the odd well-turned phrase and repeated masturbatory emblazements, yet he could not yet persuade Mr Nabokov to abandon his attempts to impose an order when there was none. I, Philip Wild, he said, slipping into the first person, hereby begin a programme of self deletion. I hate my fat stomach and the noises I make on the lavatory, so I will start by cutting off my toes. Then my hands. Then my head. Till there is nothing left. Effacement. Annihilation. 'That, too, is what faces me if anyone were ever to read this card index,' cried Mr Nabokov. 'Too bad,' said his son.

Digested read, digested: A reputation in fragments.

Solar by Ian McEwan (2010)

2000 He belonged to that Salman class of short, fat, ugly, clever men who were unaccountably attractive to women. But Michael Beard was anhedonic; his fifth marriage was disintegrating and he should have known how to behave as his philandering had ended the previous four. This time, though, it was his wife, Patrice, who was having an affair with Tarpin, a horny-handed Essex builder who knew nothing about cavity-wall insulation.

Beard waited for Aldous to collect him. Gosh, how he hated the polar bear rug in the hall. Still, everyone would soon have one, he supposed, if the polar ice-cap continued to melt. Not that Beard was yet wholly committed to the climate-change agenda, but having won the Nobel Prize for his Beard-Einstein Conflation on Photovoltaics, an idea he was very thankful he was never asked to fully explain, he had been happy to head the New Labour Climate Change Laboratory.

'I'm afraid it's not a Prius,' Aldous said. 'I'm not surprised, as they were only sold outside Japan in 2001,' Beard replied. Aldous was one of his pony-tailed post-docs who was being forced into working on the New Labour cul-de-sac of wind turbine energy. Beard nodded off. He was very familiar with the McEwan Conflation of cramming loads of dull facts about climate change into a book and calling it fiction.

'Tarpin hit me,' said Patrice. 'He hit me too,' Beard replied as he went off to visit an endangered glacier in the Arctic for 30 pages. He returned to find Aldous in his flat. 'I admit I'm having an affair with your wife,' said Aldous, 'but I've worked out that your Conflation can satisfy the world's energy needs.' At which, Aldous slipped on the polar bear rug and died, a victim of climate change.

'I could make it look like Tarpin did it,' McEwan thought. He had no real experience of writing comedy and the gags creaked as much as the plot. But it was an improvement on his previous books, so the judge mercifully sent Tarpin to prison.

2005 As his plane stacked over New Mexico, Beard passed the time unnecessarily recalling his childhood before patting his gut. He had put on 35lb. He couldn't stop consuming; it was almost as if his size was a metaphor for the world's greed for natural resources. Still, there had been something in Aldous's calculations after all, and he was looking forward to seeing the photovoltaic laboratory the Americans had built for him.

Back in England, Beard looked angrily at the man who was helping himself to his crisps and snatched them away. Only later did he realise they were actually the other man's crisps! 'That's the oldest comedy plot twist in the repertoire,' said Melissa, his new girlfriend. 'I know,' Beard shrugged, 'But Ian thinks that, like climate change, it may be old but it doesn't mean it can't happen.' 'Really,' Melissa yawned.

Beard reckoned it was time to move to the safer ground of rehashing large chunks of climate-change data and inventing an unlikely intellectual disagreement. 'I don't think the serious climate-change sceptics are fighting over feminism and postmodern relativism,' Melissa said. 'By the way, I'm pregnant.'

2009 Beard had put on another 90lb and his belly was as over-extended as the metaphor. Worse still, the plot was falling to pieces. One of his American lovers, Darlene, had rung Melissa to say they were getting married, and Tarpin had been let out of jail.

'I took the rap for Patrice,' Tarpin said. 'I know she killed Aldous because he was beating her up.' Beard looked quizzically at McEwan. 'I'm sorry,' Ian said. 'I'm OK on the climate-change stuff, but I don't really understand human psychology or comedy. Do you mind if Tarpin smashes up all your solar panels?'

'We've had enough,' said the New Mexicans. 'We don't mind you being sued for stealing Aldous's ideas, it's just we think David Lodge does this kind of story so much better.'

'Oh dear,' Beard said. 'Maybe I should go back to climate change. Perhaps nuclear power is the answer. Or how about a bit of pathos with my daughter?' 'Enough trees have died for this already,' Melissa sighed.

Digested read, digested: Solar Power: No Thanks.

So Much For That
by Lionel Shriver (2010)

Shepherd Knacker, Net Portfolio Value: $731,778. Today was the day, Shep had decided. The day 'The Afterlife' would begin. He had three one-way tickets to Pemba in the Indian Ocean and his wife, Glynis, and son, Zach, could come or not. All his life he had been a salt-of-the-earth Man of the Manual, doing his best for his family, sweating 25 hours a day, selling his business at the wrong moment in 1996 and having to go back to work for the new boss as a toilet attendant, but now it was Me time.

'Tough shit,' Glynis snapped. 'I've got terminal cancer and we need your health insurance.'

Jackson wiped his 17-year-old daughter's anus. Flicka had, of course, been born with a rare disability that meant she would die soon. 'I hate my life,' she spat. 'Why did I have to end up in a Lionel Shriver book, where everything is always shit?' 'At least you are going to croak soon,' said her sister, Heather. 'I'm fat and ugly and there's no way out.' Jackson looked up. As usual his wife, Carol, was not paying any attention. Still, at least his friend Shep had arrived.

'Thank God, I've got health insurance,' Shep said. 'That's what you think,' Jackson laughed. 'Most company schemes are rubbish and hardly pay any of the bills. Shall I go into a long polemic about Medicare?' 'Oh shit,' Shep cried. 'It was bad enough before it turned into a John Grisham saga.' 'Well, don't expect anything that well written or pacey,' Jackson said. 'Sod this,' said Flicka. 'Now I really do want to die.'

Shepherd Knacker, Net Portfolio Value: $721,778. 'There are two sorts of mesothelioma,' Dr Goodman said. 'And Glynis has the worst.' 'Obviously,' Shep answered. 'It's going to cost you $721,778 over and above your healthcare to keep her alive for a bit.' 'That's typical of the way the US rips off honest people . . .' Jackson droned for the 17th time. 'Yes, yes,' Glynis interrupted. 'Mesothelioma is caused by asbestos so you've probably killed me, Shep.'

'Enough of you,' shouted Beryl, Shep's sister. 'I need to sponge money off you and you need to look after dad because he's broken his leg. I know you'll do it because you're such a pussy. I mean so nice.' 'Jesus,' Shep moaned. 'Not even a third-rate character would come up with that plotline.' 'Too bad I'm fourth-rate then,' Beryl snapped.

'You ain't seen nothing yet,' Jackson muttered to himself, while fiddling with his apology for a penis. He had always known Carol wanted him to be better hung, so had undergone secret extension surgery – which, predictably, went wrong – leaving him with a lumpy tuber.

Shepherd Knacker, Net Portfolio Value: $000,000. 'Don't expect me to be nice just because I'm dying,' Glynis sneered. 'Why would we?' everyone sighed. It was time for the final meeting with the doctor. 'How much extra time did spending my entire savings buy Glynis?' Shep inquired. 'A good 400 pages,' Dr Goldman replied. 'They weren't good pages,' said Glynis.

Jackson showed Carol his new, deformed penis. 'I'm not going anywhere near that,' she shrieked. 'Nor am I!' screamed the prostitute he showed it to later. 'Fuck the lot of you,' Jackson wept, putting a shotgun in his mouth and pulling the trigger. 'It's sooo unfair,' Flicka said. 'How come Dad gets to kill himself and I don't?'

Shepherd Knacker, Net Portfolio Value: $800,000. 'Don't worry,' Shep said. 'None of you seem to miss him much, and I've had some luck. It turns out I didn't kill Glynis, so she's just lied to a tribunal and got an $800,000 payout from an asbestos manufacturer who didn't kill her either. So I'm going to take Glynis, Zach – we can forget about my daughter Amelia, because everyone else has – and my dad to Pemba. And you, Carol and your ugly sister can come with us.'

Six months had passed. Glynis, Flicka and his dad were rotting together six feet under the African soil, when Carol came into Shep's room. 'I bet you've got a huge penis.'

Digested read, digested: We Don't Need to Talk About Lionel.

Imperial Bedrooms
by Bret Easton Ellis (2010)

The movie was based on a book written by someone we knew. It was labelled fiction but most of it – the snuff movie, the gang rape – was true. The only bits that hurt were those that chronicled my relationship with Blair as the writer was in love with her himself, though too immersed in the passivity of writing and too pleased with his own style to bother with many commas to admit it so he wrote me into the story as the man who was too frightened to love. Make of that what you will, though the real message I want you to take is that I'm a smartass seller of banal meta-fictions.

I went to the premiere in 1987 with Blair, Rip, Julian and all the other empty narcissists who had somehow dazzled the literary establishment. The movie had been a pile of shit. Bret had hated the movie too and what follows is, I guess, his revenge. Shame he involved you in it because the real Julian didn't die in the movie, he died on the page more than 20 years later.

The jeep had been following us back from LAX to my apartment in Doheny Plaza. It's meant to be haunted by a boy who killed himself but you can probably do without that kind of banal symbolism. We're in LA everyone is shallow and on the make. Wow what insight. I nearly do some coke drink a lot of vodka take Ambien put on the Eurythmics and answer my iPhone. Julian wants to meet.

I'm back in LA to help cast *The Listeners* for which I've written the screenplay. I still think I'm being followed as I drive out to Blair's Beverly Hills mansion but I'm too detached to care so I just drink five bottles of vodka and think about Amanda whom I flirted with in New York.

'You're looking very thin, Clay. I guess it didn't work out with Meghan,' Blair says. I've no intention of ever explaining anything so I shrug in a cool sort of way and hope the critics will love the empty unreliability of my narration.

'Are you trying to fuck me?' I ask.

I meet Julian. We don't really talk so I go back to my apartment on Doheney Plaza. I'm still being followed and I drink 20 bottles of tequila do some coke and go off to the casting where a third-rate actress is auditioning. Later that evening I meet Rip at a restaurant. He looks like he's had too much surgery, then as he points out, this book hasn't had nearly enough. The third rate actress is behind the bar. Her name is Rain. 'If you come back to my place you might get the part,' I say.

We start drinking gallons of vodka and I bully her into having constant sex and she wants to know when she's going to get the part. I look moody and hit her. Messages appear on my iPhone. I'm watching you. Certainly no one's reading me. I get another call on my iPhone. Kelly Montrose has been tortured and killed. I yawn. I'd seen it on the YouTube app on my iPhone.

Someone is still following me as I have more meaningless sex. Rain says she's got to go to San Diego to see her mom. I don't believe her so I rape her but she goes anyway. Rip calls. Or is it Blair I've lost track. Rain is still going out with Julian and Julian runs a vice-network and Rain is one of his girls and she also used to go out with Kelly and Rip. Rip tells me to stay away from her but I've fallen in love in four days even though I've shown no sign of it.

So what else can I tell you? I could say that I drove Julian to be killed by Rip who had killed Kelly that Amanda lived with Rain that Rain didn't get the part that I sodomised a boy and a girl and that it was Blair who had been following me and gave me an alibi. But I guess you don't really care any more and frankly I don't blame you. If I don't give a shit about anything why should you?

'Don't worry about anything,' Blair says. 'I won't,' says Bret. 'I've come to realise I don't like anyone. Especially my readers.'

Digested read, digested: Still Less Than Zero.

Freedom by Jonathan Franzen (2010)

Patty and Walter Berglund were the middle-class pioneers of Minnesota – Patty making the cakes, Walter driving the Volvo 240 – and the very image of perfection. Yet their neighbours had always thought there had been something not quite right about them. They had two children, but we can forget about Jessica right now and concentrate on Joey, the apple of Patty's eye. Joey was 11 when he started fucking Connie. Neither Patty nor Walter were best pleased, especially when Joey moved in with Connie, and by the time the Berglunds moved to Washington it was a surprise Walter and Patty hadn't separated.

Autobiography of Patty, composed at her therapist's suggestion: Patty was unsure why she had started writing about herself in the third person, though she was woman enough to trust that the Great American Novelist knew what he was doing and she supposed it allowed him to maintain a cool, semi-detached style that would make the odd bombshell he dropped seem more remarkable for the ordinariness of its surroundings. Patty had been raped when she was 15, so she was understandably messed up when she went to college. There she spent a great deal of time with Eliza, a girl even more messed up than her.

'I shan't be offended if you forget me,' said Eliza. 'Part of the deal of the GAN is that there are too many distracting minor characters.' So the autobiographer, as Patty described herself to differentiate herself from the biographer who was more obviously pulling the strings, let Eliza go, and concentrated on trying to get the charismatic Richard Katz, who played in a band, to go to bed with her. It was inevitable she ended up with his dull roommate Walter. It was equally inevitable that after 20 years of marriage and repressed lust, she and Richard should eventually fuck. 'We can pretend we did it while we were asleep,' she said. The autobiographer resisted the desire to point out that the biographer must also have been half-asleep at this point, so dutifully displayed signs of traumatised guilt.

2004. Joey had a great deal on his mind. He was struggling to believe Connie – a woman so passive she had locked herself in a cupboard at his request for five years – was a three-dimensional character, and only a session of anal sex half-convinced him otherwise. 'Is this part of the GAN deal?' she had asked. 'No' he had replied. 'It's just this year's must-have transgression in serious fiction.' Oh, and by the way, they had got married. But what was really bothering Joey was his obsession with Jenna, the sister of his roommate Jonathan, and the side-plot which saw him joining a Republican thinktank and procuring arms for the US military in New York.

That was an improvement on Walter's situation. It was bad enough he hadn't had sex for years and his marriage to Patty was falling apart, but now he too was locked into an absurd subplot that forced him to work on a scheme to exploit all the coal from the Virginian mountains in order to create a habitat for the cerulean warbler when it was mined out. He knew the GAN needed big themes, but this was too much. Still, at least the biographer had given him a twentysomething Indian assistant, Lalitha, who had fallen in love with him.

Richard was now a famous rock star and so desperate to sleep with Patty again he left her autobiography out for Walter. 'Oh dear,' said Patty. 'We've got to have the big GAN conversation about how I always thought you needed me more than I need you and now I see it's the other way round.' 'Get this straight,' Walter replied. 'It's not the GAN, it's the G-Middle-AN. There's no real diversity here. Now get out.' So Patty left to go and live with Richard for a while, before that fizzled out and Walter started sleeping with Lalitha, until she was killed in a car accident.

The biographer might have convincingly left it at that, but the GMAN demands a more forgiving, less realistic ending. So Patty and Walter got back together and stayed friends with Richard, Joey stopped being a Republican, Connie was miraculously transformed from being a doormat and they too lived happily ever after and were reconciled with his parents. And even Jessica was allowed back into the book.

Digested read, digested: Couples 2010.

The Stranger's Child
by Alan Hollinghurst (2011)

George Sawle gathered his breath. It was the first time he had brought Cecil Valance home and he was keen to distance himself from his family's petit-bourgeois gaucheness.

'You must be Cecil!' shouted Daphne, George's 16-year-old sister. 'George is so excited to have met someone so aristocratically bohemian as you at Cambridge. Please read me some poetry about Corley, my country estate.'

'Come, now,' said Freda, George's mother. 'We must let our guest change into his pressed silk undergarments.'

'Don't worry, Mrs Sawle,' Cecil replied. 'I'm happy to read some of my own verse after dinner. But first George and I should go for a stroll to ponder the imminent war with Germany.'

'Few people ever enter this area of the woods,' said George.

'Then let me take you the Oxford way,' Cecil smiled, stripping naked.

'I thought you would never ask.'

'Your poetry was wonderful,' Daphne said.

'You're very beautiful,' Cecil gasped, forcing his tongue into her mouth.

'No, no! That's not nice!' Though in a way she felt it was.

The Sawles felt a sense of deflation in their humdrum lives after Cecil's departure. 'Oh look,' said Daphne. 'Cecil's left me a poem: 'I've written a poem / That's not very good / Though after I've died / It will give everyone wood.'

* * *

'Come on,' said Lady Valance to her children, Corinna and Wilfie. 'We must prepare for the great weekend when Sebby

Stokes comes to Corley to talk to us all for his biography of Cecil. But we must not keep Sebby too long as he has to deal with the General Strike.'

As the guests arrived, Daphne felt a sense of dread. It had felt normal in 1917 to marry Cecil's brother, Dudley, after Cecil had been shot on the Somme, but she was now embarrassed by the attention she received as the person for whom the greatest ever war poem had been written. And Dudley had turned into such a brute, and was almost certainly having an affair with Eva.

George looked sadly at Cecil's tomb, remembering the length and strength of Cecil's membrum virile. 'Ah there you are,' said his dreary wife.

'I want to make love to you,' said Eva to Daphne.

'Good lord, you're a lesbian, after all. I'm very flattered, but I shall have to decline as I'm hoping to elope with Revel, who I suspect may be a queer, but I'm hoping to turn him.'

'I wonder what Sebby will put in Cecil's biography,' Dudley sneered brutishly. 'I bet it's not as funny as my book about him.'

Daphne reflected on how the war had changed everything. It didn't matter if Cecil had been a good or bad poet, Sebby would laud him anyway. After all, he'd almost certainly fucked him as well.

* * *

Paul Bryant looked at a colleague in the toilet. Once the Sexual Offences Act was passed, he'd be able to do what he liked with him.

'I need some help in the garden,' said Mr Keeping. Paul thought this was an unusual way for a bank manager to deploy his staff, but demurred.

'I'm Corinna,' said Mr Keeping's wife. 'Why don't you come to my mother Daphne's 70th birthday party?'

Paul was transfixed as Corinna and Peter Rowe played a duet. 'I love Cecil Valance's poetry,' said Paul.

'Well, it just so happens that I teach at Corley, which is now a boy's boarding school,' said Peter, 'so if you'd like to visit, we could bugger one another behind Cecil's statue.'

'Did you know that I went on to marry Revel before marrying someone else, leaving an impossibly complicated family tree that I don't expect you to follow?' said Daphne.

'That's just as well,' said everyone.

* * *

'Did you hear about Corinna and Mr Keeping?' said Paul. 'Terrible news.'

'I can't say that I had,' Peter replied. 'And neither will anyone else, because that's the nature of other people's lives. You seldom find out everything.'

'The trouble is that now we're in the 1980s, the reader has realised we're not nearly as interesting as the characters in the first half of the book. Still, I'd better press on with my biography of Cecil. My hunch is Corinna might have been Cecil's child, even though that would mean she had a 14-month pregnancy.'

'Cecil would fuck anything,' said George, 'though you'd better not trust me, as I've got Alzheimer's.'

* * *

Rob was looking for someone to cruise at Peter's funeral. 'Isn't that Paul Bryant, the famous writer over there?' he said to a stranger. 'Didn't he make his name writing a biography of Cecil Valance, the crap poet?'

'Yes. Though I've heard Paul tells lies about himself, too.'

Digested read, digested: Cecil Gay Lewis.

The Sense of an Ending
by Julian Barnes (2011)

There were three of us and Adrian now made the fourth. I would
tell you the names of the other two, but they are of little consequence. Besides which, my memory is most unreliable and so it is
possible I have not even remembered their names correctly and it
would be a shame to burden you with even more potentially
inaccurate information.

Suffice to say we were all rather smug public schoolboys,
though Adrian's sense of entitlement was perhaps the greatest,
given as he was to making remarks such as: 'History is that certainty
produced at the point where the imperfections of memory meet
the inadequacies of documentation.' The only challenge to our
self-satisfaction occurred when a boy named Robson committed
suicide after getting a girl pregnant, but fortunately it wasn't long
before Adrian was able to put us right. 'Eros and Thanatos,' he
said. 'Camus believed suicide was the only true philosophical
question.' Or maybe he didn't say that at all.

Who knows?

Adrian naturally went on to Cambridge while I continued my
less than average life at Bristol. There I met Veronica Ford, who
was to become my first girlfriend. Though when I say girlfriend, I
don't mean that in quite the sense you may think, as though this
was the 60s. The 60s didn't really happen until the 70s for me. If
then. I'm still not too sure. But Veronica and I kissed now and
again, and she once invited me to her home in Chislehurst for the
weekend. It wasn't a great success. Her father and brother were
stand-offish, Veronica appeared ashamed of me and only her
mother was in the least bit pleasant. Though I didn't understand

what she meant when she said: 'Don't let Veronica get away with too much.' But then, she might not have said it anyway.

I could go on, but as I can sense you might quickly tire of the flatness of my prose, the absence of any emotion and the repetition of the unreliability trope, I propose to keep this short. I did eventually sleep with Veronica, after we had split up, but it wasn't very satisfactory for me so I split up with her again. In any case she had shown rather too much much interest in Adrian on the one occasion they had met. At least that's how it all seemed, though I can't really have cared too much as I went travelling to America after I left Bristol. I came home to discover Adrian had committed suicide. My sense of grief was overshadowed by one of awe for his wholehearted embrace of Camus.

There's not much to say about the next 40 years. I got a job, got married to Margaret, had a child and then got divorced after my wife left me. I'm surprised you haven't left me as well. Though maybe you have and I just don't remember. I was living on my own when a letter arrived informing me I had been left £500 and Adrian's diary in Veronica's mother's will. The money duly arrived, but the solicitor informed me there was a problem with the diary.

I called Margaret to ask for her help. 'Do you think I loved Veronica?' I said. It might seem a strange question; stranger still that I chose to ask it of my ex-wife. But the one thing I have never forgotten is that I am almost catatonically disconnected. 'You're on your own now,' Margaret replied. Which was also odd, as I was under the impression I already was.

It fell to me to contact Veronica by email. Veronica's behaviour was even stranger than my own, arranging to meet me and then leaving me without saying a word and then taking me for a drive past a group of care in the community people, also without explaining why. And as I am a doormat, it didn't occur to me to ask. Not that I can remember anyway. It also turned out I had sent a rather bitchy letter to Adrian when I realised he and Veronica were attracted to one another, and that Veronica had burned his diary, apart from one page. From this I guessed that one of the handicapped adults must have been Adrian and Veronica's child.

Even a novella requires an ending, so I suppose I had better cut to the chase. With an improbable piece of deduction based on an equation Adrian had written, I realised the handicapped person must have been Adrian and Veronica's mother's child. So Adrian's suicide wasn't so heroic. Or was it? After all, why should I be any more reliable now than I was at the beginning?

Digested read, digested: The Sense of Familiarity.

The Marriage Plot
by Jeffrey Eugenides (2011)

Let us start with Madeleine's books. Jane Austen, George Eliot and Edith Wharton. Yes, she is an incurable romantic, but there was nothing romantic about her on this, her graduation day, from Brown University. She was dishevelled from the night before; her dress had an awkward stain and she was trying to avoid her parents' disapprobation by spending time with her friend, Mitchell.

'I still don't fancy you, but I thought you should know that me and Leonard just split up,' she said. 'Why am I supposed to care?' Mitchell replied, a question readers would soon be asking themselves.

So how did Madeleine's love life get to this point? In her first year at Brown in 1979, she had had many admirers, but had remained faithful to her fictional male leading characters, but at some point during the semiotics option she had been persuaded that everything was text and that since she herself was a character in a novel there was no real need to differentiate between Mr Darcy and any of the other students. There followed 50 pages of Barthesian banter and an equally masturbatory relationship with a boy named Billy, which ended when the mirror being held up to the reader broke. For a while thereafter, Madeleine sought comfort in Mitchell, a religious studies student, and might even once have allowed him to have sex with her, had he not been so frozen by her beauty. As it was, the moment passed and she began an affair with Leonard, a dazzlingly semi-detached science undergraduate.

'I love you,' she said, as he came inside her.

'Barthes says that once the first avowal has been made, 'I love you' has no meaning,' Leonard replied. Rather than recognising that Leonard was a bit of a tosser, Madeleine fell even deeper in love with Leonard, as she had read that Barthes had also said that love is extreme solitude. So their relationship continued until he stopped going to seminars three months before graduation. Madeleine chose to deconstruct his absence as him having dumped her and so it was that she had allowed another student to come on her dress.

'We must hurry, or we'll be late for graduation,' said Mitchell.

'Haven't you heard?' said her room mate. 'Leonard has been in a mental hospital for the past three months.'

'Marry me, Madeleine,' Leonard begged, as she entered the psych ward.

Any number of thoughts might have entered the reader's mind at this point. How did Madeleine fail to realise Leonard was bonkers from the start? Why did she not bother to find out

Leonard was in hospital earlier? And was this the dullest love triangle in literature? But we cannot allow ourselves to enter the realms of sub-text or meta-text; instead we must stay with text and pursue our characters through to the bitter end.

Mitchell was alone in a Parisian hotel, pining for Madeleine, whom he had kissed just before he left New York. How had he got there? Well, he'd set off to Europe, armed with loads of books on which he would frequently discourse at length with his friend Larry, who had come to see his feminist girlfriend but turned out to be gay. Meanwhile, Leonard was trying to lose weight. How had he got to that point? Well, he'd become distrustful of the lithium and the steroids he had been prescribed and had been trying to wean himself off the drugs, both so that he could get a decent erection and to clear his mind for his research.

Madeleine wondered why she had married Leonard. A not unreasonable question, one might have thought, were it not that the narrative was going to take yet another backward leap to again fail to explain why. Like Leonard and Mitchell, she was stuck in a fictive trope and condemned to be a stylistic, one-dimensional irritation.

Mitchell too was in despair; not so much because he had been unable to persuade Madeleine to leave Leonard, but because he knew he was getting on everyone's nerves by going on for 70 pages about his religious enlightenment and Mother Teresa, yet was powerless to do anything about it because he didn't really exist. He might have felt a little better if he had known Leonard was also feeling the same way. How he longed to say he wasn't just a cocktail of drugs and bipolar symptoms and that being depressed didn't mean he had to be so depressing.

Finally, Leonard cracked. 'I'm divorcing you, Madeleine,' he said.

'I guess this is the moment in romantic fiction when you decide you're in love with the good guy,' said Mitchell. 'But this is a postmodern romantic novel, so I'm going to leave you to be happy by yourself.'

'At last,' said everyone.

Digested read, digested: The Marriage Plod.

Bring Up the Bodies
by Hilary Mantel (2012)

'It is a great honour to receive you here at Wolf Hall, your majesty,' says old Sir John Seymour, fresh from tupping his daughter-in-law's quinny. 'Though I had rather been expecting you some three years ago, when the first book came out.'

Thomas Cromwell observes Henry's eyes lingering on Jane Seymour's heaving, virginal bosom. 'The King is tiring of Anne and there is no male successor,' he thinks to himself. 'A wise Master Secretary would do well to prepare the way for a third marriage –'

'A wiser Master Secretary would do better to ruminate for a while on the death of his wife and daughters, and conduct imaginary conversations with Sir Thomas More in which he expresses regret that the former Lord Chancellor refused to swear the oath of succession and thus condemned himself to the block,' Hilary interrupts urgently.

'And why should I want to do that?' Cromwell snaps, his mind already on how much money he can make from the dissolution of the monasteries.

'Because I'm trying to rewrite you as Mr Nice Guy, you moron,' Hilary says. 'Instead of the hard bastard you undoubtedly are.'

'Come, Crumb,' yells Henry. 'I need my finest pair of ears to return to court with me.'

'Gosh, sire, you are much too kind. I just pootle around trying to do silly old me's inadequate best,' Cromwell replies. He finds maintaining this self-effacing Stephen Fry shtick annoying, though he has to admit it does make his opponents underestimate him. And Hilary keeps assuring him that the readers love it. 'But first I must retire to my house in Stepney. This present-tense narrative is making me breathless.'

His spies tell Thomas that Catherine is dying. The news is not unexpected but it is timely, for the Emperor will surely not contemplate making war with Britain once the former Queen is dead. 'Send my condolences,' he says. 'I shall miss her.'

'You could at least sound as if you mean it,' Hilary whispers.

'Would it help if I were to lament the loss of my wife and daughters again?'

'You learn fast,' she replies.

'Ah, there you are, Cremuel!'

Thomas looks up, trying to disguise his irritation. The Queen has addressed him thus ever since the King bought her the Pink Panther box set and he doesn't find it funny. 'Gosh, yes, your majesty. Pray tell me what silly old hopeless me can do to help you.'

'I require an audience with the King.'

He nods, though he has no intention of securing one. Since her latest miscarriage, her days as Queen are numbered. And not a moment too soon, though obviously he balances this thought with regret at how much he misses his own wife.

'Tell me, Master Smeaton,' Thomas asks of one of the Queen's courtiers.

'Did you make love to the Queen?'

'Oh yes,' squeals Smeaton.

'And you're not just saying that because I've put you in the Tower near the torture chamber?'

'Oh no, my Lord! Her Majesty is a right goer. She's shagged absolutely everyone, including her brother.'

The Master Secretary sighs. He does not want to see so many go to the block when his wife's death's on his mind, but if they will confess of their own free will, what can he do? He walks purposefully towards the King's bedchamber and tells him: 'The Queen's head has unfortunately become detached from her body. Your marriage is annulled and you are free to marry Jane.'

'I knew I could rely on you, Crumb,' Henry laughs.

Thomas retires to Stepney to count his royalties with Hilary. 'Please take your time over the last volume,' he begs her. 'I'd like some time to enjoy my wealth before I, too, get the chop.'

Digested read, digested: Bring Up the Booker.

Lionel Asbo
by Martin Amis (2012)

2006: Dear Jennaveieve, I'm havin'g an affair with my Gran. The sex is grea't but Im worried that my uncle Lionel will thin'k there is somefing wron'g wiv me shaggin'g hi's Mum. I dont know why cos shes only 39 as she ha'd her fir'st child when she was 12 and me own Mum had me at 12 so I is actua'lly startin'g well late as I am 15. Your's Desmond Pepperdine.

Des was less sure if he would send this letter to the Morning Lark's Page 3 Stunna Agony Aunt than he was about whether he needed help from Mart with his apostrophes. 'The thing is,' said Mart, 'I know – or care – nothing for the lower orders, so my attitude towards you is a mixture of contempt and patrician sentimentality. But I've always said that punctuation is the key to social mobility.' Des looked up guiltily as Uncle Lionel entered the room. 'I've just changed me fuckin name to Lionel Asbo,' he snarled, 'to celebrate the fact I was the youngest kid to get an Asbo at the age of three. Now wheres they fucking pitbulls? I need them to rip out the throat of your nonce friend Rory who's been taking liberties by knockin off me Mum.'

2008: Nothing had happened to the literati of west London in the intervening years, but in Diston where Lionel and Des lived, the mayhem that invariably accompanies the criminal underclasses had proceeded with gratifying regularity. Rory had gone awol, Lionel had discovered his bird Gina was getting one from his best mate Marlon and had gone berserk at their wedding, and half the residents of Diston had ended up in Wormwood Scrubs in the ensuing fracas.

'I have to inform you, Asbo,' the governor said, 'that you have just won £140,000,000 on the lottery.'

'Fuck me,' Lionel replied, 'I suppose that means Mart is going to make me owt ter be even more of a caricature of a chav van before.'

'Well that just shows what a moronic oik you are,' Mart drawled, 'because you have no concept of Swiftian satire.'

Des had long since absorbed Mart's tips on punctuation and had gone to university, so he was in a position to wonder if it was Mart who had no concept of Swiftian satire, but he kept that thought to himself as he now had a respectable girlfriend and was still worried Lionel might discover he had once shagged his Gran.

2010: 'Your Gran's so fuckin old now she's got demencha,' said Lionel. 'I've packed her off to a care home.' Des knew that even in Diston the average life expectancy was more than 43, but he had a job working for the Daily Mirror and Dawnie was pregnant, so he had other things to think about other than being patronised by Mart. 'You're a fuckin' disappointin' nonce to me, Des,' Lionel continued, 'but you're me flesh'n'blood so I'll give you a fiver.' If he hadn't shaved his head he'd have pulled his hair out at the things he was doing for Mart. Buying a mansion, calling it Wormwood Scrubs, goin out with Threnody the silicon-titted glamour model, making Marlon watch him fuck Gina ... It was like Mart had only just discovered reality TV.

2012: Des loved his baby, really loved her. Everything was going to be different now. Gran was dead, his secret was safe and he could escape his past ... 'I know you shagged your Gran,' said Lionel.

2013: Lionel hadn't topped him, the baby was safe from the pitbulls and his uncle was back inside: Des would settle for this feeble affectation of parental poignancy if it got Mart off his back. 'Tell you the troof,' said Mart from the comfort of his Brooklyn brownstone, 'Lionel is happier inside. That's the state of England for you.'

Digested read, digested: Martin Asbeen.

Umbrella by Will Self (2012)

I'm an ape man, I'm an ape-ape man ... Along comes Zachary, in the cold Friern Barnet morning Busner ... keep up, keep up, you've met him before and if you haven't then you've no place at the high table of Modernism ... heard the echoes of Rihanna as the bus passed a young man, clearly hebephrenic. The faecal smell hung heavy as Busner commenced his ward rounds with Mboya, the schizoids, the depressives, the manic depressives ... hadn't his diagnoses always been whims of his own psychiatric state? Or not his, he reflected, for was he not merely a fictive trope of a supreme narcissist, the self-proclaimed saviour of the novel, a creation to which Stephen Dedalus and Mrs Dalloway could only aspire?

The enkies ... they shouldn't be dosed with chlorpromazine or largactil ... – , –, , –, – , he wasn't sure what the dashes were for but they looked good on the page and no reviewers would admit they hadn't a clue either ... Ah there's his favourite, old Miss Audrey Dearth, all vermiculated quoins and oculogyric crisis ... Ordree, Ordree, she remembered her father shouting at her as they took the tram to Parsons Green ... Brarms Intermetzo if only it 'ad been Rihanna ven everyfink might have been OK ... She 'ad left er umbrella back at the munitions factory, she was sure she 'ad ... Ding-a ding-a-ding dong, Old Mother Hubbard ... Had it been necessary to lapse into the colloquial? ... I am the walrus, coo-coo-ca-choo, isn't that what Mrs Pankhurst had said? ... Her brother Stanley living like a troglodyte somewhere under the Messines Ridge and her other brother Albert ... changed his name from Death to De'ath, 'e wuz dead to 'er ... the puffed-up popinjay.

He had left Miriam like he had left them all, as if they were discarded umbrellas ... when did an umbrella become something to be forgotten rather than remembered? Who was it? Bernard Levin? No, Oliver Sacks ... The man who mistook his novel for an umbrella ... Awakenings ... He hadn't really believed the L-DOPA was going to work, had he? ... The hospital had complained about the cost, but the enkies had briefly come back to life. P-p-pop, d'doo-doo the engorged Looby Loos filled with two grammes of eldoughpa ... A Mars a day helps you work rest and play ... the tank to break the attrition of the spontaneous jactitations. I am-I am-I am, one equals one equals one equals one. A shprat had shpat on the shutter, Kensitas, Capstan, Peter Stuyvesant. What did you expect, Jew boy? Weren't all psychiatrists in and of themselves mental pathologies, an umbrella metaphor for war, with Miss Dearth just another of his casualties.

It's Death. It's not that uncommon. Ordree? Ordree? Are you here? … WOULD SOME CAPITAL LETTERS HELP? Probably not, especially if they were italicised. How about some more dashes then? −. −. −. −. −. It had been the blanks that had been to blame, the dud shells that Albert's factory had made that had flashed like flechettes into the Hun trenches flopping like Feydeau's manatee, if Feydeau had had a manatee. Had they exploded then Stanley might still be alive, though he might be losing his hair.

The young girl stared at him pityingly. I used to work here when it was a psychiatric hospital. A lot of patients say that. No, I did work here … the omniscient God separated from the world by Plexiglass, Tidddly-iddl-ighty. Of course you did and I expect you left your umbrella heren'all. Come and have a look at the new flats. Sir Albert … Palaeolithic Mekon … hadn't wanted to know his sister was still alive. I told you he wouldn't, and now she wasn't. Returned to oculogyric crisis. Nothing, stasis … Nothing will come of nothing … The tiger's free, the kangaroo, I'm an ape man … War, psychiatry, a nihilistic, autodidactic mess of rotting corpses … He'd said that already, but sometimes it bore repeating just to defray the onanism. You'll never guess what, Guv? I 'ad that Rihanna in the back of me cab. Left 'er umbrella.

Digested read, digested: Psy-Fi.

NW by Zadie Smith (2012)

Four gardens. North London estate. Redheaded. I am the sole author of the dictionary that defines me.

I am the sole
I am the
Deep. Doorbell! She pushes her way in.

– It's Shar. Remember me? Gimmethirty quid for me bredren.

Leah thinks she does remember her. Back from Brayton days in Willesden. She knows it's probs a scam but she gives her the money. It's what sistas do, innit?

Michel gives her hell.

– You're Irish, not a sista. She ripped you off.

No matter. Paperworkpaperworkpaperwork. Looks pretty on the page, is it? Almost as if it meant something.

Maybe she could

get away with writing a

whole

sentence that

looked

a

bit

like a tree.

There had been an attraction between Michel – Meshell – and Leah from the start. Anal before vaginal. Now they lived together. Near but not on the estate. There was a difference. Big difference. A long way apart.

– We're going to dinner at Natalie and Frank's tonight.

– Does that mean we're going to have to talk a lot about multi-culturalism and neo-modernism?

– 'Fraid so. But as long as you remember to name-drop Kierkegaard and Barthes you'll be fine.

Leah does this and then she does that and sometimes she thinks this and sometimes she thinks that but what she really knows is that she is on Zadie's home patch so she'd better go along with any old bollocks – shame about the dog dying – and let's just hope that Michel doesn't notice she's still taking the pill.

Felix dropped in on his old man, Lloyd.

'Wassup, blud. You long, or what, is it?'

'Your father is asking how you are and why you are late,' said Lloyd's neighbour Tom, who had lived on the estate since the 1970s and whose sole purpose was to supply simultaneous translation.

Felix barely noticed his section had proper quotation marks as he was on his way to Soho to meet Grace, his trustafarian junkie ex.

'Do you want some coke, babes?' she asked.

'I don do dat stuff nah more. I'm inta films n' shit more.'

'Then just go down on me as I'm having my period.'

Felix didn't quite know why he had done that. Out of his comfort zone. Far too Islington. Or Queens. If he knew where New York was. Back to Willesden. Home. Carnival. Whoops. Ironic that Nathan mugged and killed him when he wasn't loaded or nuffink.

1. Keisha and Leah had been friends on the estate. 2. Then they weren't. 3. Then they were again. 4. Keisha didn't know why she had to have everything listed in numbers. 5. On reflection, perhaps she did. 6. Sometimestimegoesveryfast. 7. S ome tim esitgo esver yslowly. 8. IS IT TIME FOR SOME CAPITALS? 9. What would James Joyce think about a black girl becoming middle-class? 10. Leah gave Keisha a vibrator and then Keisha went out with Rodney who was a nice boy. 11. Not a baaad boy. 12. Keisha changed her name to Natalie when she became a lawyer and married Frank and had

two kids. 13. People were unseen. 14. People were not people but merely an effect of language. 15. Some people do come up with some real crap. 16. Natalie couldn't cope with messing with her roots and smoked spliff and shagged a load of rude boys. 17. Frank was bare pissed.

Natalie went off to Archway with Nathan to top herself.

–You doan wann be doin tha sista.

Later, Leah and Natalie were talking.

–I'm not going to apologise for my choices, said Natalie, unaware that no one was asking her to.

–You know what? If it was Nathan that topped Felix, we ought to grass him up.

Digested read, digested: NO.

Back to Blood
by Tom Wolfe (2013)

Smack. Thadaboom. SMACK. Thahadaboom. The Safe Boat thadathunksitsfoam-filledfuckeryacrossMiami–MEEE-AH-MEE – bay. 'Dere's a fuckin' Wetfoot at da top a dat fuckin' mast a dat boat,' yelled Sergeant Kite. Officer Nestor Camacho rolled up his sleeves. His biceps were ripped. Taut. :::: What the fuck was he doing thinking like this inside this crazy, mashed-up punctuation? :::: Tappetytaptappetytaptaptap. KER-CHING! Tom couldn't believe his luck. $10,000 per page to write on steroids. :::: Like taking candy from babies. That's America, baby ::::

'¡Madre de Dios!' yelled Nestor's father. 'You're no national hero. You traidor. You betray your blood. The guy was 17 feet from freedom, and you send him back to Fidel?' Nestor reeled backwards out of the room :::: At least I have my Malena. Mia preciosa Magdalena con los grandes bazookas ::::

'Thass wat you think, Nestor,' said Magdalena, adjusting her skirt to make sure her bootycrack – HER BUM-BUM-BUM – made it into this paragraph. 'The thing is, I've just met this new man.' :::: Not quite true. She'd been dating her boss, Norman the porn shrink, for a while now ::::

Slurparlurparlurp, lubberly lubberly pussy. It felt good to be able to write dirty, as Norman's priapic pimped purple car pushed its velvet rims towards the orgy, while his billionaire patient beat on his festering, ulcerous dick for the 14th time that morning. 'Buy yourself some modern art, Maurice,' said Norman, as Magdalena bobbobbobbed on his slithery slipperiness.

'What's wrong with you, Tom?' Maurice screamed. :::: Jesus, my rancid cock aches. Can't you give your obsession with the pointlessness of modern art a break? You've been going on about it for decades, and we all get the point ::::'

'Fuck the lot of you,' Tom stompstomphuffed. 'It's my book. My advance. And I'll do what I want. WHOOP. WHOOP. WHOOOP. And leave that extra O on there, right? So I tell you what happens next. There's going to be a new sub-plot about how Sergei the Russian oligarch donated $70m of forged modern art to the Miiiiiiiiammm-oooow Gallery.'

:::: Zanks fer nuzzink :::: 'So I am anuzzer lazeee stereotype like everywon zelse,' said Sergei. 'WOW WOW WOW a rich RUSHAN with Art' said Magadelena :::: Art who? No KANDINSKY? NO KANDONTSKY! Better get my suckety-sucketysuck hypnopompic lips in gear ::::

Whoosh. Bash. Bish. Kapow. The black police chief had switched Nestor away from the Cubanas to keep him out of trouble, and now he'd only gone and taken down some black beefcake cracking crack king in a headheadheadlock, only his partner had been filmed calling the guy a nigger :::: Dios, I swear I no racist :::: 'I know that. But round here bloodisbloodisblood. You're suspended, Camacho.'

'Whoawhoawhoaza,' screeeeeched Tommmmeeee. 'I ain't finished with the badblood, city-divided shit so I'm gonna bring in Creole Ghislaine who got a brudder in pants down to his knees kinda gang stuff. And you, Nestor, are going to sort it in your UNEEEEK idididiot savant style.'

:::: Yesssiryesssirr :::: STADUNG KAPUNG. The forger was whacked. Sergei busted. LE TOUTTOUTTOUT literary monde laughlaughlaughing at the art world. Magadalena plumped her hypnopompic labioplastic lips :::: Madre. Tom. He could no be so stupido to use a word like hypnopompic twice :::: 'Get away from my white linen suit,' Tomtomtom Tomed. 'The money is mine. And I'll use hypnopompic as often as I like.'

'OKOKOK,' Nestornestornestor nestored. 'So now I'm back in da police, which broad do I get to badaboom?'

Digested read, digested: Back to bollocks.

A Hologram for the King
by Dave Eggers (2012)

Alan Clay arrived in Jeddah, Saudi Arabia. He added the 'Saudi Arabia' because otherwise Americans might not know where he was. He had taken two planes to get there. In Nairobi, Kenya, he had met a woman he would probably have gone to bed with if he had stayed. But he didn't, so he didn't.

He tried to sleep, but he couldn't. Even reading his own

sensitively pared-down sentences didn't help. Put simply, he was a complete failure. He was 54 years old, divorced and broke. He couldn't even afford the tuition fees for his daughter, Kit, who was at college in Boston, USA. He started writing Kit a letter. 'Dear Kit, here is another letter I am unlikely to send.'

This was his last chance. An opportunity to make a six-figure commission selling an IT system to the King Abdullah Economic City in the desert. Luckily, he did not stop to wonder why an American IT giant would have employed a complete idiot to sell its most expensive hardware. So the reader did not have to, either.

It was nine o'clock when Alan eventually woke up. 'Oh dear,' he said to himself. 'I've missed the bus out to KAEC and I am going to be late for the King. That's not very good, is it?' He phoned down to reception for a cab.

'Hello,' said Yousef. 'I'm your driver. Though I'm not really a driver. Tell me a joke.'

'The company I work for is called Reliant.'

'That's not really a joke, Alan. That's yet more irony about America's growing global economic dependency.'

Alan touched the lump on the back of his neck. He was sure it was cancer. Fingers crossed, it was. The heat was oppressive when he arrived at his tent in the desert. 'I'm sorry I'm late,' he said. 'Don't worry,' Karim would have replied if he had bothered to turn up. 'The King isn't coming today. Or any day soon for that matter.'

Alan touched his lump again and thought he was beginning to get the hang of this metaphor.

'Hello,' said a woman called Hanne from Amsterdam, Holland. 'Seeing as you are going to spend the next 100 pages making pointless trips into the desert, why don't you have a drink and have sex with me?'

He fumbled a bit but his cock was as limp as the subtext. 'Never mind,' Hanne said brusquely. 'Let me take you to the doctor to have your lump looked at.'

'It's definitely a benign cyst,' said the sultry Dr Hakem, much to everyone's disappointment. 'But I can take it out for you.'

Alan found himself with a lot of spare time on his hands, even after writing dozens more letters to Kit that he would never send. So when Yousef offered to take him out into the desert to go wolf-shooting, he eagerly accepted, after making a bad joke about being in the CIA. 'That's not funny, either,' said Yousef.

Alan knew he was going to kill the wolf. But he fired at a shepherd boy by mistake. 'Whoops,' he said. 'It's OK,' Yousef said. 'Luckily you missed. You'd better go back to Jeddah.'

'I've taken out your cyst,' Dr Hakem purred. 'Now I want to sleep with you.'

'All right,' Alan said, completely unaware of how improbable it was that every attractive younger woman in the book should find him irresistible.

It was still very hot when he went back out to KAEC a fortnight later. 'I'm glad you've arrived,' said Karim, who had by now bothered to turn up, 'because the King is finally here.'

'Do you think he will like my presentation?'

'Yes, but I wouldn't count on him sleeping with you as well. Or on him buying your system, as he now wants to do business with China.'

'That's symbolism for you, I suppose,' Alan shrugged. He was still 54, broke and a loser. 'Do you think it would be OK for me to stay on out here a while?'

'To be honest, we've all had enough of you.'

Digested read, digested: Alan of Arabia.

The Childhood of Jesus
by JM Coetzee (2013)

They hurry to the border guard. 'We arrived in Novilla yesterday,' says the middle-aged man. 'We need somewhere to live.'

'For you and your son?'

'He is not my son. He is a six-year-old boy who was shipwrecked with me. He has lost his parents and doesn't have a name. But I have called him David.'

'Do you have a name?'

'No. Though you can call me Simon.'

The guard feels like she has already had more than enough of this nonsense, so she waves them through and assigns them to a residence in Building C. 'Enjoy your stay here with your father,' she says to David.

'Why do you insist on calling him my father?' says David. 'Isn't it blindingly obvious from the title that this is a third-rate allegory?'

The following day, Simon goes to start work as a stevedore at the grain wharf. 'Bread is the staff of life,' says Eugenio, the foreman, as several readers throw themselves into the water to drown themselves. 'Before we start work, we must debate important philosophical questions, such as the value of labour and the meaning of Kumbaya.'

'Aren't you straying into my territory?' says Paulo Coelho.

David is playing with El Rey, the carthorse, while Simon is having unsatisfactory sex with a woman named Ana. 'I told you it wasn't a very good idea,' says Ana, wiping away unwanted secretions.

'I am going to find the boy's mother,' says a disappointed Simon. He wanders over to La Residencia where he sees a single woman.

'You are David's mother,' he says.

'I'm not, but then again I might as well be,' says the woman, who is called Ines.

Simon is not remotely concerned that he has picked someone who is obviously mentally unwell, so when she then insists she brings up the boy on her own, Simon does not hesitate to agree. 'He is so clearly the chosen one that we must do everything possible for him.'

Two weeks later, Simon begins to miss David, and asks Ines for visiting rights. 'Only if you don't mind being supervised by my psychopathic brother,' she says.

'Hello David.'

'Hello Not Dad. Have you ever considered the lilies of the valley?'

'Is that the end of the sermon?'

'No chance,' says JM Coetzee, though even he must be wondering how on earth he is getting away with such rubbish.

'Do you think the reason we are in a vaguely socialist country, where nothing is good and nothing is bad, is because we are meant to think we are in an imaginary Cuba?' David asks.

'Let's see if you have a friend called Fidel and a dog called Bolivar,' says Simon.

'Hola,' says Fidel. 'Woof,' says Bolivar.

Simon decides it's time for David to be educated. 'Let's read Don Quixote,' he says.

'Great book,' says David. 'Everything that happens in it must be true.'

'No, it isn't.'

'It is to me.'

For some reason, Simon finds this answer to be a sign of genius.

'I'm hungry,' says David.

'I'm not sure five loaves and two fishes will be enough,' says Simon.

'I think you'll find it will.'

The school called in Simon and Ines to tell them the teachers think David is an annoying halfwit who can't count. 'He's an idiot savant,' Simon insists, before being knocked over by a dockyard crane that may or may not have been Platonic.

'Forget the savant. He needs to go to a special school,' the school says.

'Whoo, scary,' says Ines. 'That school will fail to notice his beauty and purity.'

'It's OK Mummy-not-Mummy. I have escaped from the school through the barbed wire. Observe my stigmata.'

'There is no sodding barbed wire,' says the school.

Still, Simon and Ines persist with the delusion that David is the Messiah and drive him away to the north of the country.

'My invisibility cloak is working,' says David. 'You can't see me.'

'Yes we can, David, you've just burned your eyes on a magnesium flare.'

'Truly, his eyes are undamaged,' says a doctor. 'He is capable of transcendental visions. Shall we end this book now?'

'If you insist,' says Coetzee.

Digested read, digested: No hope of a resurrection.

CHICK LIT

The Clematis Tree
by Ann Widdecombe (2001)

Mark and Claire Wellings were goodish eggs, but despite being comfortably well-off, the strain of looking after their son Jeremy for seven years had taken its toll. Their marriage was an empty loveless shell.

'I've booked a holiday,' said Mark.

'We can't leave Jeremy,' Claire replied defiantly.

Mark knew his marriage was doomed.

Their daughter Pippa picked up a severe dose of gastro-enteritis. 'I hope Jeremy doesn't get it,' Mark muttered to himself. 'It could kill him.'

Jeremy spent the next two weeks in intensive care, hovering between life and death.

'That does for the holiday,' said Mark over supper one evening. 'By the way, did you know your sister Sally is planning to introduce a euthanasia bill into the Commons?' He wondered what the bill might mean for Jeremy, and whether the press would discover his link to Sally.

Mark took himself off on a week's holiday to Estoril. Lying on the beach, he was awoken by some ice-cream dropping on his stomach. He looked up to see a girl with a hideous disfigurement.

'She seems very accepting of her condition,' Mark said later to the girl's mother.

'I've taught her to be serene,' she said. 'I'm a widow, incidentally.'

They had dinner. Mark resisted the temptation of an affair, but still knew his marriage was doomed.

'I'm a shopaholic and I occasionally hit Jeremy,' Claire confessed on his return.

'I'd better talk to the vicar, then,' Mark concluded.

'I'm getting married to Ben,' said Mark's sister Ruth. 'His first wife and two children were all killed in a car crash.'

Work was hotting up at the firm of solicitors where Mark worked. They took on extra staff, including Ginny, a short-skirted Australian secretary. Mark resisted the temptation of an affair, but still knew his marriage was doomed.

Mark and Claire woke to find the press camped out on their doorstep. 'They've found out about Jeremy,' said Claire. Mark invoked the second Person of the Trinity.

As Claire's father, Sam, lay in hospital after a severe stroke, Mark waved Pippa off on her school trip to France. 'Have a safe journey,' he shouted, as the coach departed.

Reports came in of a major accident, with several fatalities, on the M20.

'I'm afraid Pippa was on the coach,' said the headmaster. Mark and Claire waited anxiously for news.

'Actually, she was on the other coach after all,' said the headmaster. 'Pippa's fine.'

Sam died of a heart attack and several months later the brake failed – or did aunt Isabel release it? – and Jeremy's wheelchair rolled into the river. Despite Mark's efforts to revive him, he drowned.

'Could I have done more,' Mark anguished. 'He looked so peaceful. But am I at peace?'

'I want a divorce,' he said firmly.

'You can't,' said Claire. 'I'm pregnant.'

Mark knew then he would stay in his doomed marriage of deepening unhappiness.

Digested read, digested: The Book of Job rewritten for High Church, High Tory matrons from the shires.

I Don't Know How She Does It
by Allison Pearson (2002)

1.37am Why am I up at this time of night distressing the M&S mince pies for Emily's carol concert when I've got to fly to New York first thing? Because I can't trust Rich to do it. And why's he called Rich when he earns less than the nanny? Come to think of it, why am I called Kate Reddy, my boss Rod Task and my email flirtee Jack Abelhammer? Oh, I see, I've got into one of those books where people's names describe their characters in a terribly amusing way.

8.52am Sorry about that, I've got a bit more time to chat now I'm in midair. So what do you need to know? I'm a fund manager with Ernest Morgan Foster; I've got two gorgeous kids, Emily and Ben, whom I feel tremendously guilty about. Ah, that reminds me. There, I've just ticked all the boxes for the Hamley's catalogue. Now where was I? Ah yes, all men are useless. Things to remember: cancel the stress-busting massage.

6.03am Just back from New York. Almost had sex with Jack. Rich tries to bully me into a reunion shag, but I pretend to fall asleep. 'We need to talk,' he says later. 'Don't you realise I've got a very important presentation in 50 minutes?' I reply. Life is so much tougher for women.

10.49am Presentation interrupted by the arrival of my dad. The loser needs some money. 'Will £10K do?' I snap. Why does every mega-woman have a useless father? Why can't I have an easy life earning the same mega-bucks churning out dreary columns or chatting to Tom and Tony?

2.42pm Momo and I won the right to manage the ethical fund. Hooray. Rich has left home. The nanny's gone AWOL. A colleague's wife has died, adding pathos and poignancy to my predicament.

7.10pm My kids fail to recognise me.

7.12am Some porno pics of Momo were found by her doing the rounds at work. Persuade hated male colleague who did this to invest in my dad's project, thereby paying off his debts and wasting EMF's money.

9.15am Resign from EMF. Sell house, move to Derbyshire to return to honest working-class roots. Am back with Rich, kiss kiss. Never did shag Jack, boo hoo. The kids have never been happier. And who's this at the door? My sister Julie saying the local doll's house factory is about to close. Do I spot an opportunity?

Digested read, digested: The column that got out of control.

Liz Jones's Diary
by Liz Jones (2005)

There are two reasons why I have never had much interest from men:

1. I've set my sights ridiculously high. Over the years I have tried to date Prince, Justin Timberlake, James Bond and Homer Simpson;
2. I am neurotic, bordering on the certifiable.

Millennium Eve Eve I think Kevin is my boyfriend because we had sex and he stayed longer than 30 minutes.

Millennium Eve I have an oily bath, waiting for him to call.

March 19 2000 The bath is cold. He still hasn't called. I ring my best friend Jeremy to find out what to do. 'Don't call him,' he says. I dial Kevin's number. 'Will you marry me?' I beg. 'No.'

April 20 2000 My three cats think I still might have a chance with Kevin. The phone rings. A man wants to interview me about my job in the media. His name is Nirpal. He is 26 years old and I think we are going to get married.

April 24 2000 He calls. 'Do you want to go out to dinner?' he asks. 'You're paying.' 'Of course,' I reply.

April 28 2000 The Boyfriend looks into my eyes. 'How old are you?' '31,' I lie. In fact, I'm 36. 'Hmm,' he says, 'your plastic surgery makes you look a great deal older.'

August 15 2000 The Boyfriend has moved in and I am being extra nice. He is allowed to sit on my £10,000 sofa without washing obsessively first and he can cuddle me in bed, providing there is a pillow between us and he doesn't disturb the cats.

September 5 2000 The Boyfriend has moved out on my birthday. 'Please come back,' I plead. 'I'll buy you a PlayStation, an Armani suit and let you write your novel at home while I pay for everything.' 'Throw in a car and I'll think about it,' he says. 'Done.'

October 10 2002 It's our wedding day. I've spent £20,000 on hiring Babington House. I've done it. I'm married.

July 17 2003 The Husband staggers into the room. 'I now weigh 17 stone,' he gasps. 'You've fattened me up because you hope I'll never be able to leave you. Women do still fancy me, you know.' I don't think so.

December 23 2003 'You treat me like a pet,' the Husband moans. This is not true. I treat him far worse. The cats get fresh tuna flakes and are allowed to sit near me.

April 8 2004 The Husband says he is feeling unfulfilled and wants a baby. 'OK,' I say, 'let's buy one.'

May 12 2004 The counsellor asks if we have considered the cultural implications of adopting an Indian child. 'No,' I reply thoughtfully. 'I've never been to the Calcutta branch of Prada.'

September 23 2004 'Not sure I want a baby any more,' the Husband says. 'Neither do I.'

November 1 2004 The Husband has been doing yoga and has lost two stone. I think he's going to leave. 'Do you love me?' I ask. 'Don't be so needy, and turn over to Sky Sports 1.'

February 12 2005 'I've got a book deal,' the Husband yells. 'I'm off travelling by myself. I'll see you around.' For the first time in years, I really think our marriage has a chance.

Digested read, digested: The untreatable in pursuit of the unspeakable.

Wicked! by Jilly Cooper (2006)

'You do realise that Larks is a failing school?' Janna tossed back her luxuriant red curls as the governors of Larkminster comprehensive offered her the job of headteacher. 'I think it's wicked,' she squealed. 'And I'm delighted to give Feral, Paris, Kylie, Graffi and other chavs the chance to succeed.'

Hengist Brett-Taylor furrowed his handsome brow. Bagley Hall had gone from strength to strength since he had been in charge, but the independent sector could always benefit from associating itself with state schools. And besides, Janna was quite a minx.

'You must be careful, Janna,' Hengist purred. 'Ashton Douglas and the LEA are looking to close Larks. But I can persuade Randal Stancombe, a local property developer, to buy Larks a minibus so we could put on a joint performance of Romeo and Juliet.'

Janna moistened. Hengist stood for everything she hated, but how could she resist his bedroom eyes?

'Oh Gawd,' drawled Cosmo Supah-Doopah, to his chums Tarquin and Xavier. 'The head's only gorn and made us do Shakespeare with the proles. How fraffly orful.'

'We think it's great,' drooled Milly and Dulcie, the Bagley Babes, their bosoms heaving in anticipation. 'The lower orders are well lush.' The production was a triumph, with Paris a sensation as Romeo. 'I must offer him a scholarship,' Hengist thought, as his fingers gently twanged Janna's suspender-belt. Janna's head was in a whirl. She wanted Hengist, yet felt guilty about betraying his wife, Sally. If only she could fancy Bagley's moody history teacher, Emlyn; but he only had eyes for Hengist's daughter, Orianna.

Hengist smiled to himself. The *Telegraph* had loved his piece, the opposition wanted him to be education minister and, best of all, the sultry Ruth Walton was going down on him.

Janna wept tears of bitter anguish. How could Hengist betray her and how could Ashton say he was going to close Larks when her working-class pets were making such tremendous strides?

An anonymous cheque for £120,000 arrived on Janna's doorstep. She could afford to keep the GCSE class open after all. A second surprise soon followed.

'I've come to teach history,' Emlyn said in his sexy Welsh lilt.

'We've got work to do,' yelled Janna, 'especially as the sports minister has taken on a bet to see if he can get a GCSE in a year at Larks.'

What a year it was. Never had Larks and Bagley Hall seen such heavy petting and frantic coupling. And how Janna's heart swelled with pride when everyone did so well in their exams.

Hengist looked up at Alex Bruce, his deputy. What an odious nonentity he was. 'I believe that you cheated on behalf of Paris,' Alex snarled. Hengist paled. 'It's true, and I've betrayed my wife, ' he said. 'I should go to prison.'

'Oh Janna, you've won the National Teaching awards, it was me who sent the £120,000 and I've discovered Orianna is a lesbian,' cooed Emlyn.

'We can be together.'

'I recognise Ashton as a paedophile,' shouted Paris, as the police arrested Stancombe and Bruce on corruption charges.

Hengist left prison a wiser man. 'Maybe we should try again,' said Sally.

Digested read, digested: Complete and utter bollarks.

Notting Hell
by Rachel Johnson (2006)

Clare: I've just seen the soignée Virginie Lacoste in the communal gardens of my £3m mansion in Lonsdale Gardens, after leaving the Avery house at 5am. Quelle scandale. My dear friend Mimi will love this.

Mimi: It's so difficult to be a Notting Hill Mummy when your husband has only inherited his £1.5m house and we're so much poorer than everyone else.

Clare: I want a baby so I can be a Yummy Mummy. I'm sooo looking forward to seeing the billionaire Si Kasparian at the Dodd Nobles' party.

Mimi: Predictably I've got three children called Casimir, Mirabel and Pretentious. How Ralph and I struggle to pay the school fees. I met Si tonight. SWOON. I've never been unfaithful before but I think I might now.

Clare: It was charming to see the Curtises – or should I say Freuds!! – and the Camerons, but I'm outraged that the Averys are building a garage.

Mimi: I pretend to poke fun at all the people I name-drop but actually this book is an homage to them. Just don't let anyone in on the secret! The Mail on Sunday phoned to ask me to profile Si. He took me out to lunch and then he, just, well, took me. How divine, but how guilty I feel. But – sob – he hasn't even called me since.

Clare: Someone else you won't care about is having an affair. Gosh! And now I've discovered the Averys are planning to use their garage as an extension. I'm going to threaten to expose his affair with Virginie.

Mimi: As I've got no money at all, I've just been shopping at Lidgates before going to Cornwall for six weeks. I do wish Si would call.

Clare: Bob Avery just laughed when I told him I knew about Virginie, but at least I told Woody Allen he couldn't film in the gardens. Guess what, Anouska, the gorgeous teacher from Ponsonby prep, has been seen with Si! Don't tell anyone this, because it would spoil what little plot there is, but Ralph and I have hatched two secret plans together.

Mimi: A supermodel saw me in my tracksuit bottoms and I'm now just over nine stone. How can I ever face the world again?

Clare: The couple you don't care about are back together. Ah! I've also got to put up a trellis to block out the Averys' view of the gardens. That'll show them. Mimi mustn't find out about mine and Ralph's plans.

Mimi: I overheard Virginie talking in a cod-French accent in Myla, saying, 'Zees lingerie ees for my girlfriend.' She's having an affair with Bob's wife!

Clare: Hoooooooray, I'm pregnant, thanks to Ralph and the turkey baster. Mimi must never find out.

Mimi: My life is at an end. Si is getting married to Anouska and Ralph has found out about my affair. He's punished me by selling our house to Clare for more than £2m and we're moving to Dorset.

Clare: Phew! Mimi still hasn't found out about me and Ralph.

Mimi: Dorset isn't so bad after all, even if you can't go shopping, and I never felt really at home with all those multi-millionaires. If this was a Richard Curtis film this would be the closing scene where he panned back from the Square. But it's not. It's even worse.

Digested read, digested: The media finally eats itself.

Handle with Care
by Jodi Picoult (2009)

Charlotte: I called you Willow. Though it's the readers who would be Weeping by the end. But not because they were sad. I felt as broken as you when Piper, the gynaecologist, saw the 28-week scan and told me you had osteogenesis imperfecta (OI), a rare condition where your bones snap easily and you never grow taller than three foot. I was so happy, though, when she told me you had Type III and you wouldn't die at birth but would have a short painful life and then die. Otherwise I wouldn't have a story.

Amelia: I'm your older half-sister. My Mom had been a single-parent before she met Sean and had you. My bits are going to show you that OI also creates difficult issues for siblings.

Sean: I'm a tough-guy cop, so I didn't cry when you were born. But that doesn't mean I don't have a lot of difficult feelings boiling inside me. I want you to know that Charlotte completed me and we both wanted you very much. We once took you to Disneyworld where you broke your femur and the staff arrested us on suspicion of child abuse. People don't understand OI is a condition that raises many complex issues, all of which you are going to hear of at unimaginable length.

Charlotte: You were a genius, which is another symptom of OI, I read on Wikipedia. Sean wanted to sue Disneyworld, but the lawyer told us their staff had only been doing their job, which relieved Jodi no end as otherwise the book might have been injuncted. But the lawyer did tell us we could sue Piper, who had missed signs of OI at the 18-week scan.

Marin: I was adopted and I don't know who my birth mother is. This means I have very difficult personal issues in dealing with Charlotte, who may not have wanted her baby – but as her lawyer I am trying to be very professional about it.

Sean: Marin says it is very fortunate that we live in New Hampshire as it is one of the few states that allows wrongful birth suits. Jodi thinks it is even more fortunate we live in New Hampshire. Charlotte and I are arguing. I don't think we should sue Piper because she was your best friend and we were planning to keep you anyway. These difficult issues are tearing the family apart.

Charlotte: Abortion is a very difficult question and I don't quite know how to answer it, as I want to keep my dilemmas open. I would just like to have had the option, not that I would have gone through with it because I don't want to alienate the Pro-Life brigade and in any case I love you very much. Will that do? Did I also mention I'm a Catholic?

Amelia: No one's been paying me any attention for a while, so I've become bulimic.

Sean: Mummy and I are getting divorced, but we still love you very much. I am testifying against her because I don't think we should sue Piper because you might think it means we wish you were dead. I've also kissed Piper, but don't tell anyone.

Charlotte: You have been having fun at an OI convention because it's important to remember that people with OI can lead fulfilling lives. Daddy and I are separating but he slept with me last night. I felt as if I was a vine. Apparently. I'm suing Piper not because I don't love you but because I want you to have some money.

Amelia: No one's been paying me any attention for a while, so I've now started cutting myself. By the way, you've also broken a few limbs at key moments to heighten the drama. Such as it is.

Marin: One of the jurors turned out to be my birth mother. She gave me away because she had been raped. Fancy that! Maybe I shouldn't be so quick to judge Charlotte. Especially as the jury has awarded her $8m.

Willow: Mum and Dad are back together and have lost all their friends. Whoops, I've fallen through the ice and have died. I should have done this 500 pages ago.

Jodi: Looks like I'm going to pocket the $8m then.

Digested read, digested: Charlotte takes the money; you should just run.

Fifty Shades of Grey
by EL James (2011)

'I've got a cold and I can't interview Christian Grey, the enigmatic multimillionaire tycoon, for the student newspaper today,' says Kate, my roommate. 'Please take my place, Ana.'

Wow! I take one look at Mr Grey and can barely speak. With his tousled hair, he is so mouthwateringly gorgeous. The epitome of male beauty. 'G-gosh,' I say.

'You seem to be struck dumb, Miss Steele,' he wryly observes. 'I like that in a woman.'

On the way home, my cell phone rings.

'Come to dinner,' says Christian.

'How did you know my number?'

'It's my business to know everything. I like to exercise control. My helicopter will pick you up at seven.'

I am unable to resist. No man has ever affected me in this way before.

'Here's the contract for our relationship,' he says, slipping an oyster down my throat. 'I will be the Dominant and you will be the Submissive. You will do everything I say and allow me to cane you, tie you up, sodomise you, clamp your genitals and fist you. In return I will buy you a car and a laptop.'

'But Sir,' I exclaim. 'I'm still a virgin, so I will have to draw the line at fisting.'

'You drive a hard bargain, Miss Steele.'

My inner goddess melts as he forces his tongue inside me. I have never been this wet before, etc. He bends me over his knee and slaps me hard. It feels wrong, but somehow very right. His enormous penis, etc. Juddering orgasms, etc.

'Sleep with me, Sir,' I beg, as I try to draw his handsome body closer to mine.

'I can't. I had a deeply disturbed childhood and S&M relationships are the only ones I can sustain.'

'Tell me about your commitment problems.'

'They are too disturbing. You will find I am 50 Shades of Grey. Yet I find myself strangely drawn to your virginal, 20-year-old body in a way that I have never previously experienced.'

My subconscious tells me I should run away from this control freak right now, but my inner goddess is telling me to stay. That I can help this poor troubled man. Christian changes into a sexy pair of faded denim jeans and leads me to his Red Room of Pain. I willingly allow myself to be chained to a crucifix while he thrashes my clitoris with a leather hunting crop. The pain is intense, but the pleasure more so. My inner goddess is panting for him not to stop until ... juddering climaxes, etc.

'I wouldn't normally allow myself to be treated like this,' I say. 'But somehow, Christian, it is OK with you as I can sense that one day we may have a loving relationship.'

'It is the Submissive who has all the power,' he witters, 'and I can feel myself slowly yielding to you.'

Oh yes please, my inner goddess yells. Does he really love me as much as Kate keeps telling me he does? And why am I so jealous of his previous Subs, and why don't I ask him a single question about his job or his life even though we have met one another's parents in circumstances bordering on the unbelievable?

Submit yourself to the greatest thrashing of your life, my inner goddess says, to prove how much you love him and to let him show how much he loves you. Torn ass cheeks/moist vagina/pain/ yet more juddering climaxes, etc.

'I love you, yet I have to go,' I sob.

'Why?'

'Because we're only going to get to the bottom of your commitment issues after you've spanked your way through the next two books.'

Digested read, digested: What every woman wants. Obviously.

Peaches for Monsieur Le Curé
by Joanne Harris (2012)

The lettre came on the wind of Ramadan. 'Ma chere Vianne, mes sales have been slipping un peu and mes publishers pensent it's a good idee if I revive mes characters from mon best-vendeur, Chocolat, pour a troisieme time. So get your witchy self along, with your deux dreary filles, back to Lansquenet as vite as possible, much amour, Joanne.' Ooh la la! Je wondered what Roux would say, but then I remembered he never dired anything anyway. As the great Paulo Coelho once wrote: 'Silence est souvent more articulate que mots.' So I packed mes tarot cartes et left Paris avec Anouk et Rosette.

Nothing is the meme in Lansquenet, Pere. A community of

Algerian Muslims have moved dans Les Marauds et ont builde un mosque avec un minaret. Toute la village est en turmoil, Pere, everyone pense qu'il etait moi who burned down the ecole run by the fierce woman who jamais takes offer her niqab. Et maintenant, le vent is bringing back my old adversary, Vianne, who once set up a chocolaterie opposite mon eglise.

The vent was warm and fast, et j'etais back en Lansquenet dans un instant. Quel horreur! The hatred and the mistrust entre les deux communautes! Je hardly recognised mon vieux manoir. Et le pauvre Cure Francis! Toute le village wants to get ridder of him parce qu'il est trop old-fashioned, mais he really a un coeur d'or. Je ne sais pas quoi I am meant to be doing ici, mes les tarots tell me to go and chat to les Muslims.

'Bonjour, tout le monde. Would you like one of my succulent juicy peches?' je dis. They respondent: 'We were told you would bring some chocolat truffles?' 'Pas this time, les chocolats were a while en retard.' 'Jamais mind, these peches are tres bonnes, so we will tell you tout what is going on with us que we have never bothered to dire anyone else.' As I listened, le vent grew darker.

Oh Pere, everything est still going seins en haut. Je was walking by the river when I saw a Muslim girl, Alyssa, try to kill herself, so I rescuer her et puis tout le monde pensent que je was essaying to faire elle dans. Et maintenant, Pere, some Muslim bloke a smashed mon visage dans, et all the village aiment le trendy new cure. 'N'inquietez pas,' Dieu whispered.

'Je comprends that it's not votre faute que you have been dumpe in le milieu d'un second rate piece of politically correct, cosy magical realism.'

Alyssa bit hungrily into my succulent peche. 'Je sais it's Ramadan et que j'ai just tried to topper moi-meme, but je cannot resist,' elle dit. 'Neither can nous,' said many autres Muslim women.

'Beaucoup de nous do not aiment being made to observer le strict Muslim orthodoxies. We want to to be Muslim and French.'

The wind is doing its work, I thought, as I decided to rustle up a few chocolate pralines, apres tout. How I yearned for Roux and quite understood why he had fathered a child by mon old amie Josephine. En effet, je comprended tout. All je needed to faire was to talk to the mysterious Inez, the femme in the niqab.

'You comprenez rien,' elle spat. 'Peut-etre mes tarot cartes on ete upside down.'

Grace pour rien, Pere. J'ai just been coshed over the tete and dumped in the cellar of the gym.

C'est un miracle. Roux a turner up out of le vent. He didn't shag Josephine so il est tout mienne, not que Roux could ever belonger to anyone parce qu-il est un spirit libre. Et le problem avec les Muslims is sorted, washed clean by the river et le vent. Les Muslim hommes sont behaving themselves again, et everyone feels tres francais.

Oh Pere, c'est bon que je suis still le Cure et que tous les muslims maintenant come to mon eglise. Mais please, Pere, ne letter that Vianne woman near Joanne's keyboard encore.

Digested read, digested: Immodium for tout le monde.

In the Name of Love
by Katie Price (2012)

Then: Charlie sobbed as she knelt beside her dying horse that had been cruelly knocked down by a speeding 4x4.

Now: 'Come on, babes,' said Zoe. 'My Premier League footballer boyfriend has forgotten my birthday. So he said he would pay for

JOHN CRACE

me to take a friend to Barbados, and you need cheering up to get over your Premier League footballer cheating on you.'

Charlie looked up to see a handsome, well-toned if somewhat diminutive hunk in white Speedos standing next to her sunlounger. Thank God she had had a Brazilian! 'Hola,' he drawled, 'My name is Felipe-Martin di Amis. Would you like to join me on my yacht?'

'You look shagged out,' Zoe observed. Charlie smiled. The past few days had been a blur as she had never come so intensely with any other man. 'I think I'm in love,' she admitted, 'though I'm not sure why I told Felipe-Martin I worked in a shop when I'm actually the world's greatest woman writer who doesn't actually write her own books.'

Felipe-Martin sobbed. He had never come so intensely with any other woman, and he had believed Charlie was The One but, even though he had told her he was an ageing author rather than a Spanish aristocrat who would be competing in the three-day event at the Olympics, he couldn't forgive her for telling him she worked in a shop when she was actually the world's greatest woman writer who didn't actually write her own books. He would have to end the relationship immediately.

Neither Charlie nor Felipe-Martin had stopped crying for two months since Felipe-Martin had abruptly ended their relationship. She couldn't believe her eyes when he walked into Chinawhite's. How fit could a bloke be! Having come more intensely and more frequently than ever before, Felipe-Martin and Charlie lay contentedly in each other's arms.

'Do you really think we can be a couple?' Charlie asked. 'You are a Spanish aristocrat, while I am only a working-class girl.'

'Don't be so silly,' Felipe-Martin cooed. 'I have a great understanding of the lower orders myself, and you write about them in a way that is so wholly convincing.'

'You do know that I don't actually write my own books, don't you?'

'Of course, but somehow that makes you even more authentic.'

'You say the sweetest things! Now give me your enormous cock again, and I will try not to let the phobia of horses that I have had since my own horse died in my arms get in the way of our relationship.'

Charlie wept bitter tears. She adored Felipe-Martin, but she knew she just wasn't able to overcome her problem with horses and that it would be unfair on him were she to jeopardise his chances of a gold medal. For his sake, she had to end it by pretending to go out with the footballer again.

'I've never been so miserable in my life,' cried Charlie and Felipe-Martin.

'I know you've never liked me,' said Darcy, 'but I've completely changed my personality since I've been going out with your jailbird brother. And I think what you need is some therapy to overcome your post-traumatic stress disorder.'

Two months later: Charlie couldn't believe the therapy had worked so well and as Felipe-Martin cleared the final fence to win a silver medal behind the British rider, she ran into the arena. 'I love you,' she cried. 'And I love you, too,' Felipe-Martin yelled, ripping off his jodhpurs and forcing himself inside her in front of the Royal Box. The Queen led the crowd's standing ovation as the couple juddered to the most intense, simultaneous orgasm.

'I always knew you would win the Nobel Prize for literature,' gasped Felipe-Martin.

Digested read, digested: In the name of God ...

It by Alexa Chung (2013)

Horses were my first love. When I was six I REALLY, REALLY, REALLY wanted one. So my parents got me one. It was my first fashion accessory.

I loved everything about the Spice Girls. Their clothes, their music, their manufactured artificiality. But I especially loved the fact they showed women could become celebrities without having any talent. Here's a couple of photos of me completely naked.

My favourite book is *Lolita* because I just adore the pubescent teenaged girl look. It rocks. I also like the Edie Sedgwick look. How many drugs can one girl take? Never enough, because taking drugs looks really, really cool. Kate Moss is the hippest woman alive. Fact. Here's a photo of my best friend, Misty.

Getting dressed in the morning can be the most difficult thing ever. You have to, like, remember where you are, get out of bed and decide what to wear. My tip is to get someone to phone Chanel and get them to send over a selection of their latest collection. That way you can be sure what you're wearing is clean. You're welcome. Here's a rubbish doodle of mine.

When buying new Converse, make sure to get the sales assistant to rub a bit of mud on them. Though obvs only Cotswolds mud. Anything else makes you look common. Isn't it strange how my hair always looks best the night before I have a hair appointment booked for the following day? Though, on reflection, this could be just because I have a hair appointment every day. Then I expect you do, too, so you know how I feel. Here are some more photos of me looking amazing.

I love men. By men, I mean famous men. Jeremy Irons is dreamy. And I fancy all the Beatles equally, but if I had to choose one of them it would be Mick Jagger. Here's a photo of him that

I didn't take. My biggest influence has been Jane Birkin. Probably because she has never done that much either. Here's a photo of her.

This book is beginning to completely fall apart, isn't it? But I haven't really got anything to say. Have you noticed how many pop songs are about break-ups or being generally bummed out? How weird is that? The thing about being heartbroken is that it feels like your heart really has been broken. When I don't feel I have the answers to all life's problems, I type my questions into Google. It's uncanny how often you can find out something useful. When I last typed in 'Help! I'm really, really unhappy' the first thing that came up was: 'Go to the Caribbean and get wasted with your really cool friends for three weeks.' Here's a photo of me in sunglasses. CRA-ZEE!

My mum is the coolest mum in the world. Whenever I break up with a boyfriend, she tells me to go out and shag someone else. How cool is that? I don't seem to have a photo of my mum.

Sometimes my male friends get really depressed. That's because they don't have enough leather jackets. You can never have too many leather jackets. I've got 25 at least. I really do believe that if everyone in the world had 25 leather jackets, no one would be unhappy again ever. Here's a photo of me in one of my leather jackets.

Some people become doctors. Others win the Nobel Prize and shit like that. The woman down the road does my nails, though I find it very annoying I can't update my Twitter status to #having-manicure when I am actually having a manicure – because I can't use my phone and have my nails done at the same time. Someone should really think of a gadget to get round that. We all have to realise what we are best at and go for it wholeheartedly. I do nothing. Here's a photo of me doing nothing.

I so love Karl Lagerfeld. He is literally the funniest guy in the entire world. He needs to be looking like the way he does.

Digested read, digested: Anyone know what Alexa Chung actually does?

Bridget Jones: Mad About the Boy
by Helen Fielding (2013)

18 April 2013
Years since last book:15; Money in the bank: too much to count
9.15am Funny buzzing in my pocket. Decide to ignore it.
9.20am Knock on the door. It's Talitha, telling me she's been Texting me. Look blank. 'Your phone,' she says. So that's what that BUZZING was! Not sure why I capitalised that. Must have a drink.
9.30am Talitha says it's her 60th birthday on May 24th. OMG. That's the same day as the Roxter's 30th. 'You can bring your Toy Boy if you like,' she says.
9.45am Agent phones to say my Hedda Gabbler screenplay has got the green light.
9.50am Having second thoughts about mis-spelling Hedda Gabler. Editor says it will make me look cute and ditzy. 'Just like the old Bridget!' I think it just makes me look dim.

23 June 2012
Alcohol units drunk: not enough; pages to fill: too many
8.30am Late getting Billy to school. Mabel has diarrhoea. HELP!!! I do miss Mark. Shame he had to die, but couldn't have written another book if he'd been around and we'd been, like, really

happy and smug oldly-weds!! And going through a messy separation would have made Elizabeth Bennet VERY, VERY cross. Hope she approves of his hero's death.

9.30pm Miranda comes round and says it's time I stopped being so boring and had a jolly good shag. Drink three bottles of wine. Miranda brings out this odd metal thing. Says it can send messages to people by something called email. Note to self: must get one. She finds Leatherjacketman on Slipyoualength.com.

11.30pm Try to stick my tongue down Leatherjacketman's throat. Leatherjacketman makes a run for it. WHOOPS!!

7 December 2012

Weight: miraculously slim; worries about the menopause: none

9.47am Letter from school. Atticus and Hero have Nits. Really, really scared. What are Nits? Are they like Aids or something?

11.21am Have discovered Twitter. It's totes amazeballs. Can't understand why no one laughs at @JonesyBJ. AAAGH! Have accidentally twittered 'I really fancy the Roxter' to everyone!!! Could die with embarrassment. The Roxter twitters back and invites me on a date.

12.57pm DISASTER!! Weird Mr Wallaker who lives up the street caught me buying condoms from the chemist. Gave me a very funny look. Especially when I asked him which way round they went on!!!

11.58pm The Roxter is a dream boat. Chiselled jaw, firm six-pack. I think I might have just died myself!!! Mmmmmmmmmmmmmmmmmmmmmm!!!! I heart the Roxter.

14 June 2013

Designer dresses bought: 8; style: overwrought

8.01am No text from the Roxter. Panic.

8.02am Still no text from the Roxter. DOUBLE PANIC!!!

8.03am Text from the Roxter saying he had left his phone downstairs which is why he hadn't texted earlier. PHEW.

10.35am Catch sight of myself in the mirror. Think, 'I'm 51 years old FFS. I'm too old to be writing like a hyperactive ingenue'. Phone editor to say wouldn't it more interesting to write something rather deeper and more reflective about grief and getting old. Feel I have rather more to say about that. Editor says no. 'Readers like you just the way you are. But if you want to say you miss Darcy a bit, that is OK.'

10.57am I miss Darcy. Don't we all.

3 August 2013

Ferraris bought for the Roxter: 3; sense of reality: nearly all gone

11.09am CATASTROPHE. The NITS are back. Worried they might have hopped from me on to the Roxter.

12.33pm Have a near Brazilian!

2.22pm A gnawing sense that the ongoing NIT gag is falling flat. Face it. No one really gives that much of a toss about them. Editor says that all the Mums at her daughter's North London private school are obsessed with them. So NITS stay.

3.51pm Call from agent. Hedda Gabbler screenplay not going to work after all. Could I try Madame Ovary instead? Heart sinks.

5.33pm Weird Mr Wallaker gives me a funny look when I ask him if he has any moisturiser I could use as my bush is very red after waxing.

9.38pm Just had five – FIVE – shags with the Roxter. He could be the ONE!! 'I heart you Jonesy,' he texts me while we are in bed. Am beginning to wonder if this relationship is going anywhere.

17 November 2013

Bottles of vintage Dom Perignon drunk: 23: advance: banked

3.28pm GUESS WHAT! Mr Wallaker isn't so weird as I thought. He's my age, single and a bit of a hero like Darcy.

3.29pm Mr Wallaker has moved in with me!!!!!

Digested read, digested: Bridget's arrested development.

LAD LIT

A Long Way Down
by Nick Hornby (2005)

Martin: Can I explain why I wanted to jump off a tower block? I'd been to prison for having sex with a 15-year-old girl – yeah, I know what you're going to say, but she told me she was older – I'm separated from my wife and kids, I lost the big TV job and all in all I'm a bit unhappy.

Maureen: I picked New Year's Eve because it seemed like a good idea. I told Matty I was going to a party, but he looked blank.

Jess: Like, I was at this party looking for Chas who had dumped me, like, and I remembered the block was called Topper's Tower, so I, like, thought, whateffer.

Martin: These two women appeared next to me and we sat and chatted for a bit about jumping and then this other bloke turned up.

JJ: I don't know why I decided to kill myself, really. Sure my girlfriend had left me and my rock band had split up, but this was everyday stuff for a superannuated everybloke from north London. In the end, I guess it was just that I didn't think the book would work with only three voices as we'd never sell the film rights unless I pitched up, too.

Maureen: After so many years of looking after my disabled son by myself, it was quite nice to get together and chat about killing ourselves.

Jess: Like, I persuaded them dull fuckers to go to this party where I thought that bastard Chas would be.

Martin: I might have guessed that idiot Chas would recognise me and tell the papers that we had all met up on Topper's Tower.

Jess: Fuckin' fantastic. I persuaded some fick journo it was an angel wot had persuaded us not to jump and she's like given us all loadsa money for the story.

Maureen: It was quite nice to talk to a journalist. I still feel a bit guilty about Matty, though.

JJ: I haven't said anything for a while, so I thought I'd check in. I've been making lists of pop groups, you know. I find that very interesting.

Martin: Oh God, the story just gets worse. It turns out that Jess is dead posh and is the daughter of the education minister. I should have topped myself when I had the chance.

Jess: Like, I hate my parents. And they, like, hate me too. It's soo unfair. I suggested we all spend the dosh going to Tenerife, and I got well smashed for a week.

Maureen: I loved Tenerife. I'd never been abroad before.

JJ: Jess arranged for us all to meet up with the important people in our lives. I now go busking and am happier than I've ever been.

Martin: I realised my life was shallow and I now help disadvantaged kids to read. It's so cathartic, I'm never going to think about killing myself again.

Jess: I've got a new boyfriend and I adore my parents.

Maureen: I go to quiz nights and we're all going to remain really good friends.

Digested read, digested: The only genuine despair is the reader's.

My Favourite Wife
by Tony Parsons (2008)

The first thing that struck him was the noise. The people. The contrasts. The clichés. 'Welcome to our new life in Shanghai,' Bill said, pulling his wife, Becca, and their three-year-old daughter, Holly, close to him.

The alarm went off at six the next morning. Bill groaned. Surely no one in their right mind started a new job the day after arriving in a new country? But then he remembered. He wasn't in his right mind. He was in Tony's. A parallel universe of unbelievable stupidity. And short sentences.

And paragraphs.

Becca felt sad as she left Holly at the school. Less than a day in China. And she had never felt so alone. I'd better get used to it, she sighed. After all, it had been her idea for them to get out of London after Holly had been diagnosed with asthma. It was just that she'd hoped that at least one person might have told her that Shanghai was even more polluted.

'Good to have you on board, Bill,' said Devlin. 'We do things differently out here. Play your cards right and you'll make partner in two years.'

This, Bill thought to himself, was what it was all. About. Back home, his accent, his chip on his shoulder and his obvious lack of intelligence had counted. Against him as a lawyer. But here, he could earn enough. To buy a house in Islington.

Becca and Bill watched the single women polish their new cars outside their gated community in Paradise Gardens. 'They look like kept women,' Becca exclaimed in surprise.

'Modern China is a complex country,' Bill replied, sagely. 'And everyone has to make difficult choices.'

'Well, they seem like whores to me.'

'I suppose they are,' he nodded, knowing he could never be. The type of man who had a mistress.

Or could he?

He remembered Li Jin Jin, the pale Chinese woman he had met briefly. And felt a pang. Of guilt.

'Listen, Bill,' said Devlin. 'We're working on a big development. It involves a stereotypical, ruthless Chinese businessman and oppressed peasants. People are going to lose their limbs. So don't go squeamish on me.'

Bill gulped. China really was another world. But wasn't it good that some of the Chinese were getting rich? And didn't all new economies need to make compromises?

'I'm lonely and my dad's ill,' Becca sobbed. 'I'm going home with Holly for a while.'

Bill nodded. He would be lonely. But it was the right thing to do. And he wasn't the type to have an affair. Was he?

He held Jin Jin in his arms. He wasn't like the others. He truly loved her. And she loved him. Though they both knew she came second. He checked his mobile. Twelve missed calls.

'Your dad's dying,' Becca said.

He felt guilty. He was the loneliest man in the world.

'I'm glad we could have some catharsis,' he said as he sat by his father's deathbed. 'I'm going to be a proper husband and father now.'

And he meant it. But it wasn't easy. Even when Becca rejoined him in Shanghai.

'How's your Chinese whore?' Devlin's wife shouted, drunkenly.

'I'm never going to speak to you again,' Becca shouted. 'But I love you,' Bill pleaded. 'OK, I forgive you. For Holly's sake.'

'Thank you, darling. But before we can be a happy family again, there are things I must do first. There is the long goodbye with Jin Jin involving a nauseating attempt at pathos with a breast cancer scare. Then I must get fired from my job for exposing corruption in China.'

'Then do you promise that this nightmare will finally be over?'

'That's no way to refer to my book,' Tony snapped.

Digested read, digested: Our least favourite writer.

Meltdown by Ben Elton (2009)

Jimmy Corby graduated from Sussex in 1993 with five friends: Robbo, David, Rupert, Henry and Lizzie. They were to remain friends throughout the 90s and most of the noughties. Mates. Proper mates. Through good and bad sentences. Except there were no good sentences.

Jimmy was tired. Really tired. Dog tired. Tired as a very tired person. How was he going to provide for Monica and the kids?

Eighteen months earlier the stars had twinkled like diamonds. 'Rupert's just saved me a fortune,' Jimmy had said to Monica. 'Tipped me off that Caledonian Granite is going belly up.' 'Haven't you got a more imaginative alternative for Northern Rock?' Monica had replied. 'Apparently not.' 'Well it sounds like insider dealing, and as I am the book's voice of morality, I think you should give it all to charity.' 'Tell you what, babe,' he had laughed, 'I'll put it all on the gee-gees.'

Henry blew-dry his blond curls. He needed to make a good impression now he was a junior minister. 'Maybe I can claim the hairdryer on expenses,' he thought. 'Is the whole book going to be this telegraphed?' his wife Jane groaned. 'It's by Ben Elton,' he snapped.

'Mwa-ha-ha-ha,' Rupert cackled, in the manner of the archetypal villain. 'Everyone else is broke but I'm fine, thanks to my Fred the Shred pension and my Tony Blair knighthood.'

Even Monica was astonished by the banality of both the insight into the banking crisis and the characterisation, but she wasn't going to miss out on her own clichés. 'Everyone has been very greedy and naughty,' she observed.

'Oh, Mon,' Jimmy wept. 'You are so right, and I regret not saving sensibly while I was making a fortune as a banker. Now I'm out of a job, it's very hard to keep up the mortgage on our huge house in Notting Hill, and my property investment has gone belly-up. We might have to take Toby out of private school.'

'Hang on,' Monica said, 'luckily, Lizzie has agreed to lend us £2m.'

'Robbo and I have always been careful with money and put all our savings into premium bonds,' Lizzie said. 'And our luxury cushion shop is still making millions.' 'Hooray. We're saved,' Monica and Jimmy smiled.

'Oh dear,' Lizzie wept. 'Robbo has just killed himself by driving into a wall and it turns out he inexplicably invested all our money with a character who resembles Bernie Madoff, so now we're broke too! Though obviously there was no connection between him crashing the car and our being broke, because that would be morally complex.'

'That's awful,' said Jimmy. 'Toby will have to leave private school after all.'

'Don't worry,' Toby replied. 'Some state schools are awfully good, and I will do good works by befriending the son of a Somali asylum seeker.'

'You know,' said Monica, who never missed an opportunity to be annoyingly sanctimonious. 'I can't help feeling that we lost our moral compass while we were making all that money.'

'At least we didn't resort to writing *We Will Rock You*,' Jimmy replied.

'Fancy that,' said Henry. 'The expenses scandal has broken and I've had to resign my seat.'

'Fancy that,' said Rupert. 'Everyone hates me, I'm being investigated for insider trading and I've had to leave the country.'

'We believe your husband committed suicide to give you an insurance payout,' Inspector Knacker growled to Monica.

'No I didn't,' yelled Jimmy, appearing from nowhere. 'That was some crap arson subplot to make you think the book was more interesting than it is. I've decided to be a plumber.'

'My man of the people,' Monica drooled, the only person apart from Jimmy who had failed to notice bankers were now paying themselves huge bonuses again.

'And the bet I made two years ago has won me £5tn. But I'm giving it to charity. Which is more than Ben will do with the proceeds of this trash.'

Digested read, digested: Totally bankrupt.

Round the Bend
by Jeremy Clarkson (2012)

There are many ways to tell if someone is a bit thick. You can ask them if they believe in global warming. You can ask them if they live in Newcastle. But there's another, easier way of establishing whether someone is two spanners short of a tool box. You can ask them if they are a presenter of *Top Gear*. Which brings me nicely to the Subaru Impreza. Who but an idiot would pay £25,000 for a car that comes with fewer toys than an Ethiopian birthday boy?

The Scottish chief constable recently lambasted me for encouraging everyone to drive fast. My only crime? I like Lamborghinis. He would too if he could afford one. But as he can't, he wants to spoil my fun. It's killjoys like him that are turning Britain's roads into a haven for health and safety geriatrics. If there's one thing that would improve my life more than being able to burn up the M40 at 135 mph, it would be having the freedom to take out a few cripples in wheelchairs along the way.

All Jaguar's problems stem from the days when the communists took over the shop floor at British Leyland. If the government had just had the nerve to have every striker executed in front of his family, then we wouldn't be depending on an Indian manufacturer to bail the brand out now. Just what we need: An It Ain't Half Hot Mum advertising campaign. I'd rather have a sedan chair carried by four greased Egyptians.

Who on earth do you know who actually washes their car? Other than the homosexuals of Gerrards Cross? The whole point of a car is that you should drive it aggressively off road, spilling dirt and gravel over the bunny huggers who are traipsing around National Trust properties, while nibbling on their falafel and ciabatta sandwiches. Which brings me to the Renault Clio. If you're the sort of limp-wristed L'Oreal man who spends hours in the gym doing botty-clenching exercises, then you're going to love this. Me? I'd rather get my local village idiot, Dave, to clean my rims!

So cars are making all the polar bears drown, are they? Oh, diddums. If they spent less time posing for David Attenborough and more time learning to swim, they'd be fine. Which brings me to the eight-seater Mitsubishi Outlander. The ramblists say cars like this are destroying the planet, when it's their nasty little Priuses that are really doing the damage. Not that global warming is a reality for anyone but a few scaremongering communists who want us all to eat nettles and live in middens. How else am I going to get my kids to school than in a 4x4? You can't expect me to use a bus, as the drivers are always out on strike.

As a major celebrity I get photographed countless times a day – all too often with a woman who isn't my wife. All speed cameras should be burned, preferably using traffic wardens, council officials and gays as lighter fuel. Which brings me to the Porsche Cayenne, the car with the most pointless rear seat ever made. So small it can't even fit the 8-inch Hammond, a man who gives dwarves a bad name. Talking of which, how come the over coiffed homosexualist had his crash on the one day in the century when the entire NHS wasn't on strike?

What is the point of a bicyclist? Answer: to die. The only reason any beardy vegetarian or lesbian gets on a bike is because they secretly want to commit suicide. Which is fine by me. I want them all to die, too. The world would be a much better place without them. But what I don't want them doing is holding me up and tempting me into doing their dirty work for them. If you haven't got the balls to phone Dignitas, then don't make me late for dinner at the Ivy by forcing me to crush you under my front wheels. So run along and get a gun and top yourselves in private, losers.

Thanks to the utterly useless Gordon Brown, we're apparently all going to be so broke we'll have to drive a Fiat 500. Frankly, I'd rather die. Who wants a car that can only kill its occupants? Which brings me on to Sarah Brown. Did she look at Gordon before marrying him? I mean, she's not much of a looker, but she didn't need to stoop that low. Why is every politician's wife – with the exception of the divine Samantha Cameron – such a munter? Talking of which, the reversing mirror in the Range Rover allowed me to look right up Sam's skirt.

Lots of people write in to me asking if Mays is 'a bachelor'. What I can say is that he is right at home in the Jean-Claude 'Durz ma bum look beeg in zis' Citroën Diane. As for me I'm staying with my Mercedes XLR-BIGCOCK. Fritz may have made a few minor errors with the Poles in the war, but he was dead right about the communist workshy scum. Thank God for my mate Dave. Boxing Day as per usual?

Digested read, digested: Car crash of a career.

AUTOBIOGRAPHY/MEMOIR

Experience by Martin Amis (2000)

I write both to commemorate my father and to set the record straight. This will involve me in the indulgence of certain bad habits. Name dropping is one of them. But I've been indulging in this, in a way, ever since I first said, 'Mart'.

There will be no point-scoring, valued reader, though if you're reading this, Jules, I'd like to say that it was you who turned away from me, not I who turned away from you. So you can fuck right off for a start. And as for you, Thersites Eric, who demeaned and defiled our family after Kingsley's death, I'll deal with you and the toiling small-holders of the Fourth Estate in a 10-page appendix.

Rather, this is the journey through the unconscious, the 'un' conscious, the un, of how the fledgling Osric became Hamlet, Prince of Westbourne Grove. It is here in the world of un, that murky novelist's landscape, where experience is collected, connections are made and communion is Freely given and received. Here we will find the pain schedule, the climacteric collision of the missing and the lost, the Delilahs and the Lucys, and the loves that come and go. There is no morality. What must be, must be. All we can do is rage and hurt and pay the bill.

It is the late 1970s. The gross of condoms that Kingsley gave me and Phillip have long since been used. Many times over. I am looking at a photo of a two-year-old girl, another version of myself.

'Do you think she might be mine,' I asked my mother.

'Definitely.'

'What shall I do?'

'Nothing.'

But I didn't do nothing. I didn't see her or take an interest in her, obviously. No, I did something more profound and important. I wrote about her. In scribendo veritas. A careful reading of my novels, from the publication of *Success* in 1978 onwards, will reveal a stream of lost or wandering and putative or fugitive fathers. So Delilah and I were always together, our inner-selves linked in un-ness, un-needing of a corporeal presence.

The mid-90s were my lurid years, using lurid strictly according to the condensed epic poem of the Fowlers' article in the COD. A mid-life crisis is critical in a man; a man who reaches his forties without one has no concept of the continuum of being. The beginnings and the endings. And all things must end. My marriage to Antonia was ending, my teeth had prematurely resigned and Kingsley was creeping to his reluctant adieu. Only Saul, the world's other great novelist, could truly comfort.

But in the endings there are also joys. There is you, Isabel, and Delilah, who have come back to me. Immenso giubilo. I worried that you and the boys would not get on. Ridiculous. And even with no genetic barrier between me and my own mortality, there is a freedom in being orphaned. My tennis has got much, much better since Kingsley died. There. My experience is told. Now there is the living to be done.

Digested read, digested: Brilliantly written, highly selective, episodic portrayal of a life well-thought but only half felt.

Things My Mother Never Told Me
by Blake Morrison (2002)

Hark! Dost the gentle wheezing from my mother's chest grow ever softer?
Is that her spirit passing now or has it passed long since?
Still her breath and let it ne'er be said
I missed a chance to be a poet of the dead

The phone rings. It's the nursing home to say my mother's end is nigh. We have been here before, so many false goodbyes, that I find myself wondering whether I have time to finish a review. But duty – such a mean-spirited word, but surely none else will do – forces me out the house. I make it to her bedside with just 40 minutes to spare.

Later that evening, my sister Gill and I go to our mother's home. We drink too much and row as orphans often do.

'Mam always loved me more than you,' pouts Gill.

'Well I'm going to write a book about her,' I reply. 'Then we'll see who the public thinks loved her more.'

Looking through my mother's possessions, I am struck by how little I knew of her. Unlike my father who loved attention and would have adored my bestselling book about him, my mother was a shadowy, private figure who liked nothing more than not to be noticed. So obviously she would have hated the idea of this book; but that should not stop me, I thought. Would William Leith fail to exploit his family for a large cheque? Of course not. And am I not a man of equal sensitivity and depth?

Why did my mother not tell me she had so many siblings? Was she ashamed of them and of her roots? Or was she merely worried that if I discovered I had so many relations I would write about them, too?

I feel guilty reading through my parents' love letters. Have I mentioned how guilty I feel about invading their privacy? See how my father refuses to call her Agnes, or even Gennie. 'I will call you Kim,' he says, and she accepts it.

There are times in their courtship when their love seems to be waning and I feel my very existence coming into doubt. But of course I was, so even a few literary stylistic tics cannot generate much excitement in the story. I know as little of my mother now as when I started. She let my father walk all over her and now she's let me do the same.

Digested read, digested: Attention all Morrisons. If you value your privacy don't even think of dying before Blake.

A Round-Heeled Woman
by Jane Juska (2003)

My teeth are not as sparkling as they used to be, and what was once firm is now loose. But all things considered I look good. I like men's bums and penises. At 67 years old, I am what you might call an easy lay.

'Twas not always so. In the fall of 1999 I was watching a French art house movie, when I reflected both on how little sex I'd had over the past 30 years and how unfortunate it was that I had never been published. I resolved to do something about it by placing an advert in the *New York Review of Books*.

I took my time composing the ad before settling on it. 'Before I turn 67 next March, I would like to have a lot of sex with a man I like. If you want to talk first, Trollope works for me.' I thought hard about mentioning Trollope as it added $30 to the cost, but I reckoned it would establish me as an intellectual and I would be more likely to sell the book. After all, no one would publish a book about geriatric sex among the lower orders.

Over the coming weeks, I received 63 replies, which I divided into yes, no and maybe. Only those from people on life-support machines or with little sense of literary appreciation made the no pile.

My first meeting in down-town San Francisco with Danny was not a success. He was rude and I told him so. My next was with Jonah, who flew in from the east coast to spend the weekend with me. He poured the champagne and I could feel myself get wet. He thrust himself inside me and I came for the first and last time. I sensed his withdrawal, his reluctance to touch me.

'What's the matter?' I asked.

'I need a paper bag.'

'Why?'

'In case yours falls off.'

Worst of all, he stole my champagne flutes. With two strike-outs you would have thought I might have called a halt. But, as my therapist reminded me, I had a book to write, which is why I am now going to bore you with a load of details about my family life that you can't possibly want to know.

Fifty pages later I arrived in New York to see Robert. He was old, slightly decrepit, but formidably literate. I loved him intensely, though he didn't want me and rejected physical intimacy. I took time out to see Sidney, instead.

'Take my cock,' he said. I did as he asked, enjoying the power, even though his penis was slightly sub-standard.

Matt proved enigmatic, refusing to meet me, though I shall be forever grateful for his introduction to the Berg Collection. John talked dirty beautifully.

'Margaret Fuller.'

'Atwood.'

'Roth.'

'Updike.' We collapsed in a mutual orgasm on the last syllable. He then told me about his suspected liver cancer.

Graham was just in his mid-30s, though he adored Willa Cather. 'I've got to have you,' he said. He's arriving next week. I, meanwhile, have already arrived.

Digested read, digested: Shagging for New England.

Broken Music
by Sting (2003)

Rio 1987. It's the weekend before I'm due to play the world's biggest ever gig, and Trudie and I are being driven deep into the rainforest to partake of the sacred ayahuasca. I have momentary misgivings and picture the negative headlines. Trudie reassures me and gulps the potion. I do likewise. I feel violently sick and then my mind fills with strange hallucinations: the first world war, my mother groping another man in an alley, my father's look of hurt, my alienated childhood. And when I come to, I have just one thought. All you need is love. Deep.

* * *

This is not intended to be a straightforward autobiography. Rather it will be like my music: a series of atavistic, yet profound and moving sounds that combine to create something utterly predictable and dull.

I was born in the north-east. My father was a milkman and my mother felt constrained by the routine of their lives.

'Oi, Gordon help your mum with the shopping,' my father barked.

'My name's Sting.'

'Next you'll be telling us you think you can sing.'

'We are a family cloistered in silence,' I replied smugly.

I was far more intelligent than all my friends, and their resentment fuelled my inner sense of loneliness. My search for understanding drew me further into my music, and I remember hearing the Beatles for the first time and thinking that one day they might even be nearly as influential as me.

Alone in my bedroom at home, I lovingly practised on an old acoustic guitar, until there was no tune I hadn't mastered. With my talents it was hard to know what instrument to play. I found myself drawn to the understated, yet more complex, demands of the bass.

My accomplishments rapidly brought me to the attention of all the musicians at the Newcastle YMCA and I played in a series of bands in the early 70s that didn't get the credit they deserved.

Naturally there were many women drawn to my presence – Megan and Deborah to name two – but it was the actress Frances Tomelty I chose to bless with marriage. Until I was famous, of course, when I left her for Trudie. But Trudie did look exactly like Deborah who had died, so there was a cosmic reason for us coming together.

I was eventually invited down to London to practise with a drummer called Stewart Copeland. He was extremely impressed with me, though he was later rather annoyed that our first album contained many more of my songs than his. As the Police we became the most famous band in the world, and then I split it up, as I had always known I would, because I needed to do my own thing. And for no good reason I'm going to stop here.

Digested read, digested: The Tantric autobiography – goes on way too long and is only of interest to the writer.

Chronicles, Volume 1
by Bob Dylan (2004)

Lou Levy, top man at Leeds Music Publishing, took me up in a taxi to West 70th Street. Outside the wind was blowing.

'Columbia have high hopes for you,' he said.

I'd met John Hammond at Columbia the previous week.

'Howdya get to town?' he asked.

'Jumped a freight train.'

It was pure hokum. But who wants truth, when you can buy the dream?

I was staying in The Village with Ray Van Ronk. Outside the wind was blowing. Ray was like a wolf, living like he was hiding out. It was said that the second world war spelled the end of the Age of Enlightenment, but I wouldn't have known it. I was still in it. I'd read the stuff. Voltaire, Rousseau, Locke ... it was like I knew those guys.

I usually started a book at the middle. It was like I was looking for the education I never got. Thucydides, Gogol, Faulkner. They were like a freeway to my mind.

I wanted to cut a record. But not a 45. I went down to play a song for Woody Guthrie. 'You brought that song to life,' he said.

I'd been in a motorcycle accident. I just wanted out of the rat race. Journalists, promoters, fans: they were all calling me the tortured conscience of America. I never planned to be an icon. I was just a singer writing songs that made some kind of sense to me. Outside the wind was blowing.

People told me what my lyrics meant. It was news to me. One album was supposedly intensely autobiographical. Let them think so. I knew it was based on a bunch of Chekhov short stories. I just wanted to escape with my wife and raise my kids like any other American.

I was on tour with Tom Petty, but I felt I was going through the motions. I couldn't connect with my songs or find a voice. I'm gonna retire at the end of this, I thought. I'm burnt out.

My manager told me to take time out to rehearse with the Grateful Dead, but I had reached the point when I opened my mouth and nothing came out. The terror was overwhelming, but then, from nowhere, a sound emerged. It wasn't a pretty sound, but it was one I recognised. My songs had come back to me.

I was having lunch with Bonio. We looked deep into each other's reflector shades and liked what we saw.

'God wants you to record with Daniel Lanois,' he said.

It was the first Danny had heard of it, but we started to lay some tracks. Outside the wind was blowing. But we stitched and pressed and packed and drove.

John Pankake told me I was trying to be too much like Woody Guthrie. I changed my style. You're now trying to be too much like Robert Johnson. The folk music scene was a paradise, and like Adam I had to leave.

Digested read, digested: The answers are still blowing in the wind.

The Intimate Adventures of a London Call-Girl
by Belle de Jour (2005)

The first thing you should know is that I am a whore. Prostitution is steady work. I open my legs. And then I close them. It beats working in an office. After leaving university, I applied for a number of jobs that I never got and watched my savings steadily dwindle. So when a friend gave me the phone number of a madam, I decided to become a call girl. Like you do. And that's really all there is to me, but since I've been overpaid to write a book I'd better witter on.

Samedi, le 1 novembre. French is so sophisticated and sensual. It also reminds you that I'm middle-class and respectable, because no one's really interested in working-class or foreign prostitutes.

Did I mention that I am actually rather clever? Oh, I did. Well, Martin Amis is cool.

Vendredi, le 12 décembre. My nipples are clamped and a bald-headed man is pissing on me in the bath. I knew that would get your attention.

Mardi, le 27 janvier. I have some wonderfully fascinating ex-boyfriends. Let's call them A1, A2, A3 and A4. We talk about sex all the time. A2 was telling me about his new girlfriend who is into latex. 'Must be very hot,' I observed.

Mercredi, le 18 février. My parents wouldn't be very happy if they knew what I did for a living. I went to see them in Yorkshire last week and we went for a walk before watching *Countdown* on the television.

Mardi, le 9 mars. My publisher tells me the book needs more smut. Anal sex is the new oral. My friends have been doing it for years and I scarcely raise an eyebrow when a client asks for it.

Lundi, le 22 mars. Went shopping for lingerie with A3. I love buying knickers. Even call girls have their favourites. Had dinner with A4, and my latest lover, The Boy, walked into the same restaurant. The Boy repeatedly told me he loved me. Our relationship is over.

Jeudi, le 8 avril. I can tell you're waiting for me to say something profound. Dream on. I don't have any difficult feelings about being a prostitute. Everything's just fine. Got it? I'm just as happy fucking an ugly stranger as I am a handsome lover. The only difference is that I never come with my clients, even when I'm being fisted.

Dimanche, le 2 mai. Sometimes I lie about my age to clients. Sometimes I even lie to my friends. I guess you must be wondering whether I'm lying now.

Mercredi, le 16 juin. More smut. I always wax. The clients prefer it and it's much better for lesbian sex. A4 asked for a threesome when I mentioned this.

Samedi, le 26 juin. The madam has been giving me less work, but I don't mind because I never mind about anything. A client told me he didn't pay me for sex. He paid me to go away. I wonder if book buyers have the same attitude.

Digested read, digested: A new variation on taking the piss.

Don't You Know Who I Am?
by Piers Morgan (2007)

Introduction: For more than 20 years I worked in Fleet Street, but everything changed on May 14 2004, when I was sacked as editor of the *Daily Mirror* for publishing hoax photographs that could have been real if they weren't faked. Having no obvious talent, there was only one thing I could do. Become a celebrity.

August 2004: ITV invite me to appear on *I'm a Celebrity… Get Me Out of Here!* 'That's just a step too far,' I reply grandly. 'You might be right there,' the researcher says. 'Forget it. You're too much of a nonentity even for us.'

November 2004: Michael Ancram is the first guest on my new hard-hitting political-interview TV show, *Morgan and Platell*. I think it could be huge.

February 2005: Star-studded turn-out for the launch of my autobiography, *The Insider*, for which I was paid a £1.2m advance. Jade Goody is there. 'I never read mine,' she says. 'Who wrote yours?' I blush. 'I did it all myself.' Did I mention I got an advance of £1.2m? Go on to dinner at the Ivy but nobody famous is there so it is a waste of time.

March 2005: Get drunk and name-drop some famous people. Michael Parkinson calls to invite me to lunch; on discovering I'm not Pierce Brosnan, he rings off quickly with, 'Got to go. Some other time.' What a star that man is.

April 2005: Matthew Freud rings to suggest we buy the *UK Press Gazette*. 'With you as editor,' he laughs, 'we can run it into the ground in next to no time.'

June 2005: There will be no new series of *Morgan and Platell*. Take everyone famous I know to lunch at the Ivy. They all promise to be my best friend so long as I continue to pay for everything.

August 2005: That fat, talentless fool Jeremy Clarkson has been rubbishing me to the media again. Just let it go, Jeremy. Face it, you are never going to be as famous as me.

October 2005: *GQ* editor Dylan Jones has come up with a cracking idea. He wants me to get really pissed with some minor celebrities, chat to them about sex and stuff and then write about it as if it were vaguely interesting. First up is the ridiculously beautiful Telegraph diarist Celia Walden. 'Why are you so utterly clever and gorgeous?' I swoon incisively. 'Will you shag me?' She smiles radiantly. 'Only when I'm really desperate,' she slurs. I'm definitely in with a chance then!

December 2005: Send five lorries full of red roses and 25 cases of the finest Cristal champagne to Celia. 'You're acting like a D-list celeb,' she texts sweetly. 'Keep it up.'

February 2006: Take everyone famous I know to lunch at the Ivy. They all still promise to be my best friend, so long as I continue to pay for everything.

March 2006: One of my best friends, Simon Cowell, tells me he is going to try and get me a job as a judge on *America's Greatest Talent*. 'You're not very bright, you're overweight and you're hopelessly in love with yourself,' he says. 'You'll be perfect.'

May 2006: Invited on to *Question Time* and come up against Jack Straw. 'So what about WMD?' I deftly point out. Straw is skewered. 'Tu es le Paxman de nos jours,' Celia coos afterwards as we embrace. We are now an item.

June 2006: I am now the biggest star in America. I'm on TV with David Hasselhoff and someone else and I've even got my own trailer. Thank God my kids got in to Charterhouse so they don't interrupt my celebrity lifestyle.

August 2006: How come no one in Britain apart from Sharon Osbourne has heard of *America's Greatest Talent*? Simon Cowell invites me to lunch at the Ivy where someone recognises me. 'Aren't you Diarmuid Gavin?'

October 2006: Bump into Michael Winner in the toilets. He tells me what brand of sweets he likes. What a scoop for Celia's award-winning diary.

December 2006: Celia rings to invite me to Tatler's Brain-dead, Nonentity Couple of the Year Awards. I remind her we don't have a ticket. 'They'll let us in anyway,' she simpers. Hooray. I'm now officially a celebrity.

Digested read, digested: Yes, but we still don't care.

Snowdon by Anne de Courcy (2008)

On May 6 1960, Antony Armstrong-Jones, known as Tony, stood on the balcony of Buckingham Palace and waved to the cheering crowd. He was at the peak of his powers and yet there was only one thought on his mind. Why had he married the Queen's dwarfish sister when he could have had the fabled society beauty and sometime Daily Mail feature writer, Anne de Courcy?

There was nothing in Tony's upbringing to indicate the extraordinary and unselfish life that he himself would lead. His parents, both commoners, divorced when he was five and it was only Tony's resilience and talent that carried him through the hardship of his early years at Eton. 'Tony was a spiffing chap,' says his old school friend, Freddy Cholmondely-Bowles-Binkerton. 'He always made us laugh in Latin lessons.'

Tragedy almost struck when Tony was diagnosed with polio when he was 16. Without his strength of will and exquisite good looks, he might have succumbed to the disease, yet Tony pulled through, and vowed to dedicate his life to helping the handicapped.

Tony decided to become a professional photographer and with no help at all from his favourite uncle, the celebrated designer Oliver Messel, or his extensive network of upper-class dilettantes, he soon made a name for himself as the most pre-eminent artist of the London scene. He was also wonderfully tolerant in his attitudes. When the Kabaka of Buganda booked a sitting he told his assistant, a cheerful cockney, that although the Kabaka was black, he was royal and therefore should be allowed to use the toilet.

Tony moved in a fast set in the 50s, and his animal magnetism made him irresistible to both sexes. I wouldn't want to be so vulgar as to say categorically that he might have been a homosexualist but I'm happy to infer that his relationship with the gloriously effete Jeremy Fry might have strayed beyond the bounds of normal aristocratic platonic idealism. And if it did, it was far removed from the vile buggery of the lower orders.

Women also threw themselves at Tony's perfectly chiselled body, and his sense of noblesse oblige led him into a lifelong string of affairs, one of which continues to this day. In order not to cause any distress to the living, I have chosen not to reveal this woman's name, though once she has croaked I will be happy to expose her in the *Mail*.

Princess Margaret was overwhelmed by Tony's physicality. 'I'd have shagged him a great deal sooner,' she once joked over a pint of gin and 60 Gauloises, 'if I hadn't thought he was queer'. They became the golden couple of the jeunesse dorée de leurs jours and no social gathering was complete without Ken Tynan or Peter Sellers fawning at their feet.

Tony's talents were etched deep into the global memory with his timeless handling of the Investiture of the Prince of Wales at Caernarfon Castle. Possessed of such gifts, Tony was forced into more affairs with some of the world's most beautiful women. Margaret had no such excuse for her squalid cavortings with Robin and Roddy, and Tony was deeply hurt by her betrayal. 'I've only ever wanted what's right for my children and the Queen,' he said when the separation was announced.

Enduring the pain of the title forced on him, Tony sought solace in his second wife Lucy and any other woman lucky enough to meet him. Sadly, Lucy failed to understand how Tony's artistic genius and tireless work for the handicapped excused his affairs, and the couple separated. Melanie Cable-Alexander, a journalist half his age, tried to trap his restless creativity by getting pregnant. 'I'm extremely proud to be Jasper's father,' he said through gritted teeth, after being forced into a DNA test. Another DNA test revealed that Tony had also fathered a daughter with his best friend's wife more than 40 years before.

Yet, despite these trifling annoyances, Tony remains the gentlest, most handsome and greatest of living Englishmen. And as he moves serenely towards his 80s, he continues to shag anything that moves. Except me. Sadly.

Digested read, digested: Please shag me too, Tony.

Going Rogue: An American Life
by Sarah Palin (2009)

It was the Alaska State Fair, August 2008. I passed the Right to Life stand with my daughter's face on their poster. 'That's you, baby-girl,' I said to Piper. 'There's no member of this family your momma wouldn't sell out to promote her career.' As we watched three commy abortionists being burned to death, Senator McCain called my cell phone. Would I like to help him lose the presidential race?

My parents moved to Alaska when I was three and I fell in love with the outdoors and killing things. Swearing the Oath of Allegiance in school gave me a sense of civic pride and I vowed to serve America and go to church a lot.

After coming runner-up, and last, in the Miss Alaska pageant, I married Todd Palin, a guy with his own snow mobile. Todd blessed me with five children: Track, 'we'd have called him hockey if he'd been born in the winter'; Bristol, 'Todd said he hoped she'd have a rack like mine'; Willow, 'we misspelled pillow'; Piper, 'after our light aircraft'; and Trig, 'short for the trigger on our AK47'.

'Dang it,' I thought, 'this election campaign is getting mighty dirty.' But Todd told me God had a purpose for me and after praying for his guidance, I was duly elected mayor of Wasilla by nine votes to six. Various stories have been told about how I dismissed a librarian for stocking anti-American literature on evolution and how I tried to get my brother-in-law fired from his job as a state trooper. Well I don't have space in this 400-page book to go into this in any detail, but if I did I would say that anyone who messes with God or my family has to deal with this pitbull in lipstick!

My proudest moment in office was seeing off an attempt by the police chief to introduce gun and alcohol controls. I hate liberals who don't understand how things work in the 49th State. It is a God-given right for any Alaskan to get drunk and take out anything that moves. Why else did God create guns? Would He have made animals out of meat if He had wanted us to be vegetarians?

Having served on the Oil Commission, I realised that Alaskan politics was rife with corruption and the waste of public funds, and when I was elected governor in 2006 by 73 votes to 59, I vowed to end pork-barrel politics. Mysteriously, though, I find I have omitted my initial support for the 'Bridge to Nowhere, Jobs for the Boys' scheme, a $300m construction project to build a bridge to reach 11 people. I would rather now concentrate on my vice-presidential campaign.

'Tell me what you know about American foreign policy,' McCain said, when we met at his ranch in Arizona.

'About as much as the average American,' I replied. 'So that's nothing, then.' 'Hell, Senator. I don't need to know anything about the history of the Middle East to know the Iraqis are all a bunch of Russian Czechoslovakian Shiites.'

'Where do you stand on God?'

'Sarah Palin won't hold back on God, Senator. I'm proud to believe in the book of Genesis that says the Garden of Eden was in Alaska. Jeez, every December I even go out hunting dinosaurs.'

For some reason I didn't get to see much of Senator McCain after this and although there were great moments, such as talking to President Sarkozy of Paris, Texas on the phone, our campaign never really took off and we were narrowly beaten by 250m votes to 23.

The mud-slinging started in earnest once we returned to Alaska. Rumours about my marriage circulated – dang it, why would I want to divorce a man with the biggest skidoo in Anchorage? – but most damaging were the complaints about my ethical conduct, all of which have been dismissed except the ones that haven't. So I won't be standing for governor again. But if the American people are as stupid as I think they are, it's Palin for president in '12!

Digested read, digested: Going Rouge, An American Embarrassment.

Must You Go?
by Antonia Fraser (2010)

1975: I meet Harold at my sister's. 'Must You Go?' he asks, as I get up to leave. We talk until dawn. Harold: I am loopy about you. Me: I would make a very good secretary. Harold: The same thought had occurred to me. Harold sends me a poem. 'My darling Antonia/I just had to phone ya.' I am thrillingly in love, though it is terribly awkward as I am heppily married to Hugh, and Harold is heppily married to Vivien except when he is having affairs. Luckily our children Orlando, Pericles, Immaculata and Stigmata just want me to be heppy.

1976: Take Harold to meet my uncle, the writer Anthony Powell. Tony asks me if Harold is one of the Northumberland Pinters. I shake my head. 'Oh,' says Tony, before circling the table in a clockwise direction to pour himself another glass of port. Harold sends me another poem. 'My heart goes va-va-voom/When you walk in the room.' His genius is irresistible. He and Hugh have a naked wrestling match in front of the fire while reciting Orlando Furioso, after which Hugh gives us his blessing to move in together. I am the heppiest woman alive.

1977: Harold and I have a long chat about money. Frankly, we are down to our last two castles and we are flat broke. We open a bottle of champagne and go to dinner at the Connaught to cheer ourselves up. The phone rings. It is Melvyn, Larry, Ralph and Trevor all calling to say Harold is a genius. I have to agree with them. We get home and Harold recites Eliot. He does so brilliantly.

1980: To Sissinghurst where Harold learns bridge, confirming my theory he has a naturally brilliant brain. We then join Tom Stoppard for a game of cricket. Harold scores a scintillating 1 before writing me another poem. 'Your radiance divine/Is mine, all mine.' If he wasn't such an outstanding playwright, they would have to make him poet laureate.

1982: I continue to beaver away at my little histories while Harold creates his masterpieces in his Super-Study. He is in a furious temper because he can't make the second act of A Kind of Alaska work. He says he can't write any more. I glance at his notes. Me: You really haven't lost it at all. Harold: That was my shopping list.

1985: Harold is in New York to direct a production of *No Man's Land*. He rings to say he has a slight cold. I can't bear the thought of him alone in his hotel room. How I long to mop his fevered brow! Luckily he recovers and the reviews for the play are, of course, marvellous. He sends me another poem. 'Such beauty, such grace/The smile on your face.' I really do think it's the best thing he's ever written.

1988: At some point in the last few years, it appears that Hugh and Vivien have both died. But I do not want to dwell on unheppy things. And Harold and I are both so very heppy. We have Daniel Ortega and Vaclav Havel to dinner and are heppy to hear both plan to stage *The Homecoming* once democracy is restored to their countries. Salman was also present. His fatwa is too, too awful, but he is such a handsome man.

1995: Harold and I are the heppiest we have ever been now Dada has finally accepted our marriage. Harold has decided to return to acting and is quite brilliant in *Betrayal*. Jeremy Irons and Claire Bloom say it is terribly unfair he should be the world's greatest actor as well as the world's greatest writer. I am the luckiest woman alive.

2005: Every theatre in the world is performing one of Harold's plays. It is no more than he deserves. Harold is increasingly angry about the war in Iraq and he sends me another poem of transcendent beauty. 'Without you at my feet/I am incomplete/Just like the widows in Baghdad/Whose husbands have been murdered/By that fucking war criminal Blair.' So sweet!

2008: Despite filling the house with the scent of freesias, I am very, very unheppy. Harold is dying. He writes me one last poem. 'My heart is all yours/My death just a long pause.'

Digested read, digested: Hark the Harold, angels sing.

A Journey
by Tony Blair (2010)

I wanted this book to be different from the traditional political memoir. Most, I have found, are rather easy to put down. So what you will read here is not a conventional account of whom I met. There are events and politicians who are absent, not because they don't matter, but because they are part of a different story to the self-serving one I want to tell!

No, seriously guys, this is going to be well different. How many other world leaders use so many exclamation marks! And it is as a world leader that I'm writing for you about my journey. And what a journey! When I started in politics I was just an ordinary kind of guy. And you know what? I'm still an ordinary kind of guy – albeit one who has become a multi-millionaire and completely destabilised the Middle East!

You know, I had a tear in my eye when I entered No10 for the first time in 1997, though it wasn't, as the *Daily Mail* tried to claim, because I was choked with emotion at how far I had come since I was a young, ordinary boy standing on the terraces of St James' Park, watching Jackie Milburn play for Newcastle. It was because Gordon had hit me. Ah, Gordon! He meant well, I suppose, in his funny little emotionally inarticulate way.

I guess some of you will find it hard to believe, but I never really wanted to be a politician. But sometimes courage is about taking the difficult decisions and when Cherie said, 'God is calling you to fulfil your destiny', I knew I had to listen. So it was with a heavy heart that I outmanoeuvred Gordon over the leadership of the party after John's death – and whatever Gordo says there was never a deal struck at Granita where he could definitely take over after my second term. Because I had my fingers crossed!

The first year in office was pretty exciting and it was great fun having my old mates like Anji in the office. (I'd tried to get in to her sleeping bag once when I was 16 but she kicked me out! Her loss!) The death of the People's Princess came as a blow – I always found the Royal Family a bit freaky! – but I had a real sense the public were willing me to succeed. A pity the same couldn't be said for the media, who were only too willing to see the worst in the Bernie Ecclestone and Peter Mandelson affairs. Looking back, I feel bad about forcing Peter to resign. But at the time it was him or me. So what the hell!

I find also that Mo Mowlam's part in the Northern Ireland peace process has been rather overstated. So to put the record

straight, it was all down to me. The talks had reached an impasse
and I said to Gerry and David, 'Look guys, we're on a journey,'
and they said, 'Cool Tony, we're with you.'

If only Iraq had been that simple. I know there are some of you
out there who want me to apologise, but life isn't that simple
when there's a war crimes indictment at stake. Look, I feel the
deaths of our servicemen every bit as keenly as if the bullets had
pierced me like stigmata, but sometimes one has to just stand up
and do the right thing even if the evidence isn't there. OK, I will
admit I did have a bit of a wobbly – Cherie had to give me big
cuddles, know what I mean! – when it turned out Saddam didn't
have WMD, but I honestly never lied about them. It was just one,
small, teeny mistake and everyone tore me to pieces! Give us a
break! And for the record I didn't always have a plan to go to war.
The first I heard of it was when Statesman George – Top bloke!
Top thinker! – phoned to say US troops were going in!

I was pretty fed up when everyone failed to see what we had
achieved in Iraq, but an audience with the Pope, who said, 'It is
you who should be baptising me', soon cheered me up. And I felt
a sense of duty to protect the country from Gordon's incompe-
tence. 'You're just waiting until everything's about to go pear-
shaped,' he would yell. As if! It was only my darling John Prescott's
desire to be out of the limelight as my deputy that prompted my
resignation. Selfless little old moi!

Yet, though I feel proud of my achievements and sad at the
direction the Labour party is now taking, my journey is not over.
It continues ever onwards into farce. May my blessings rain upon
the Middle East!

Digested read, digested: A journey ... along the path of self-
righteousness.

Life: Keith Richards
(2010)

Man, I only sleep two hours a day so I've been conscious for several lifetimes. Shame I've missed most of them by being completely out of it. But hey, this is my best guess at what happened so you cats better chill and come for the ride. It ain't free, but we've all gotta pay our dues to the Man, man.

Dartford. Town of short sentences. It was hard, man. When I got kicked out of the school choir, I thought, 'Fuck these cats.' That was me done with authority. My guitar. I slept with it, man. You've gotta. It's like running a whorehouse. Fats, Muddy. Music, I was on the black side of town. Mick. He was the greatest R&B singer I ever heard. And I don't mean maybe. Charlie, Bill and Brian. When we were playing Alexis's club it was like we were on another planet. We moved to Edith Grove. Man, that was poverty. Pooftahs living above. Bank robbers below.

Andrew Oldham threw Mick and me together. Said, 'Write songs, dudes.' Man, my guitar was a mangling, dangling, tangling kinda thang. Tuned it to C. Played a couple of minor breaks. Bobby twiddled some knobs. Charlie hit some back beats. Bill stood in another room. Guess you kinda had to be there.

Satisfaction. Wrote it in my sleep. Then it was hard to tell. They don't make downers like they used to these days. Mandies, reds, Tuinal. Yeah! And the acid. I was tripping with Johnny Lennon. What a lightweight. The chicks. Anita was some sexy bitch. She made the make on me. Then Mick and his small cock made the make on her. Couldn't resist. He was like that. So I had the boinky-boinky-boing with Marianne. I guess we're quits. And she never had the Mars bar. Get me, brother?

We'd had enough of Brian. Long before he died. We heard later some motherfucker said he killed him. Who knows? But even if he did, it would only be manslaughter. Cos Brian was a whining son of a bitch. He could take his narcs, mind. Heroin. Man, it was all around. Gram Parsons. You couldn't find a nicer cat to do cold turkey with. Then, like, it was we gotta get out of town. The pigs were out to bust us. The Man wanted all our cash.

France. Mick was starting to fuck us all off. He got off on flattery. I got off on smack. And how. Exile was epic. Anita looked after Marlon. Yeah, I had a kid. Cool. Perfect accessory for stashing my drugs. I had discovered open tuning. So I played these chords. Mick would sing something in the basement. Bill and Charlie would be in the kitchen. Someone else would be twiddling knobs somewhere. Then someone would move a mike a quarter of an inch. Yawn.

The 70s were hard, man. I hung out with rastas. It is because I is black. And Toronto. Man, what a fuss about an ounce of smack. And it ain't like I was mainlining. Strictly skin-popping. Bill bought me some gear in Canada. One and only time he did anything. It was emotional. Late 70s. Had to stop the heroin. Killing me, man. Luckily, I still had the coke, spliff and Jack Daniels. So I still didn't have a clue what I was doing.

The Stones almost died in the 80s. Mick and me weren't talking. Mick was sucking establishment ass. Anita was just being heavy. So I dumped her. First time I met Patti was in Studio 54. Surrounded by faggots. I was trying to escape Britt Ekland. Nice chick. But Britt, my agenda is full. With Patti I felt safe. It takes a special kind of chick to put up with a rock star only really capable of thinking about himself.

Mick and I kinda made up in the late 80s. Though he's basically still a tosser. And the last 20 years get written off in just a few pages: we haven't made a decent record in years, and the Stones have become kinda dull. But I'm still that dude. Fighting authority. Playing with guns and knives. Hanging out with crims. Counter-cultural in the way only some tax-exile stoner with several hundred million in the bank can be.

Digested read, digested: Inside every ex-junkie… is a trainspotter waiting to get out.

Bird House
by Annie Proulx (2011)

Driving through the wind-blown volcanic ash of Wyoming, it seems impossible not to ask why anybody would live there. I live there. The best way I can describe the otherworldliness of the river by Bird Cloud, with its towering 400ft cliff, is to invoke Uluru in Australia's red centre. Where else could a woman who carries centuries of Native American tradition in her little finger set down her roots?

During the 1980s, my sister and I were kept talking by a man in a shop and avoided being possibly involved in a fatal car accident as a result. It turned out the man's name was Proulx. It turned out he was no relation. I have since done a lot of research into previous generations of people named Proulx and none of them are relations either. Ah well.

I have lived in many of the wildest and most spiritual parts of North America. I had to leave Newfoundland when the local restaurant stopped serving turbot cheeks and I now find myself drawn away from Centennial because many of the inhabitants are too working class and watch American football on the television. So it is to Bird Cloud I am drawn, to create a sensitive eco-mansion with a $10,000 Japanese soak bath. All for just me.

There were difficulties finding an architect capable of realising my vision in the backwoods of Wyoming, as most could not conceive of anything but the most basic lumber dwelling. Eventually, I came across Kevin McCloud. 'Annie has a dream,' he said. 'She wants to create a defiantly modernist Bauhaus structure that will breathe in the ancient spirits of the region. And with the reclaimed metal sheeting on the outside walls, that glows in the same blood-red of long dead Sioux warriors during the three hours of annual sunlight, I think she might achieve it.'

It was also hard to find the right craftsmen. We tried Idle Ian and Bodger Brian, but it was clear when they arrived on site five minutes late that they were not up to my exacting standards. Eventually, Kevin found Patronised Pete and Put-Upon Paul, and the build got under way in late 2005. I had to go away to Capri for the winter and didn't return to Bird Cloud until the following spring. I was horrified. Not only were the tatami prayer mats made of unsustainable rice-straw, but the window in my bedroom had been positioned three inches too far to the left and my view of the eagle's nest was blocked by the cliff. It took three tonnes of dynamite and several hundred thousand dollars to rectify that problem.

The subsequent three years followed a similar rhythm. I would go away somewhere important and glamorous for the winter, while Patronised Pete and Put-Upon Paul would work round the clock in the snow, and then I would come back and scream at them for having got nearly everything wrong. Imagine my fury to discover that the concrete floor sloped 2mm from the door to the wall and that it was not the precise shade of umber I had specified. That cost a further $70,000 to put right.

Worse was to come. My Japanese soak bath flooded the downstairs living area, ruining its recycled teak flooring, the cupboard drawers didn't open noiselessly, the temperature control for my library was faulty, the deer antler door handles had not been polished and the Polygal windows arrived with the wrong kind of non-abrasive dirt. I couldn't write a word for weeks.

During the rare lulls between catastrophes, I would take to the outdoors, removing the cattle that had wandered on to my estate and communing with the sublime, while giant eagles soared above me, repeatedly yodelling, 'Thank Christ someone as deep as Annie has come to live in this Godforsaken land' as they patrolled the desolate skies. And then, disaster once more. Not only had Moron Martin, the landscaper, planted non-native species of chenopodium throughout my 700 acres, he had used non-organic compost to do so. I had to remove three feet of topsoil throughout to avert an environmental disaster.

In 2009, after an agreeable six months in Germany, the work was complete and I was able to soak in my Japanese bath after a tough hour searching for prehistoric relics from the 19th century, congratulating myself that the project had only come in $4m over budget. And then Patronised Pete called to remind me that they didn't bother to clear the snow from the minor roads in winter, so I had really just built myself an expensive summer house. So my restless spirit must move once more. Luckily, Kevin has identified the perfect plot in the Yukon.

Digested read, digested: Grande Dame Designs.

Mud, Sweat and Tears
by Bear Grylls (2011)

The air temperature is −20. I'm clinging on to the mountain by my fingernails. Beneath me a vertical drop. A camera comes loose. I tumble 1,000 feet on to the rocks below. Another close shave. I pick myself up. There is work to do. I love my life.

My great-great-great grandfather was Samuel Smiles who wrote the first self-help book. The gene pool has been rather diluted since then. I can only write in trite aphorisms. God helps them who help themselves. If at first you don't succeed, try again. That sort of thing. It works for me.

I was always a bit wild as a child. That is posh for a bit thick. Luckily that didn't stop me going to public school. Why would it? Eton seriously lacked girls. But that was good for me as I had already decided I wanted to remain a virgin until I got married. My faith has always been very important to me. I have a very simple belief. If you ask, so shall you be given. God has never failed to find me a parking meter. Note to self: no need to pray after 6.30pm.

My mother found my constant need for attention quite tiring. But my Dad totally got me. He said, 'Bear, you are a Bear with a very little brain. So go out and do Bearish things like climbing on to the school library roof.'

I was seriously broke when I left school. University didn't appeal so I went travelling. Because I've always believed that life is out there to be lived. And I wanted to go out there and grab it. India was amazing. I saw some incredible sights and met some truly awesome people. I came home feeling truly humbled. I've learned never to grumble about anything again.

On my return to England I was even more seriously broke. But

I still didn't get a job because I wanted to take on a bigger challenge. I planned to join the SAS reserves. The training was brutal and there are aspects of it I can't mention due to the Official Secrets Act. You will probably wish there were more bits covered by the Act after you have read more than 100 interminable pages about wandering around the Brecon Beacons.

The disappointment I felt at not making the grade was intense. For a while I was at a loss what to do next. Then I remembered my faith. Had God not said unto me, 'Go forth and learn how to kill people?' So I went back with my good mate, Trucker – top bloke, the best bloke a bloke could ever want – and told the recruiting officer, I wanted another go. The beasting was almost unbearable. Yet I was determined not to break. It was the proudest day of my life when I was given my beret.

I was seriously, seriously broke by the time I had finished my training. So I went to South Africa, as life is about taking the chances on offer. I was determined to grab any that came along with both hands. Then my parachute failed to open properly. My back was broken in three places. It was a low point. For months I was lost in self-pity before I remembered the story of Lazarus. 'You can get it if you really want, but you must try and try,' God said. And on the third day I rose again.

It was around this time I met Shara. She is the light of my life. I couldn't do without her. Like my Dad, she is seriously not bothered by how dim I am. I needed to be with her, but I had other things to do. 'You are my rock,' I told her. 'But I must climb another rock.'

Everest is seriously high up. It can get bloody cold and dangerous up there. Apparently some people have died there. I came close myself. I had to push myself to the limit to reach the summit. But that's what life is for: pushing yourself to the limit. So that's what I did.

I was seriously, seriously, seriously broke when I came back from Everest. I prayed for guidance. And I got it. A producer said, 'We're looking for a thick bloke to take a lot of unnecessary risks.' 'You've found him,' I replied. I see I've already written 400 pages, so I've run out of space to tell you about the bits of my life that might have been more interesting. I will just say I forgive those who claimed my TV shows were put-up stunts and that I stayed in five-star hotels. Everyone needs a little quality time with their family.

Digested read, digested: Do Bears bullshit in the woods?

A Walk-On Part
by Chris Mullin (2011)

1994: John Smith is dead. To London for tea with Tony Blair. He is seeking my support for his leadership bid. 'It would be great to have you on board, Carl,' he said. For some reason, I got the feeling my political career was over. But I will back Blair as there isn't anyone better. To Sunderland, where a constituent asks if I am still on holiday. Why does everyone assume every MP is just having lunch? I have worked tirelessly for the past three months to get new windows for the local community centre. It's not my fault nothing has happened. To Blackpool for the party conference, where Tony has taken on clause IV. I fear we'll be out of government for another generation. I wrote to Tony asking him to make sure my campaigns to limit Murdoch's media empire and expose the Masons in public office will be a priority for a new Labour government. 'Of course, Keith,' he replied. Maybe we aren't doomed after all.

1995: To Sunderland for a constituency surgery. No one comes. It appears I've turned up on the wrong day. The opinion polls suggest we have a 41-point lead. They are quite wrong of course. We will be lucky to get a single figure majority. Anji Hunter calls to say Tony will be ringing me soon so will I stay by the phone? I don't move for five days. It turned out he wanted to talk to Charles Clarke. I am still very hopeful of making headway with my bill to limit the Masons. To London for a meeting with Michael Green, who was waited on hand and foot by a pushy, fresh-faced public schoolboy called David Cameron. If ever there was a man going nowhere, it's Cameron. To the House, where John Major puts in a good performance at PMQ. I get sixth question and ask what he proposes to do about the Masons. I get a good laugh and am invited on to *Loose Ends* but somehow I can't help wondering if I'm wasting my life.

1996: *The Economist* predicts we will have a 45-seat majority. They are wrong, of course. The best we can hope for is a hung parliament. Much discontent within the party about the influence of Peter Mandelson. I fear we are in danger of alienating our supporters by trying to out-Tory the Tories, but I'll keep my powder dry for now as I am increasingly hopeful of getting Murdoch and the Masons at the top of Tony's agenda, having written to him once more. 'You're at the front of my mind, Charles,' he said. A respectable showing in the elections for the shadow cabinet, but somehow I get the feeling that the post of 'Token Left Winger Who Can Be Bought Off With Promises of a Big Office and Lots of Lunches with Tony' has been earmarked for John Prescott. To Sunderland, to sign some Christmas cards. Unfortunately I left them all in London.

1997: Made a new year resolution to engage in less pointless activity, before writing to Tony Blair to ask what progress he was making on Murdoch and the Masons. 'A lot, Kevin,' he replied. It's sounding hopeful. The opinion polls are predicting a landslide victory for us, but they are clearly wrong. Waited by the phone for four months to hear whether the Man was going to appoint me to ministerial office. In September he invites me to chair a select committee. 'May I ask what you are doing about Murdoch and the Masons?' 'Bad line, Clint. Must go.' To Sunderland where every major industry is being closed. In truth, there's nothing I can do about it, but I ring Peter Mandelson anyway. He tells me not to worry as it's only the working classes who will lose their jobs.

1998: The Man put in a brilliant performance in the House. It's just a shame it was on behalf of the Conservatives. Jack Straw is proving to be slightly more able than anyone imagined. He told me the secret is to lower people's expectations and then surprise them. I asked him to put in a good word for me with the Man about the Masons and Murdoch. He assured me he would. Perhaps this government will be one to remember after all. Or perhaps not. Prescott is incoherent, Mandelson has been sacked already and Gordon is the worst chancellor in living memory. We will certainly be voted out at the next election.

1999: To the House to escape the children, who are keeping me awake. John Prescott soon puts me to sleep. Bumped into the Man in the lobby. We have made a huge error over Bosnia and he is in thrall to the US, so I asked him about the Masons and Murdoch. 'Any minute, Claud,' he said. I told him I had had enough of chairing the select committee. 'Then I'll give you a non-job as parliamentary under-secretary, Chip.' Things are looking up.

Digested read, digested: Diary of a Nobody.

May I Have Your Attention, Please?
by James Corden (2011)

Where do I start? I've never written a book before and how do I begin to tell you about my life? Especially as I'm only 32 and haven't done very much. In fact, I've just realised you may not actually have purchased this book and are just reading the first page to see if you're interested. I'm guessing you're not overly impressed so far, but then I'm not that bothered as I've already banked more than £1m as an advance and there's no chance of the book earning out.

To be honest, I'm a bit all over the place. My gorgeous wife Jules, the most gorgeous talented wife in the world, was due to have a baby in a week's time and I had been planning to get the book knocked off before the birth but she's gone into labour early so I'm going to have to get a bit of a bend on and bash it out before they both come home from hospital. Have I told you I haven't written a book before? What shall I do? Hey, just had an email from my publisher saying that any old drivel will do as long as I make the word count. So is this OK? I really hope so, because I really, really want you to like me.

Hey, that's one chapter down. This book writing is easier than I thought. So let me tell you a funny story. On second thoughts, let's just call it a story. My parents were both in the Salvation Army and I knew from the first time I stood on a chair at my sister's christening that I was going to be a performer. Fascinating. So what else can I tell you? We lived near High Wycombe and we were the happiest family ever.

It may surprise you to know that when I was 11 my parents sent me to secondary school. I wasn't the brightest kid on the block, but somehow I always had this faith in my acting talents and when I left school I got a part in the West End musical *Martin Guerre* – definitely up there as one of the best musicals ever written, in my opinion. I was the happiest person on the entire planet as I was working with some of the most talented people I have ever met.

After a year in the West End I got a part in a brilliant movie, *The Church of Alan Darcy*, starring Bob Hoskins. I don't suppose many of you saw the movie, but it is definitely one of the best films ever made and Bob is one of the most iconic actors of his generation and taught me more about acting than anyone else apart from all the other extremely talented actors I went on to work with later. I should also mention that it was at this time I met Shelley, the most talented and beautiful girl in the world, and we stayed together for eight of the happiest years of my life.

'Are you sitting down, James?' It was my agent on the phone. 'Mike Leigh wants you to star in a film alongside Alison Steadman.' Can you believe it? Me, working with Mike and Alison the two most talented people in the world. Ever. I was like, 'Yes. When can I start?' it was just such a totally mind-blowing experience working with such talented people and I wondered if I would ever get to work with such talented people again, but luckily I got to work on Fat Friends and Teachers with some more of the most talented actors and directors in the world. Ever, ever.

Would you believe it, I then got a call saying would I like a part in *The History Boys?* Hello! Alan Bennett, Nick Hytner and the National. Try and keep me away! It really was the happiest two years of my life working with the most talented people in the history of theatre ever and I was so thrilled when Alan sent me a letter saying Dear _____, Thank you for working on *The History Boys*. You are the best actor ever. Yours, Alan.'

While I was starring in *The History Boys*, my good friend Ruth, the most talented woman ever, and I knocked up a pilot for *Gavin & Stacey* over a weekend and getting that series commissioned and working with Matt Lucas and Rob Brydon, two of the most talented actors I have ever met, was the happiest time of my life. Sadly Shelley and I had split up by then, but luckily I almost went out with Lily Allen. Well, I would have done if she'd fancied me! What a talent she is!

I have to admit success may have gone to my head and for a year I wasn't as nice as I should have been. But then I met Jules and my agent suggested doing some work for Comic Relief to improve my image and I haven't looked back. And, best of all, Jules and the baby are back from hospital and my editor says I have exceeded my word count by 5,000, so job done.

Digested read, digested: You'll have to try a lot harder than this...

Vagina by Naomi Wolf (2012)

Spring 2009 was beautiful. I was emotionally and sexually happy. But then I noticed a change: my orgasms, which I had always previously timed at 22 minutes 47 seconds, had petered out to a pitiful 13 minutes and two seconds. I immediately barged my way to the head of the queue to see Dr Deborah Coady, the world's pre-eminent vulvaologist. Dr Coady shook her soft light brown hair that falls to her shoulders and sighed deeply.

'I regret to say that several millennia of patriarchal oppression are causing your vagina to lose consciousness,' she said. 'But if you agree to a simple 38-hour procedure, I can restore your Inner Goddess.'

Within minutes of coming round after the operation, I heard a faint whisper speaking to me from between my legs. 'On behalf of women everywhere,' it said, 'I thank you for giving me back my voice. So tonight, Naomi, just for you, I'm going to sing 'I Believe I Can Fly'.

My mascara began to run as I wept plangent tears of joy while I tried to locate my reborn G-spot with my perfectly manicured index finger. 'Left a bit,' groaned my Inner Goddess.

I checked the stopwatch and smiled: 21 minutes and 39 seconds. My vagina was back in business. I owed it to her and womankind to celebrate her recovery by writing her biography.

As I began my research – I cannot recommend the findings of Dr Pfaus's MRI scans of the cervix too highly – I began to make some remarkable discoveries. A vagina that is neglected can easily fall into a deep depression; indeed, I encountered several that had self-sealed in an act of suicide. Meanwhile, a pampered vagina is capable of acts of great creativity. It is a little-known fact that Edith Wharton wrote the House of Mirth with her clitoris. And while it is true that the vagina may sometimes become addicted to her own happiness, this is something society ought to celebrate, rather than control with a strict 12-step programme that insists on submission to a male God.

Throughout history, men have sought to subjugate the vagina through whatever means they have available and as Dr Nancy Fish, whose luscious auburn curls cascade dreamily over her angular shoulders, points out in her seminal work, *The Vagina Songbook*: 'The Delta Blues actually originated from the Venus Delta, as women began to protest at 'Waking up in the morning/ With a penis in my bed'.'

I had experience of this directly when a male friend, whom I shall call Neanderthal, offered to host a party in celebration of my vagina. 'I've made some vulva-shaped pasta that I've named cuntini,' he laughed. I gasped as I noticed he was also serving champagne out of deliberately phallicised bottles and had not even had enough respect to circumcise the sausages. My vagina went into a three-year spasm during which I was unable to do anything except write to Ban Ki Moon and insist that verbal insults to the vagina be considered a war crime.

To say I was astounded by the degree to which the Goddess Array (as I now choose to call my vagina) reacts to oppression is an understatement, not least when I conducted my own experiment on mice with Dr Here Shite, whose neat bob perfectly offset her generous smile. You should have seen the look of terror on the rodents' faces as we shouted: 'Watch out for the pussy!'

Many decades of detailed exploration of the inner contours of the Goddess Array ensued, until I was finally able to conclude that a happy vagina is one that is equally respected by men and women. And as I pondered this brilliant conclusion, I lay back in the Greek countryside where I was on holiday, and realised that the Earth was a Goddess, too. The hills enveloped me in their bosomly embrace and the trees bowed down to my vagina and cried: 'Come, Yoni.' For three hours, 57 minutes and 28 seconds, I did as they commanded.

Digested read, digested: The Holy of Holies.

Margaret Thatcher:
The Authorised Biography, Volume I
by Charles Moore (2013)

Lady Thatcher was not a woman prone to self-examination and so it was with great humility I accepted the task of protecting her legacy while maintaining a veneer of even-handedness and objectivity. Margaret Hilda Thatcher was born in 1925, the second daughter of Alderman Alfred Roberts and his wife, Beatrice. Her elder sister, Muriel, who has never previously spoken of Margaret, remembers that her mahogany desk was always tidy. Her dentist, Geoffrey Marks, recalls her having near perfect molars. Margaret did not get on well with her mother and there was a terrible family row over whether she should study Latin.

In 1941, Margaret bought her first pink uplift bra which she wore when reading the poems of Rudyard Kipling. She also bought a skirt for £3 16s to celebrate her admission to Oxford to read chemistry. There, she met her first male friend; one hesitates to call Neil Findlay a boyfriend, though I have ascertained to my satisfaction they once went to the 'flicks' (her word, I should never be so vulgar). Upon leaving Oxford, she went to a Conservative party conference in Llandudno, where she came to the attention of the Dartford constituency that first adopted her as a candidate. At about this time, realising she was on the rise, she palmed off her new dreary farmer beau, Willie Cullen, on to her sister Muriel to whom she once paid the singular compliment of saying, 'You are the only person I know who is more rightwing than me.'

Even though Margaret was defeated at the 1950 election, she did far better than anticipated and decided she ought to marry Denis Thatcher, a man to whom she was not particularly attracted, but had the advantage of both a minor public school education and sharing her fondness for a tipple. They honeymooned in Estoril where Margaret observed many Jews. Margaret was very fond of The Jew, observing that 'The Jew is a natural trader', an empathy that stood her in good stead when she was selected for East Finchley.

The arrival of twins, Mark and Carol, took both Margaret and Denis by surprise, but they reacted with characteristic pragmatism. A next-door neighbour, Brigadier Arbuthnot, remembers Margaret handing them over to a nanny, while muttering 'that's the last we'll hear about those brats for 500 pages until Mark gets lost in the desert'. 'It was an act of tremendous love,' the nanny later said, when I twisted her arm.

Margaret was universally acknowledged to be the most attractive of all the women in parliament in 1959 and her sexual charisma would later work to her considerable advantage, not least for Tory grandees such as myself who are still aroused remembering the occasional sightings of Matron's stockings. She was much taken aback to find herself in opposition in 1964. 'I'm not a natural attacker,' she explained with her customary insight.

She first went to America in 1968 where her good manners were much commented on and, having failed to attend the funerals of either her father or mother, she was much perturbed to find many Marxists working within the Department of Education when the Conservatives returned to power. She was deeply hurt by the sobriquet Milk Snatcher and blamed Ted Heath for fostering the politics of consensus.

After the 1974 election, it became clear to Margaret that Ted had to go. It is hard to understate her bravery in putting herself forward against him, as so many people have testified to me and, faced with the prospect of 'a filly or a gelding' as leader, the Conservatives stepped into the unknown.

It was still far from clear whether the country would accept a woman prime minister and it was her stylist Gordon Reece and her advertising guru Lord Saatchi who came up with the brilliant idea of keeping her away from the cameras as much as possible.

The strategy worked and in May 1979, she strode into Downing Street with the immortal words, 'Where there is discord, let me drive a permanent wedge.'

Of the final 300 pages, almost anyone who is remotely interested in monetarism, Ireland and the Thatcher government will have read them countless times before, though I shall attempt to add nuance by saying 'on the one hand this' and 'on the other hand that'. I can confirm, though, that while she had a deep distrust of black Africans, she was not racist. In private, she only made jokes about the Germans and the French.

How the country roared with laughter when Margaret said, 'You turn if you want to. This lady's not for turning' but her good humour aside, she could be steely when required. Several people I have interviewed remarked that she could be quite critical. Yet she felt her criticism was justified and as she was right about almost everything, history may find in her favour. Mine will, certainly.

Margaret was greatly displeased that Ronald Reagan did not back her unequivocally over the Falkands crisis and felt that Francis Pym was pusillanimous as foreign secretary. She also reported that the deaths of British servicemen caused her the worst moments of her entire life, a reaction that showed her characteristic natural maternal sympathies. Unfortunately, there was no space in this volume to record Carol Thatcher's comment of 'Are you kidding?'

Ultimately, the Iron Lady was proved right to hold firm and, as the Argentines surrendered, the clamour went up: 'Rejoice. There's another volume to come next year. It's a licence to print money.'

Digested read, digested: The Dead Thatch Bounce.

A Man in Love
by Karl Ove Knausgård (2013)

2008: The summer has been long, and Linda and I have been quarrelling for longer. I still haven't finished the second novel I haven't started and we are taking our three children, Vanja, Heidi and John, to a rundown theme park.

'This is boring,' Linda says.

'Really boring,' I reply.

'Do you want a sandwich?'

'Only if it's stale.'

We switched tenses and went home. I tried to write, but Linda wanted me to make dinner. I could have told her to do it herself, but I preferred the sullen silence of martyrdom. I put the children to sleep by reading extracts of Dostoyevsky and Holderlin. If they were going to bore me, I was going to bore them. I then sat down and thought of the first and only time I had been happy.

I had left Tonje and come to Sweden at a day's notice. 'Why are you leaving me?' she had asked. I didn't know. I just had this vague feeling I'd never write anything interesting again if I stayed with her. So I shrugged. I arrived in Stockholm and called my old friend, Geir.

'Can I stay with you?' I asked. He laughed. 'OK,' he replied eventually. 'As long as I don't have to listen to you talking about the book you aren't writing.' We talked about Nietzsche and his book about boxing before I went to the lavatory to write a paragraph about toilet paper. We then tried to see Tarkovsky's *The Mirror*, but were too late. It had been an agreeably pointless day.

A month later, with my second novel still unwritten, I met

Linda, a woman I had once tried to get into bed several years earlier at a symposium for people who didn't write. 'I don't write books,' I had said. 'I don't write poems,' she had replied. She also didn't fancy me. Something had changed, though. Maybe she had become a little more desperate, because Geir told me she fancied me.

'There's something I have to tell you,' Linda said.

'What?' I replied, impatiently. 'I have a book to write and cigarettes to smoke.'

'I once tried to commit suicide.'

I perked up immediately. 'That's fantastic. You're just the woman for me. Let's get married and have three children.'

Those five minutes were the happiest of my life. Happier even than when I was reading Schopenhauer as my father died. Linda's pregnancy provided plenty of interruptions for my writing: we argued constantly about whose turn it was to read the latest Rachel Cusk, and it was typical of her selfishness that she chose to go into labour while I was putting the finishing touches to the first sentence of my second novel.

Vanja was a stroppy, demanding baby who constantly required attention. After giving her a week of my time, I told Linda I needed to go to my apartment to write for several months. Much to my amazement, I did manage to finish my novel – a torpid affair about sheep and angels – which the critics predictably praised, failing to recognise its inherent mediocrity.

'I'm so fed up with Sweden,' I screamed when I returned to Linda. 'All our friends are petit-bourgeois writers and artists who have never done a proper day's work in their life.'

Geir returned from not writing his book in Iraq and reminded me I had once told him I had been a paedophile. I slapped him. 'You failed to understand my use of Hamsunian infantilist metaphor.'

Somewhere down the line, Linda got pregnant again. Heidi's birth was even duller than Vanja's. I can barely bring myself to mention John's.

'Where have we gone wrong?' Linda cried. 'We used to be in love. Now I'm the world's worst parent.'

'That's typical,' I replied. 'It's always got to be about you. I'm the world's worst parent. Now stop moaning while I fly to Norway to give a lecture to seven people about my two shitty novels.'

As I landed in Oslo, my phone rang. My mother had had a serious heart attack. I smiled. Maybe now I'd have something to write about in my next book.

Digested read, digested: A man in love with writing about not writing.

Girl Least Likely To
by Liz Jones (2013)

I went to visit Mum today. Her dentures were out and she was dribbling. She hadn't even moisturised. The staff at the expensive, run-down care home that I have been bankrupting myself to pay for on my own because my brothers and sisters are too dead or too tight-fisted to contribute towards, don't know her name. They even put full-fat milk in her tea. I can't help weeping, and I pray that when my dear horse Lizzie is dying she isn't so degraded.

When I was 11, my father told me a joke. That was the last time I ever laughed. At school I was the ugliest girl in my class. My hair was long and greasy, my face pitted with acne, and my whole body covered with matted fur. The only boy to snog me was Kevin, and he was so disgusted he vomited down my throat.

I immediately rushed to the lavatory to make sure I hadn't accidentally swallowed any unnecessary calories.

By the time I left school, my skin was so bad as a result of my anorexia the doctor prescribed me hormone tablets. These caused my breasts to balloon from a 32B to a 32C. How I hated those pendulous dugs and was delighted when I found a plastic surgeon willing to remove them for just £20,000! I asked if he would also amputate my legs while he was about it, so I would never have to set eyes on my hideous calves again, but when I came round I was shocked to discover they were still attached. Since then, I've never been able to trust a man.

I'm not sure why I was appointed editor of *Marie Claire*. Everyone hated me there. They couldn't cope with my perfectionism and workaholism, and I couldn't stand their idleness. 'There's no need to go to the toilet to throw up your lunch,' I would say. 'Just stay at your desk and use the wastepaper basket like I do.' I also couldn't understand their uncritical attitude towards the fashion industry. 'Can't you see it has a negative impact on women's self-image?' I said, as I hailed a taxi to take me home, laden with freebies from Mulberry and Prada.

In my late 20s, I nearly had sex for the first time after I paid a man called Chris £1,500 a week to live with me, after bargaining him up from his initial request for £1,000. But I'd mown my extensive pubic area and he declared that my vagina was completely sealed – then went to the pub to watch football. In the end, I got a doctor to treat me rough and came home to tell Chris I was now fixed. But he had left, taking all my credit cards with him.

When I did have sex for the first time with my husband, I remember thinking how messy it was. My cats agreed. 'By the way,' said Sweetie, 'did you know he brings loads of other women back here while you're out at work? I can't get a wink of sleep with all the noise they make.' Straight away I told Nirpal he could pack his bags with all my belongings and leave.

I decided to move out of London to live among the small-minded bigots on Exmoor who couldn't tell the difference between a Gucci original and a knockoff. 'Why does everyone hate us?' Lizzie sobbed, when I brought her three-course dinner to her stable. 'Have they never seen a horse with a Brazilian before?'

The £3m bill for building a dog jacuzzi left me nearly bankrupt, and what little grasp I once had of reality deserted me for good. I no longer knew quite who I was, what I was or even if I had a Rock Star boyfriend. All I knew for certain was that no matter how badly everyone treated me, no one could hate me more than me.

Digested read, digested: The girl least likely to stop writing about herself.

An Appetite for Wonder
by Richard Dawkins (2013)

I was christened Clinton Richard Dawkins. By a strange quirk, Charles Darwin also has the initials CRD. I often think how proud he would have been to share them with me. Although, by reductio ad absurdum, everyone must be related to one another if you go back far enough, I propose to start this memoir with my grandfather, Clinton Evelyn, the first Dawkins to go to Balliol College, Oxford. The eulogy I wrote for his funeral still brings tears to my eyes.

My father also went to Balliol. My mother, being of Cornish origin, didn't, though I have often wondered about the evolution of the Cornish dialect. Her father wrote a book, Short Wave

Wireless Communication, which was legendary in our family for its incomprehensibility, but I have just read the first two pages and find myself delighted by its lucidity in comparison to my own.

I was born in Nairobi in 1941, my father having been posted to Kenya by the colonial service. By all accounts, I was a sociable child and I have a clear memory of all the friends I made by pointing out the nature of their second-order meta-pretends while we were playing together. I also had a fondness for poetry and have only recently realised that some of the early, rhythmic verses I invented for myself are highly reminiscent of Ezra Pound.

After several peripatetic years, my family returned to England where I was sent to Chafyn Grove, an unremarkable preparatory school, where I frequently pretended to know less than I actually did. This, I now see, was early evidence of my peculiar empathy towards individuals who are much stupider than me. There was, of course, life beyond Chafyn Grove and I spent many happy holidays sorting out my father's collections of coloured bailer twine and serpentine pebble pendants.

My father had intended me to follow him to Marlborough, but his application on my behalf was too late and I was rejected – a sleight from which he never fully recovered, as I explained so movingly in my speech at his funeral. Instead, I went to Oundle boarding school and I shall never forget the shame I felt on my first day as a fag, after ringing the five-minute bell five minutes too late. For my many thousands of American readers, I should point out that fag in this context does not mean homosexual. Of course, some boys did make advances towards me, but I firmly believe there was nothing sexual about that. Likewise, Mr GF Bankerton-Banks whose preferred method of teaching was with his hands in a boy's pockets. No doubt in these more suspicious times, he would have been dismissed as a paedophile.

Some years ago, I was invited to give the inaugural Oundle lecture, in which I playfully invoked the ghost of a long-dead headmaster. I would like to make clear that this was just creative use of poetic imagery and in no way implies a belief in the supernatural. I may have once, shortly after my confirmation, been foolish enough to believe in the possibility of an intelligent designer, but I have long since exposed the pathetic fallacy of that belief.

Having taken up my anointed position at Balliol, I quickly became one of the most remarkable zoologists of my generation, and it was a surprise to find my work on chickens pecking at eggshells and crickets reacting to light sources didn't receive greater international acclaim. Not that Balliol was all work and no play. I did achieve my first sexual congress with a cellist and it was most gratifying to discover how biomechanically efficient my penis was.

I married my first wife Marian in 1967, though that's the last time I propose to mention her. Far more interesting are the two computer languages I invented to determine hierarchical embedment. Who would have guessed that $P=2(P+P-P*P)-1$?! In the early 1970s, I started work on *The Selfish Gene*. I had no idea when I was writing the first chapter just how remarkable the book would be, as it had seemed self-evident for more than a decade to me that panglossian theories were erroneous and that natural selection took place at the genetic level. What I hadn't then realised was my remarkable ability to be right about absolutely everything: the consequences of that realisation will follow in a later volume. Though you may be hoping a process of natural literary selection prevents that.

Digested read, digested: Me me meme.

LETTERS/DIARIES

The Letters of Kingsley Amis
(2000)

My dear Philip,

So very sorry not to have written earlier, so very sorry. I haven't done much of anything since my wife left me. Not for anyone, she just buggered off. I think she did it partly to punish me for stopping wanting to fuck her and partly because she realised I didn't like her any more. Even so, not having her around is infinitely crappier than having her around. I did feel better for 20 min today, though, as I have just found and installed the couple who will look after me. They are Hilly and her third husband, Lord Kilmarnock.

I'm still working on the Welsh novel, *Iv dn bggrll*. I'm so painfully slow. I have to keep checking the Welsh dictionary, and have come up with the not particularly Taffy suggestion that the reason women live longer than men is that a good number of women knock off their husbands with rage-induced coronaries. What do you think?

I saw your piece on Waugh. It sounded a fucking dreary book. The more I think about it the more I reckon he wrote one good book and then went off when he became a Catholic. The thing that really gets me about him is the way he toadies to the upper classes, droning on and on about how wonderful everything about them is. Still, he isn't as bad as Bron, I suppose.

Bin reading the new Tony P. It starts OK but then falls apart. Pissy as it is, though, it's not half as bad as the bunch of new books by the leading young novelists I've been sent. Not that I've read them all. As if. One William Boyd short story goes on and on, and just when you think something is about to happen it ends.

And then there's M**t** *m*s. Don't know what to say about him, though I bet you do. He made £38,000 last year. The shit. The little shit.

NB: Have you read the new Dick Francis? He's back to form with *The Danger*. I went out to lunch with the Penguin publicity girl yesterday and quite enjoyed it. It would have been bloody brilliant if I had actually wanted to fuck her. It wasn't her fault. My sex drive just isn't what it was.

My damn fool doctor has told me I ought to give up the booze as I've been getting spasms in my arm. But what's left if you can't drink? So sod him. I am on my New Alcoholic Policy of four to five drinks per day. It allows me to eat, sign my name and follow films on TV. But it doesn't stop the nightmares. I'm piling on the pounds. I now have a 42-inch waist rather than the normal 38. Growing old is hell. What a feast future generations will have when they read our letters.

Happy and prosperous new bum,

Kingers.

Digested read, digested: Grand old curmudgeon turns out to be consistently more entertaining as a letter writer than as a novelist.

The Diaries of Ken Tynan
(2001)

June 1971 Chronically idle since my return from France. I used to take Dexamyl to give me confidence to start work. Now I take it to give me the confidence not to.

April 1972 I talk to John Dexter and Frank Dunlop about LO's willingness to sell us all at the National to P Hall. Hall is one of those curious types with no enemies and no friends.

October 1972 One difference between the London theatre today and 20 years ago is the relative paucity of queers.

February 1973 I have been seeing a fellow spanking addict, an actress called Nicole. Her fantasy is to be bent over with knickers down and caned, preferably with the buttocks parted to disclose the anus. She also enjoys spanking and exposing me. Really there is no sport to touch it; it is not just a nocturnal relaxation, it is a way of life.

April 1973 My birthday. Noel is dead and Muhammad Ali has broken his jaw and I am 46. God and bugger and fuck.

September 1973 For lunch and dinner at Tony Richardson's villa near St Tropez. John Gielgud asks me about *The Joint* by James Blake. KT: It's about a masochistic convict who gets himself imprisoned because he likes being sucked off by sadistic Negro murderers. JG: You can't quarrel with that.

May 1974 What is my current profession? Drama critic: not since 1963. Impresario: not since Oh Calcutta. Nabob of the NT: not since last December. Film director: untested. Journalist: extinct. Author: blocked. I have no professional identity and have ceased to exist.

July 1975 General depression due to persistent bronchial infection.

March 1976 At last able after many months to make love to Kathleen again. But my potency vanishes after she spends another night with her lover, Dan Topolski. Debts now mountainous; yesterday the telephone was cut off. I can't write without smoking and if I smoke I shall die. Vicious circle or double-bind. Compare and contrast.

November 1977 A cheque for $22,000 – three times the amount agreed – arrives from the New Yorker. For a day I am surely the best-paid journalist in the world.

January 1980 Debts in excess of $75,000 and health failing rapidly. From Maugham's *The Summing Up*: He leaves out his redeeming qualities and so appears only weak, unprincipled and vicious. Shall I fall into this trap?

Digested read, digested: High angst, top gossip and lashings of S&M from the final years of one of Britain's most talented theatre critics.

Alan Clark: The Last Diaries
(2002)

Saltwood/Albany, February 1991–September 1999

Still obsessive about 'X' but haven't the nerve to end it. Darling Jane is looking strained, she knows something is up. Tension headache, my pulse up to 87. I'm not at all well. How much longer have I got? Five years? Ten years. Finances in a total mess. Don't want to get rid of Big Red so might have to sell the Degas; 300 would clear the tax bill. State of abject depression. The party is in a mess and I feel now is the time to step down. But I can't bring myself to do it yet as ACHAB*.

Slept very badly. Had to get up three times for a tinkle. I must book a PSA. 'X' is ignoring me and I'm taking it out on Janey. Cleared my office at Westminster and said my goodbyes; my health is good, my stamina is up, but my mood is black. I SHOULD NEVER HAVE LEFT THE HOUSE OF COMMONS. I really need to organise a car cull and get on with my life. God has been good to me; I've had a great career, sex-life with Janey has never been better and there's the prospect of grand-children on the horizon.

Is it too much to ask for one last chance at power and 10 more years? Richard Ryder isn't returning my calls – little shit. How I miss the thrill of power. JM is almost isolated, the party rudderless. Publication of my diaries has caused something of a stir. It's nice to still be famous. Or should that be infamous?

Desperate to get back into the House. Had an approach from Kensington & Chelsea but Nick Scott is hanging on. Am I too old? Still, ACHAB. My vision is going. Cancer of the optic nerve? Scott enquiry still rumbles on, find it increasingly hard to trust Tristan G-J. See in the *Sunday Times* my name has been put forward as possible leader of the Tory party. I feel marvellously young once more. A miracle. K&C have adopted me against all the odds. But how long will I be alive to enjoy it? Disastrous general election, but my seat quite safe.

Alastair Campbell phoned twice to offer me a K. BB published but poor reviews. My headaches are getting worse. The doctors say there is nothing wrong with me.

The fact is I have a brain tumour and I'm going to die.

* *Anything can happen at backgammon.*

Digested read, digested: AC's observations both on his health and his fellow politicians remain spot on to the last.

Primo Time
by Anthony Sher (2005)

2 November 2002: I wonder if Nelson Mandela knows Primo Levi. I'm on my way to meet Nelson and I'm planning to adapt Primo's *If This is a Man* as a one-man show; it would be a remarkable coincidence if there was a tangible connection between three of the most iconic figures of the 20th century.

7 November 2002: At Grayshott health farm with my dear friend Richard Wilson. I mention the project to him and he replied, 'But of course you must play Primo.' I immediately see he's right.

8 November 2002: Sod it. I start writing tonight.

9 November 2002: Finished. It's far too long, but I could sense Primo's presence guiding me. I am wrung out; I have cried so many tears.

27 November 2002: Dearest Greg says it's the best thing I have ever written. Richard, too, has been terribly affected by the script and has agreed to direct me.

10 January 2003: I am bereft. Nick Hytner has said he's not sure Primo is right for the National and my agent says Primo's estate is extremely reluctant to give permission for his work to be adapted for the stage. Don't they understand Primo is not just theirs? He belongs to the world. How many more bitter tears do I have to weep?

20 July–18 October 2003: I am doing *I.D.* at the Almeida and The Fear is gripping me. Will I walk off stage? No.

5 January–17 July 2004: The six months of *Othello* are far too big a story to tell here. I will publish my diaries on this later.

18 July 2004: Rehearsals start today. The Levi estate adore my script and Nick H promised me the Cottesloe, yet I feel flat. Is The Fear returning?

27 July 2004: Richard has suggested some punishment exercises to try to access Primo's psyche within the concentration camp. I am deeply apprehensive.

30 July 2004: I haven't been able to write about myself for several days. Richard forbade it. That was my punishment. It may not be quite the same as Auschwitz, but I have been shaking with terror. I can almost sense Primo talking to me.

18 August 2004: First costume fitting and my shoes from Harrods are perfect. Richard wants me to be more restrained. It feels strange not to over-emote.

23 August 2004: The day started badly with Greg spilling my champagne but ended well after a session with my therapist. We were talking about The Fear when I said, 'It wasn't Auschwitz that made Primo commit suicide: it was his depression.' 'You're so wise,' she smiled.

15 September 2004: I have started writing letters to Primo. Dear Primo, I hope you like my play. Love, Tony.

29 September 2004: A red light came on in the dress rehearsal. How can I work with such distractions?

30 September 2004: The first night. Everyone thinks I'm marvellous. If only Primo would write back to me ...

Digested read, digested: If This is an Actor.

The Letters of Noël Coward
(2007)

1915

Dear Darling old Mummy-snooks,

You are SUCH a DARLING and I know you don't love Daddy and Erik nearly as much as me.

It really is heavenly here and I was a great success in *Charley's Aunt*. I just know the West End beckons. I will write every week.

Your ever ever ever loving Noël

1921

Dear Ackie Wackie Weeza,

Thank heavens the beastly war is over. It played havoc with my nerves. It's wonderful to be here in New York and I've just met Lynn Fontanne. Do you remember her? She played some small parts in London but now she's become a huge star with her fiancé, Alfred Lunt.

All my love, you wicked, grasping old bitch,

Noëlie Wolie Polie

1925

Darling lamb,

GBS has been a little tart with me, but I think *Hay Fever* and *The Vortex* will show I have talent. Have met Joyce Carey and Gladys Calthrop; they really are terribly gay even though Paris at this time of a year can be a little de trop

Your darlingest Snoop

1928

Dear Virginia Woolf,

I am hot and glowing after reading Orlando and I am completely at your feet. It is the finest book *de nos jours* and if I continue to flatter you like this will you agree to become another of my top 500 bestest chums?

Yours, Noël Coward

1935

Darling Marlene, or should that be Darling Achtung? How are you my Prussian cow?

The Baybay has been managing my accounts very badly and I fear I am in danger of developing a German sense of humour about it all.

Love and kisses, Noël

1941

Darling Stoj,

It's just too, too horrid. Everyone is being nasty, accusing me of doing nothing for the war effort and I'm not allowed to speak out and say that I'm one of the government's top-secret agents.

Don't they realise that getting the Americans onside by writing

Don't Let's be Beastly to the Germans has shortened the conflict by several years?

Your miserable Poj

1947

Dearest Toley Coley,

So glad to be back in New York with Marlene. London is so fearfully drab at the moment and no one seems to want my work anymore. I've dug out a few plays from the bottom drawer and bashed out some numbers for a revue, but the critics are determined to hate me. Ecris-moi often, ma petite Tolette

Le Maître

1952

Darlingest Queenie,

When I heard the news that the king had died I thought of your loss and cried and cried. But even though your husband is dead I'd be willing to bet you live to a hundred.

Your humble servant,

Noël Coward

1958

Dear dear Larryboy,

Did you not think that Johnny Gielgud was completely underwhelming in *Nude with Violin*? I hate to be a bitch but it's a shame to see even a moderate talent wasted.

I am also involved in a nasty squabble with John Osborne and Ken Tynan. How can they imagine that people want to see the great unwashed on stage? Isn't it obvious that what the world needs now is a revival of Blithe Spirit? So how about it, Larrikins? Kisses to Vivien,

The Master

1966

Darlings,

Switzerland and Jamaica do pall, I'm coughing myself into a Firenze.

But how things change! It seems that in my dotage I have become a national treasure. Everywhere I go I am feted and CBS have offered me $450,000 for three 90-minute specials. I sense it is time to dust off a few more old manuscripts. But most of all, how I long for a gossip.

   Noëllie

Digested read, digested: His Master's Voice.

Ever, Dirk: The Bogarde Letters
(2008)

Clermont 1969–1987
Cadogan Gdns 1987–97

Darling Josie Posie, Patreeecia, Dilys, Luchino, Penny Lope, Norah and Kathleen,

   Pleese excuse the nastie Basildon Bond Paper and my terribul speling. Tote and I are quite ALOAN here ... we had to leeve all our possesshuns (Is that rite?) in London apart from the Rolls. I'ts so boring that peepul just want the Doctor films. But I will not do that rubbish any moore.

   Do'nt be grumpy Josie Posie*. I was meening to be funny when I told a journlist that you were hideiously pissed most dayz

* *Joseph Losey, the celebrated auteur.*

and I have never been the slytest bit upset that you never asked me to do *Death in Venice* ... Espeshally as I'm now doing the fillum with Luchino. SO THEIR! (Tha'ts ment to be funnie two). You know I LOVE you reely. Luchino, sweetie, I NEVER, EVER said that I was miscast or that you coul'dnt direct me ... Does one want to be a Burton or O'Tool? One must have some self-respect. Everything is terribley expensive here ... I do'nt know how wheel manidge.

I'm feeling rather mouldy today ... Do'nt menshun another word about the unspeakable Redgrave or Two-Inch Todd. The reviews for *The Night Porter* have been dissappointing. They were cleerly hopping for some Pekenpaish violence. I DO'NT CARE. We made that fillum for ourselves, not the great UNWASHED. I've bored you stiff again. Tote is in the garden and I'm starting to write something.

I do hope it does'nt turn out like that ghastly Evelyn War.

The MOST IMPORTUNT DAY of my life ... A Postillion Struck by Lightening is published and it was onederfull to see so many cueing to meetme at Hatchards ... Reiner* dearest, how lucky you are to share your tallent with me. Your lether gang is tres amusant. How I hate the Jappunnese. Their voices still terrify me†.

Lord Next-Door‡ has been shatturd by the critics reaction to *A Bridge Too Far*. Do you think I am becuming a littul mannered? I certainly look middle-aged ... Went to an awards do wear Ustinov was talking ... H'es quite funny, I suppose, if you hav'ent hurd the

---

* *Rainer Werner Fassbinder, the celebrated auteur.*
† *This is an exaggeration. Dirk never actually fought the Japanese in the war.*
‡ *Richard Attenborough, the celebrated auteur.*

patter befour. Agent sent me a Michael Winner script. Coul'dnt possibly do it. Its AWASH with sperm. The Connaught has become ridiculously expensive. I do'nt know if Tote and I can visit London again.

I was very good in Despair ... This is not conceit, merely a statement of fact. Had to appeare at nasty Cannes Festivul ... I do detest Americans and Australians ... but it is luvvly to know one is ADORED. Tote's tests are costing me a fortune ... I fear we'll have to move back to London. It will feel like an amputation ... But as long as its not Kentish Town.

Tote's chemio therepy is hard to bare ... I suppose it must be for him two. So the Patient is dead ... And Ive had a stroke. FUCK, FUCK. But wun must go on. Am stuck on chapter 8 of my leightest book. My others are on the bestseller lists so I must be doing something rite! I hate this new typewritur ... It tries to correct ure speling. Penny Lope, we are not estranged ... Im just not riting to you much. Its me Im interested in, not you. BUT I STILL LOVE YOU. John, Did you read Penelope's latest book? It's awefull.

I am not at all unhappy. I want to get pissed and my charitee work talking about the Holocaust is very demanding. Why is their so much hate in the world? A Chinese familee has moved in downstairs ... I wish they'd go back to Singapore. What's so good about being 70? No one can act any more. No wun CARES about my ground-breaking work. But at least Penguin want some more of my recycled memoirs ...

Love and Love, Dirk

Digested read, digested: I wus Mwahvellous, darling.

The Pursuit of Laughter:
Essays, Articles, Reviews & Diary
by Diana Mosley (2008)

In as much as we had a home, I suppose it was a small estate called Gloucestershire. My father often used to tell us we were ruined. At times we wondered anxiously where the next party was coming from. 'You realise that, unlike me, you children are going to have to work,' he told us. Our blood ran cold; we'd rather marry a duke or a Nazi. (*Sunday Times*)

Evelyn Waugh was a much misunderstood man. People say he was a snob, but he was happy talking to anyone, from royalty to landed gentry. The reforms of Pope John XXIII were a great sorrow to him; he couldn't bear the idea of sharing his Catholicism with the lower orders. This is a very good book. (*Letters of Evelyn Waugh, Evening Standard*)

Mr Wildeblood's book about Lord Montagu's indecency trial reminds me not just that I once spent a very enjoyable summer at Beaulieu but also that I was unlawfully detained during the 1940s. Prison was horrid; the toilets were revolting and the staff were extremely surly, seldom observing the everyday niceties of please and thank you. This book is very good. (*Against the Law*, Books & Bookmen)

With the shooting of the (I do so hate the word fascist) slightly-right-of-centre Dutch politician, Pim Fortuyn, some socialists have suggested that all people who oppose immigration are queers. Not so. A great many sensible people oppose immigration and even though Hitler and that great orator, Sir Oswald Mosley, were both keen on dressing up and homoerotic activities, there was nothing queer about them. (*Spectator*)

Many people enjoy porn and the Marquis de Sade was just a flamboyant eccentric who liked orgies and whipping prostitutes. Had he been alive today he would have made a fortune. He may even be head of formula one. This book is very good. (Marquis de Sade, *Evening Standard*)

The last time I was in London, some foreigners asked me the way to Harrods. Why does that store say it is in Knightsbridge when it is in fact in the Brompton Road? (*Diaries*)

Typically, the *Observer* censored my letter about how beastly we were to imprison Sir Oswald Mosley during the war for being a patriot by siding with Hitler. We should have a national day to celebrate Britishness. Perhaps it should be on the feast of St Oswald. (*Diaries*)

I note that I have chosen not to publish any diaries of my wonderfully happy time in Germany in the 1930s. What a curious oversight. (*Diaries*)

Hugh Trevor-Roper makes a number of errors editing Goebbel's diaries. He describes his villa as palatial. It wasn't. Unity and I stayed there. This lack of attention to detail perpetuates the misconception that the Nazis were wrong. Otherwise, it's a good book. (*Goebbel's Diaries, Evening Standard*)

Michael Bloch has written a silly book about Wallis Simpson. She was a great friend and everyone knows her first marriage only failed because of her husband's drinking. Her love for King Edward VIII was one of the great events of the 20th century and had he not been forced to abdicate, Britain would not have entered a ruinous war with Germany. Not a good book. (*Wallis Simpson, Evening Standard*)

AN Wilson is a fearful snob, which is why he always asks me to review books for him in the Evening Standard. He has now given me biographies of Ibsen and Mann, both of whom I have never met. So I will do what I always do under these circumstances; summarise the main points and say they are good books. (Ibsen and Mann, *Evening Standard*)

There is an error in the biography of Georgiana. She wasn't the fifth Duchess of Devonshire. Some might say this is only a small slip, but these things do matter. Especially to my sister, who wrote the foreword to my book. (*The Two Duchesses*, *Evening Standard*)

Digested read, digested: We are family, I got all my sisters with me.

God Bless America
by Piers Morgan (2009)

October 2008, sorry, I mean **October 2006.** My editor suggests we doctor the 'diary' to make it look like I was the first person to spot Barack Obama's potential. 'It'll make you look even more of a heavyweight,' he says. Who is he calling fat? I still don't see what was wrong with my original fascinating entry about having lunch at the Ivy with Cheryl Cole and Jason Donovan.

December 2006 Simon Cowell phones. He's looking for a not very bright, attention-seeking brown-noser with no self-awareness whatsoever to join him on the judging panel for *America's Got Talent*. I look through my Rolodex and shake my head. 'Can't think of anyone,' I reply. 'You've got the job,' he smirks.

February 2007 I have been asked to appear on *Celebrity Apprentice* with Sir Alan Sugar. Alastair Campbell is also a contestant so it's clearly an A-list event. Alastair and I bond with some competitive arm-wrestling and boasting. These charity events are great for the career. Shame about the viewers.

April 2007 Ever since I opposed the Iraq war, some people have confused me with a serious political commentator. Gordon Brown is one of them. He invites me to Downing Street to ask what his first move should be when Tony Blair steps down. I tell him he should appear on *Strictly Come Dancing* and bomb Zimbabwe. I can see he's taking it seriously.

June 2007 A nightmare journey to LA. I was dozing in first class when I was pestered by the Duchess of York, Shania Twain, Naomi Campbell, Sharon Osbourne, Fern Britton and Peaches Geldof – all desperate to give me a blow job. Then I woke up. Celia wasn't best pleased that I had dribbled on her black PVC jeans. Still, it was nice that the TV company had sent a stretch limo to collect me at the airport, though it was the first time anyone had spelled my name Pierce Brosnan on the noticeboard.

Get to the Beverly Wilshire hotel and phone my agent for the viewing figures for my landmark TV series on Sandbanks. 'I can't find them anywhere,' he says. 'Then ring ITV,' I reply. 'I meant I can't find any viewers.'

August 2007 Hillary Clinton has thrown her hat into the presidential ring. I've always been a great admirer of hers, unless she doesn't win the nomination, in which case I will say I've always had my misgivings. Tonight is the grand finale of *America's Celebrity Apprentice*, the TV show with famous nonentities that no one in the UK has ever heard of. And I win after getting myself filmed next to some crippled war veterans! This is the proudest day of my life.

October 2007 The government is having to bail out Northern Rock. I always said the financial system was inherently corrupt, ever since two *Mirror* journalists were done for share-price fixing. Brown phones to say he should have made me chancellor of the exchequer. I tell him he couldn't afford me and put a block on his calls. His stock is falling and I can't be associated with failure.

February 2008 My divorce with Marion is turning nasty. I hoped we would be able to split amicably, but now I'm making loads of cash her lawyers inexplicably feel she is entitled to a share. No way am I parting with the mid-life Maserati.

June 2008 An invite from Sir Alan Sugar to his 40th wedding anniversary party. No one seems to notice me, so I heckle the speeches. 'Oh look, it's that twat Morgan,' Simon Cowell says. Everyone stares at me. Result! My boys ask if I can bring along some celebrities to their prep school. I pull out all the stops and turn up with Amanda Holden and Gordon Ramsay. 'We said celebrities, Dad,' they moan.

August 2008 I'm disgusted that Jonathan Ross has been leaving vile messages on an answerphone. He's the worst kind of sycophantic sleazeball. He should be doing cutting-edge interviews for *GQ*, like asking Nick Clegg how many birds he's shagged.

November 2008 Gordon's ratings are up. I might start taking his calls again. And Barack Obama's been elected president. I'd better ring Sly Stallone, Arnold Schwarzenegger and Lily Allen to remind them I said he'd do it.

Digested read, digested: Piers of the Brain Dead.

JOHN CRACE

Letters to Monica
by Philip Larkin (2010)

My dearest Monica,
Your letter arrived while I was eating breca in Rabbithampton.
I have spent the past three months thinking about a poem I
haven't written and I am utterly disinclined to work. What did
you think of the Test squad? I am furious the selectors have left
out Laker. Increasingly I find that Thomas Hardy and DHL are
the only writers worth reading. I am due to meet E.M. Forster
tonight. The only thing I really want to ask him is whether he is
a homo. Do you think he cares about rabbits as much as we do?
I found the pessimism in your last letter totally inspiring, though
I'm sorry you were upset when we last met. I've never been very
good at the sex thing. If it's any consolation I was just as bad at
it with Patsy.

How lovely to get your letter when I was alone at home. I'm
sorry you were so upset about me and Patsy. It's just that I found
myself in an embarrassing situation for several years in wch it would
have been rude to say no and you wouldn't want Mr Pussy to be
rude. Read *Lucky Jim*. I can't believe Kingsley has got away with it.
The dialogue is awful and all the best gags have been lifted straight
from me. I doubt he will ever see fit to recompense me. I suppose I
shall have to make do with a flithy bottle of Bo-Jo and a pittance
from the Spectator. Tried to write another line of *Wedding-Wind*
and failed. I'd be better off listening to *The Archers*. Don't you
think Walter Gabriel would be happier if he killed himself?

I am sorry to hear your mother and father died within a couple
of months of one another. Still, it could have been worse. I have
had a terrible haddock for a couple of days and the coal man

187

hasn't delivered so I am freezing to death. Count yourself lucky. I do find you quite attractive even though I rarely pay you any attention and am uninterested in the sex thing. You can blame my Mum. Bob Conquest came round; he's basically a cheerful idiot. I can't read another word of Jane Austen or CP Snow. Give me Beatrix Potter any day.

Thank you for your letter. I am sorry to hear you feel I am ignoring you but I have had a great deal to do even though I haven't done any of it because I am so bored. The renovation of the library is almost complete but I doubt anyone will ever use it. I certainly hope not, because then I will be left alone. Don't you think Blake and Byron are quite dreadful? Does anyone care about them any more? The University of Cincinnati offered me 200 guineas a week but I turned it down as it's a long way away and I might have had to do some work.

Thank you for your letter. I am sorry that you inadvertently discovered I had been having a long-term affair with Maev by reading about it in a poem wch I had published in the Spr. To make matters worse I was only paid 3/-. I'm sure Betjeman gets more. Still, I think it might be for the best that it is now out in the open as your Mr Pussy has now told Maev it's over. Don't you think Leavis is a frightful old bore? And isn't Pinter a dreadful prick? A CBE at 42. I ask you.

Thank you for your letter. I am sorry you are upset that my affair with Maev hasn't ended after all. It's just she made such a terrible fuss, I felt obliged to go through with the sex thing again. I did, though, spend the whole time thinking about how I could keep your name as small as possible in the acknowledgements for the *Oxford Book of English Twentieth Century Verse*. I hope that reassures you of my undying affection for my darling graminovore.

Thank you for your letter. I have been extremely unwell and

very frightened and all my other friends have deserted me. You can come and live with me now, if you want.

Yours affectionately, Philip.

Digested read, digested: He fucked her up…

PG Wodehouse: A Life in Letters
(2011)

Dear Willyum, Snorkles and Denis,
Fiend of me boyhood, here's some dread news. My parents haven't got enough of what they vulgarly call 'stamps' these days to send me to Varsity. It really is a terrible bore as I shall now have to send a few pomes to editors and hope to pay my own way. But at least Dulwich beat Haileybury so all is not lost.

Good tidings! I managed to sell my first novel for £2/2/6d and several American magazines have asked me to write for them. Only trouble is that they don't want my usual public-schooly stories, so I'm fresh out of plots. Any ideas? Dear old Jeames of Jermyn Street has made me the most spiffing pair of cream golfing bags. You really should see me. Quite the man about town, I'm told. Toodle-ooo for now.

Would you believe it? I've just happened to arrive back in New York at the very moment the war in Europe has started! I suppose I could go home, but it seems rather unnecessary as from what I've heard the Kaiser will come to his senses soon and all the nastiness will be over by Christmas. In any case I've been struggling with the Psmith story, so I should probably wait till that is finished before doing anything rash.

The restaurants in New York are quite magnificent and I've met this charming actress called Ethel with whom I'm smitten. Ethel has quite the sweetest daughter, Leonora, so I suspect I shall be staying out here for a little while longer, especially as I have to write another 15 novels by the end of next year. I hear that London has been hit by something called Zeppelins. They don't sound very terrifying to me. More like the name of a popular beat combo!

Now the war is over, it just so happens that we might be back in Blighty for a while. I can't tell you how much I've missed the cricket; it's been deuced difficult to get any of the Dulwich scorers at all. Though I did hear we drew with Harrow. I'm sorry you are having so much trouble getting your books published. The last effort sent me was quite brilliant, apart from the plot and the characterisation. I've come up with a splendid idea for a series of stories about a gentleman and his manservant. Everyone frightfully excited and I dashed off the first 30,000 words before brekkers this morning. Must go. Some frightful do at the Waldorf to attend.

Here I am in Los Angeles being paid $30,000 to do next to nothing and still I'm finding life rather dull. How I wish I was back watching Dulwich as I hear we've got a demon offie this term. But since my new play is opening on Broadway and I also have nine Jeeves books coming out, I don't think I will make it back. But do give my love to Binky and don't worry about the Nazis. All this talk about war is just fooey. Much more pressing is how on earth I'm to pay my $100,000 tax bill. How does the government expect a man to live?

Well, I have to confess the war rather took me surprise, but I can confidently predict it will all turn out to be a lot of fuss about nothing. It is damned inconvenient, though, as there isn't a decent bottle of claret to be had in Le Touquet.

I'm sorry not to have been in touch for a while, but there's been this awful confusion. Some awfully nice Nazi asked me to do a radio show so I thought I'd keep everyone's spirits up by making a few jolly remarks about the food in Germany and now I hear everyone back home thinks I'm a collaborator. Nothing could be further from the truth. I'm having a perfectly miserable time in the Hotel Adlon in Berlin. It's almost impossible to write more than 20,000 words at a time before the air raid warning goes off. Can't the RAF give a man a little peace?

It's wonderful to be back in New York. The Americans are so much more forgiving about my Nazi misunderstandings, though their magazines are refusing to run any more of my stories. They say they are too Edwardian. I ask you! But at least the hoi polloi are still dipping into their pockets for Jeeves. I'm sorry you are still having trouble getting published yourself. Your last 37 rejected manuscripts were triumphs ahead of their time. Talking of which, have you read the new Kingsley Amis and Evelyn Waugh? Insufferably boring, though I've written to both to say how much I admire them. The critics say they are the future: if so, it's a future of which I want no part.

Everything going marvellously well here apart from Snorks, Bill and Denis all dying and Dulwich losing a close run chase against Charterhouse. Next we will be playing grammar schools! Still, chin up and all that.

Much love, Plum

Digested read, digested: Don't mention the wars.

Public Enemies
by Michel Houellebecq
and Bernard Henri-Levy (2012)

Dear Bernard-Henri Levy, We have *rien* in common except that we are both rather contemptible individuals. A specialist in farcical stunts, you dishonour even the white shirts you always wear unbuttoned to the waist. You are an intimate of the powerful, you wallow in immense wealth and are a philosopher without an original idea. *Moi*? I'm just a redneck. A nihilist. An unremarkable author with no style. These, then, are the terms of the debate.

The debate, *cher* Michel Houellebecq? There are three approaches. 1. You've said it all. We are both morons. I agree that is the most likely, but then we have no *livre* and we generate little publicity. 2. You are a moron, but I am a genius. This, I must admit, I also quite *aime*. 3. We are both geniuses and we debate why we are so misunderstood and hated. This one is more tendentious, I think, but for the purposes of mutual masturbation and knocking out a *livre*, it has, as they say, *plus de jambes*.

Dear Bernard-Henri, it is time that I quote Baudelaire, Schopenhauer and Musset to establish my credentials as an *intellectuel*. I think you must enjoy the hatred: why else would you Google yourself *vingt fois par jour*? For *moi-même*, my desire to be hated masks a desire to be loved. I want people to desire me for my self-disgust. Perhaps.

Cher Michel, Yet again you misunderstand me. I do not Google myself out of self-hatred, but out of *amour propre*. I can assure you that nothing can dent my preening narcissism and self-regard. Those that do hate me do so purely because I am Jewish and drop *mort* gorgeous. *Toujours les petits gens* want to bring down the colossus who has it *tout*. *Regardez mon bon ami* Dominique Strauss-Kahn. Is it his fault that *chaque femme* who comes near *lui* gets all moist? It's a cross he and I have to bear. And while I'm about it, I can also quote philosophers and *artistes*. Cocteau, Sartre and Botul. So there!

Dear B-H, I must confess I have never read Botul and cannot access my library as I am now living in Ireland. I can't say the *pays* has much to recommend it as the inhabitants are *trop* dense to *parler Français* but at least the taxes are minimal and my hard-earned cash doesn't get spent on Muslim illegal immigrants. Shall we now be a little more daring in our exchange and enter the arena of the confessional? Let me *commencer* by saying how much I hate my *père et mère*. Along with everyone else.

Mon cher Michel, the confessional is not my style. *Oui*, I write a daily diary of 10,000 *mots*, but that is for *moi seul* and is the bare minimum required to record my breathtaking insights. I hate the fact that people jump to conclusions about me, based on what I write. They call me a disaster tourist. A fraud. How dare they? Even Jesus was treated better than me. But let me get one *chose* straight. My own *père et mère* were *parfait*. For only from perfection can come perfection, as Spinoza and Hegel might have said if they had been as clever as me.

Dear B-H, We have more in common than I thought. We are both *horriblement* misunderstood by a *monde* that refuses to accept our own estimation of our talent, and I see now that I, too,

193

have Christ-like qualities in the suffering I endure for portraying the world as it is and not how people would like it to be. Not that I believe in anything but my *oeuvre*. As for your onanism, I am not sure I quite understand your position.

Michel *mon cher*, it is monadism, *pas* onanism! Though I admit it's a *facile* mistake to make. Try to think of my faith as Judaism but with no god and *moi* at the centre of the *univers*. And *quel univers*! While ordinary *gens* were born to work in *magasins* and places *comme ça*, I was born to write and make love *avec mon coq enorme*. That *est ma vie*. As I said to *mes amis Nicolas et Carla* the *autre jour*, I write for 12 hours *et puis* I pleasure women for 12 hours.

Dear B-H, sex is immensely disappointing for me as on the few occasions I manage an erection I always suffer premature ejaculation. So that just leaves writing. I know that whatever I write will be canonical, but I am unsure what to write next. Perhaps *poésie*? My biggest fear is that the pack will win and I will die unloved and unregarded.

Mon cher Michel, the pack will never win and our names will live on with Kant, Nietzsche and Camus as the greatest *penseurs* of our generation. It does not matter what you or I write next. It is *assez* to know that whatever we do it will be brilliant and far too good for the little minds who will tear it to pieces. You *et moi*, we will live for *jamais*!

Digested read, digested: *Pensant* in the wind.

Liberation, Volume 3: Diaries: 1970–1983
by Christopher Isherwood (2012)

Wrote three sentences of *Kathleen & Frank*. Totally exhausted. Sent Gore a thank-you letter for having us to dinner which was not even acknowledged. Don the Angel says that's the height of bad manners. Saw Swami and meditated very badly. Arrived in London. It's terribly cold, and my temper was not improved by being taken to see a terribly pedestrian performance of Hadrian VII. Wrote four sentences of *Kathleen & Frank* before getting a near-fatal nosebleed. Still freezing cold, so went to Strand Sauna where two men exposed rather ordinary cocks. Weighed myself. 150 pounds. I am extraordinarily obese.

Journeyed to St Tropez and New York where we dined with Morgan, Wystan, Stephen Spender and a host of young men dressed in way-out clothes. My weight has dropped to 149 pounds, and I have a small bump on my hand from where I slipped on Santa Monica Boulevard. This can only mean I have cancer. Poor Don. I do hope he will manage without me.

Dodie Smith has asked me to read her latest book. It is cuntily pitiful, but I shall have to be polite about it. Was just settling down to write another sentence of *Kathleen & Frank* when I was interrupted by the extreme shortness of Michael York's shorts. My weight has ballooned to 151. Went to the opening of Don's exhibition of portraits of famous people he has met through living with me. I think they are brilliant, but everyone else is very bitchy about them. Crossed out a sentence of *Kathleen & Frank*. Sometimes I feel as if I am going backwards.

Worked with Don on a screenplay of *Frankenstein*. The studio says the title is very promising. Dinner with Anita Loos and

Truman Capote, before going on to several film premieres, none of which was better than mediocre. The mood in Hollywood is still against homosexuals. Why can't the Jews be more tolerant? I have a twinge in my upper buttock. Unquestionably, it is fatal.

Eventually got round to reading *Travels with My Aunt* and surprised myself by staying awake. More than can be said for Claire Bloom in *Hedda*. She's really not up to it. Went to see Swami to discuss my meditation but he had died. *Kathleen & Frank* finally published and sold 172 copies, while the play I let Don write with me has had six performances in a bus shelter. That's a success, I suppose. Not that I care because I have a spot on my neck which is almost certainly cancerous. Tried to read Philip Roth but gave up as he is too Jewish.

Larry phoned me to say Wystan had died, but seemed oddly perturbed I wanted to talk more about my headache. Angel agreed Larry has no sense of time or place. Ed says he loves our version of *Frankenstein*, but could we do a screenplay about a mummy instead. Read Byron and Wordsworth for inspiration before having several lunches with Tennessee to discuss how boring *Urban Cowboy* is. Rushed to hospital with rectal bleeding. Turned out I had just eaten beetroot. My weight is 149 and a half pounds.

Have just written a book about Swami which no one likes. I feel I should trawl through my diaries for another autobiographical novel, but I really can't be bothered as I feel a bit dizzy. Kathleen asked me to say a few words at Ken Tynan's funeral. So I got up and said: 'A few words' and sat down again. Don has another exhibition of portraits of famous people he met through me. Why is it only me who thinks he's a genius? I have a lump that is definitely cancerous. I lie down and wait to die. The biopsy reveals it is benign. But fuck it. I'm

78 so I'm going to lie down and wait to die. I'm waiting. I'm still waiting…

Isherwood died four years after writing his final entry.

Digested read, digested: Goodbye to LA.

Counting One's Blessings: The Selected Letters of Queen Elizabeth, the Queen Mother
edited by William Shawcross (2012)

Having been fortunate enough to write hagiographies of both the Queen and the Queen Mother, I was honoured to be asked to edit this collection of the Queen Mother's letters, which reveal her as one of the most important letter writers of the twentieth century.

A Palace Somewhere, 1914–2001:
Dear Medusa, Mama, the Queen, Bertie and Assorted Crawlers, Mama tells me there is a war going on. It sounds too, too terrible. So many balls have been cancelled. Last night Glamis Castle caught fire and one of the staff got a bit burned trying to put it out. I now know what our men must have gone through at the Somme.

Thank God the war is over. There have been so many parties this summer that I feel I have scarcely spent an evening at home. Bertie keeps sending me flowers and has proposed at least twice, but I do rather think I can do better.

How happy I am to be your wife, Bertie, though I do find the political situation worrying. Taxation is very high and Daddy

says he might have to sell a painting or two. Gosh, the Labour party are awful <u>SNOBS</u>.

It is most trying being away from baby Lillibet for several months at a time, but Bertie and I are absolutely loving our tour of Africa. Bertie shot <u>a lion</u> yesterday and this morning I bagged a <u>rhinoceros</u>. What very odd creatures they are. I do so miss Cowes week, but the benediction of the Archbishop <u>of</u> Canterbury does help with the loss.

Thank you <u>so</u> much for sending me your latest poem, Mr Sitwell. It has been a great comfort while the Trade Unions have been behaving so <u>badly</u>.

<u>A Certain Person</u>, whom I cannot bring myself to name, has <u>been</u> very difficult. I do hope David comes to his senses.

How strange, though not unagreeable, it is to find <u>myself</u> Queen. Bertie has just <u>awarded</u> me the Order of the Garter. I want you to know, David, that I <u>continue</u> to uphold you at all times and I have absolutely no idea how <u>my</u> reply to your previous letter went unposted. I shall have to fire the servants.

Your book fills me with hope, Mr Sitwell. How fitting it should arrive on the day Mr Chamberlain should return from Munich and we can all rest safe once more. Bertie has just <u>told</u> me we are to tour Canada. Why Canada again? How I long to go somewhere else.

So we are at war with the idiotic <u>Germans</u> again. Buckingham Palace has been bombed. <u>Ghastly!</u> But some good news at least as Mrs Greville has left me her <u>jewels</u>. Mr Churchill has committed a grave faux-pas by congratulating the Indian troops. They are Bertie's troops to congratulate. How I <u>miss</u> Mr Chamberlain.

Thank you for the copy of your new book, Mr Sitwell. I know it will help me recover from the loss of my husband.

Life is awfully difficult without <u>an</u> equerry, Elizabeth, but thank you for my annual 48-hour stay in Balmoral. The <u>fishing</u>

was magnificent. Charles is a most amusing young man, and gave me the most super towel for my birthday.

Thank you for your poem, Sir John. I couldn't agree more about Slough. One of my horses pulled up lame in a hurdle race at Lingfield. At least the racing does keep one so busy that I find I have nothing to say about the family divorces or the death of Diana.

If I may say so, Elizabeth, I do think we should reward the nice Mr SHAWCROSS with a knighthood. *(This important letter has only just come to light.)*

Digested read, digested: Queen Zelig, the Queen Mother.

The Letters of TS Eliot: Volume 4: 1928–1929 edited by Valerie Eliot and John Haffenden (2013)

Dear Mrs Woolf,
Thank you for sending me your new short story. I read it with great interest, but feel it is, perhaps, too frivolous for inclusion in *The Monthly Criterion*. Have you thought about sending it to *Grazia*? Yours, etc.

Dear Messrs Methuen,
I note with alarm that the paper for the new setting of *The Sacred Wood* is below the standard I expect. Please correct soonest. Yours, etc.

Dear Master,
I trust that nothing will interfere with my stay at New College on the 9th proxima and that I will be accorded the same suite of rooms as previously. Does five guineas sound reasonable for my expenses? Yours, etc.

My dearest Ottoline,
I'm so grateful that Valerie managed to find room for a few of my maddest letters. La – la – la. Otherwise no one would have any idea how much of a saint Tom was to put up with me for so long before having me committed to an asylum. Such a wonderful Christian man! Anyone else might have been tempted to have an affair by my madness. The cat stood on the mat. Much love, Vivienne.

My darling Emily,
(Regrettably, all the correspondence between TS Eliot and Emily Hale has been embargoed until 2020, so readers will just have to take the chaste nature of their relationship on trust – Eds. PS. I've always hated that bitch – Valerie)

Dear Cummings,
Thank you for sending me your new ditty. Unfortunately it is not quite suitable for *The Monthly Criterion*. Have you thought about taking remedial lessons in grammar and punctuation? Yours, etc.

Dear Leonard,
It was a rare honour to meet someone, such as yourself, with more money than sense. As you know, *The Monthly Criterion* is struggling financially and with your help we could re-establish the magazine on a quarterly footing. Thank you also for your offer to publish an edition of my poems in Latin. Once I have fulfilled my contractual obligations to Faber, of which I am now a director, I shall be happy to accept. In the meantime, I submit my invoice for 300 guineas. Yours, etc.

Dear Faber,
I note that 12 paper-clips are missing from the office inventory and that my papers had not been placed perpendicular to the

inkwell on my desk. This state of affairs cannot be allowed to continue. Yours, etc.

Dear Aldington,
Thank you for sending me your latest verses. If they can be called that. I confess that I found them disappointing in the extreme – an opinion that I must make clear has nothing to do with your outspoken assertions that Vivienne is not really that mad. Have you tried The People's Friend? Yours, etc.

Dear Prince de Rohan,
Thank you for your appreciation of the German translation of my essay on Machiavelli. So often, one feels one is putting pearls before swine. Vivienne is doing as well as can be expected and I get enormous comfort from my faith. Yours, etc.

Dear Auden,
I am sorry I kept you waiting in the Faber ante-chamber for several hours. I had a very important meeting with my secretary. Do call the office to arrange another appointment some time next year. Yours, etc.

Dear Faber,
The paper-clips are still missing. Yours, etc.

Dear Spender,
Thank you for your invitation to speak at the Oxford Poetry Society. Regrettably, I must decline as I am exhausted. Having read a few lines of your latest work, dare I suggest that poetry is not your forte? I submit my invoice for 15 guineas for the expenses that would have accrued, had I accepted. Yours, etc.

Digested read, digested: A publisher's thank you for being kept afloat by *Cats*.

Distant Intimacy
by Frederic Raphael and Joseph Epstein (2013)

Dear Freddie, Twenty-five years or so ago, I proposed to my friend John Gross who was then editing the *TLS* that he might care to engage in a self-regarding, grumpy-old-man correspondence with America's greatest essayist. To my surprise he turned me down, but having just watched yet another repeat of The Glittering Prizes on PBS, I wondered if you might be a man of sufficient neglect and vanity to say yes instead. Best, Joe

Dear Joe, I confess I had no idea who you were when your letter first arrived, but having looked you up, I discover that though you are a lesser Jew than me – *la chose juive c'est aussi importante que la chose génitale* (as Charcot would say – there might be some $$$$ in my extravagantly parenthesised *bons mots* reaching a wider audience). *Tout à toi*, Freddie

Dear Freddie, I am delighted you have entered so fully into the spirit of my *grand projet*. I agree that Jewishness is the sine qua non of human existence, and I regret deeply that my Jewishness is not as realised as your own. Yet still I find I am a remarkable Jew. Talking of which, do you loathe Gore Vidal and Susan Sontag as much as me? Best, Joe

Dear Joe, I will only return to the subject of Jewishness and the evil of antisemitism in every other epistle. How much we have in common! I cannot stand GV. A homosexualist – homosexu-A-list – of limited talent. As for La Sontag. She had the pleasure of meeting me once. The pleasure was all hers. *Tout à toi*, Freddie

Dear Freddie, *The New York Review of Books* has offered me only $20,000 for 3,000 of my best words on the Essays of Montaigne, and Columbia University is refusing to fly me business class to deliver a lecture on hubris. I fear for the recognition of my genius. Best, Joe

Dear Joe, It was always thus, thus it always was. When I worked in Hollywood with fools such as Kubrick, I found it best just to take what was on offer while retaining *un détachement supercilieux*. Have you seen the pitiful new poem has Harold Pinter for the LRB? *Tout Londres rit!* As for the new offerings from Ian McEwan and Julian Barnes, these are books you don't want in your wood-panelled library. I once felt the same about the pathetic criticism of Clive James, but then he was nice about my daughter. *Amitiés*, Freddie

Dear Freddie, Did you ever meet Vladimir Nabokov? A more overrated pedlar of leaden phrases it is hard to conceive. It is all very well to have one's daughter praised by an Australian, but thank God she did not miscegenate with him. I have another 300 of my 500-word essay on the impact of the Astronomica of Marcus Manilius on Roger Federer still to write. I should be finished by next week, though it's hardly worth the $15,000 I am being paid. Best, Joe

Dear Joe, I have just read your piece for the journal with a circulation of two. Quite the best-written and most incisive *obiter dicta* I have read since I went through the page proofs of my latest novel. Not that it will sell, because these days there is only room for the middle-brow ennui of Hollinghurst and Byatt. Alan Bennett has a talent but it is a very limited one. *Tout à toi*, Freddie

Dear Freddie, We come to the end of our little experiment. I have enjoyed it beyond words and believe we have left a lasting monument to those writers who would dare to trace our footsteps. Best, Joe

Dear Joe, While I miss *la gloire, comme on dit*, of not having been tested in physical combat, I take pleasure that those of our persuasion – if indeed we are persuaded! – will look sympathetically (simper-thetically) on our efforts. If only Michael Frayn would Re-Frayn. *!E basta;* What is our legacy? *Un palimpseste de bons mots*? Or the ramblings of two solipsists who have trashed what little remained of their reputations? *Figure-toi*. Either way, *c'était une joie complète*.

Digested read, digested: La Vieillesse Dorée.

Here and Now: Letters
by Paul Auster and JM Coetzee (2013)

Dear Paul, I have been thinking about how so many novelists have been cashing in by writing letters to one another which are then later published in book form. I wondered whether you might agree to be my correspondent for such a venture. We could start by discussing the nature of friendship as I note that Aristotle had something to say on the subject.

Dear John, I can't say I have hitherto given the semiotics of friendship much thought, though for the purposes of publication I am prepared to do so now. My feeling is this: a friendship should always be of a non-sexual nature.

Dear Paul, A response to your last letter. I couldn't agree more that our friendship should remain non-sexual. Much looking forward to seeing you in Estoril.

Dear Paul, I haven't heard from you for a while. Did you receive my last letter?

Dear John, Many apologies for my failure to reply. As you know, I refuse to engage with modern technology and Siri inadvertantly unplugged the fax machine for several weeks so I have only just received it. I feel we have exhausted the subject of friendship. Perhaps we could turn our attention instead to the banking crisis which seems to have consumed the attention of everyone in New York.

Dear Paul, It seems to me that if only financiers could grasp a few simple Platonic and Borgesian truths then there would be no panic. The truth is that nothing has changed but the numbers. So why don't they merely susbstitute some more pleasing numbers for the ones that have caused such alarm? My publishers are insisting I go to Tuscany. Perhaps we can meet in the same palazzo as last time?

Dear John, Your prescription for the economy seems eminently sensible to me. Let me tell you a story. I once met Charlton Heston on three separate occasions in as many weeks. What does that say of the signifier and the signified? My Italian publisher is insisting I, too, fly business class to Tuscany so Siri and I are much looking forward to seeing you again. In the meantime, I am watching baseball on the television.

Dear Paul, As it happens I have been watching a great deal of cricket on the television. Perhaps our intercourse should extend to why two such brilliant minds should be so fascinated by sport. It is my contention that sport satisfies a very primitive need for heroes.

Dear John, I truly believe you may be on to something with your insight about sporting heroism. Did I ever tell you about the time I once nearly met Willie Mays? I'm also finding the situation in Israel immensely complex, but we can talk about that when we meet in Canada where I am to read from my new novel.

Dear Paul, Congratulations on your new novel. It is, as ever, a masterpiece. I am looking forward to seeing you in Canada. For my session, I have insisted that members of the public should not be allowed to ask questions as they rarely have anything worthwhile to add. In the meantime, I have been asked to write something on Beckett.

Dear John, I too have been asked to write about Beckett. The reviews of my novel have been generally favourable, though I am increasingly irritated by those who insist on linking my own identity to that of my characters. How can they so fail to appreciate the imagination of the artist?

Dear Paul, The paucity of the critic in the modern age is lamentable. I am also tired of my work being subjected to that conflationary scrutiny. It is not as if either you or I have ever written books in which the characters have been named after ourselves or are in any way autobiographical. Ah well, such is the lot of genius, I suppose. I'm also having tremendous difficulty sleeping. On a lighter note, has your new typewriter arrived?

Dear John, I am disturbed to hear about your insomnia. Siri suggests that continuing our correspondance may improve matters greatly.

Digested read, digested: Hither and Thither.

Building: Letters 1960–1975
by Isaiah Berlin (2013)

Dear Important Person,
Thank you for your illuminating monograph on Tolstoy which perfectly reflects my own anti-existentialist interpretation of his character; one that I iterated some years ago, I recall. I wish I could say more, but I have a busy few decades of intense social-climbing ahead, starting with an irksome but necessary trip to America to have dinner with the new president. It will mean I have to miss Joan Sutherland's magnificent Lucia at Covent Garden, but I will be back for Callas.

You ask me for my thoughts on the Cuban question. I regret they are at present unformed, as I have spent the past month wrestling with the seating plan for the All Souls Dinner. Freddie will not be happy unless he is at high table. I know I ought to be able to find a way of making this happen, but sometimes the Kantian 'ought implies can' is fallible. I have also not had time to commit my apercus on the construction of the Berlin Wall. It is, of course, a great honour to have such a landmark named in recognition of one's achievements, but I am not sure I have done quite enough yet to be worthy of such a legacy.

What a terrible business the president's assassination has been! It quite knocked me off my stride for the lecture series I was giving at Harvard and, combined with the ongoing furore about admitting graduates to All Souls, has left me feeling quite out of sorts. My sciatica is unbearable. For what it's worth, I think Sparrow's position as warden will be untenable unless the college is seen to move with the times as the Franks Report suggests. But I dare say no one will heed my opinion. So be it. Thank God I have five months' holiday in Portofino and Jerusalem with Aline coming up.

It was with a deep sense of shock I found myself implicated in underhand dealings to ensure Hannah Arendt's book on Eichmann was reviewed badly in the *TLS*. Although it is my habit to retain a carbon duplicate of every letter I send, it has never occurred to me that the correspondence of such a minor luminary as myself would ever be placed on record; and thus my passing remarks, unfortunately committed to paper, suggesting Arendt was a minor figure with an inferior intellect who deserved to be ridiculed in the *TLS*, were never intended to be seen as something to be actioned. I also find it extraordinary that evidence has come to light that I voted against the admission of graduates to All Souls. Needless to say, I contest this with the utmost vigour, but not so much that I am prepared to have the matter aired in public.

I am honoured to have been asked to contribute to AJP Taylor's festschrift. I consider him to have been one of this country's foremost historians, despite his hopelessly misguided Marxist deterministic analysis of the origins of the second world war, which I have exposed on more than one occasion. Unfortunately, I am, like Rousseau, in a state of chaos having one lecture and two books to write over the next 30 years and am therefore unable to commit to the project. However, I would like to offer £10 for someone else to write it instead.

The Arab-Israeli war is causing me some distress, not least because I have been so preoccupied with deciding which architect should build Wolfson College, that I have not been able to give it my full attention. Here at Oxford, the hippies and the beatniks have been demonstrating against the Vietnam war. There was a time when I might have had some sympathy, but now I have ingratiated myself as an establishment lackey I am inclined to let bygones be bygones.

I cannot end without voicing one minor irritation. Having invited 12 of my closest intimes to the Royal Box at Covent Garden, it was extremely embarrassing to find we were moved to less prestigious seating at short notice by the Prince of Wales. Please can you ask him to ensure this does not happen again? Yours ever, Isaiah.

Digested read, digested: Climbing.

SELF-HELP

The Privilege of Youth
by Dave Pelzer (2004)

My heart was racing. I hadn't slept in days. I didn't even know what city I was in. I had never felt so lonely. But then it's tough when you're on a two-month lecture tour. The phone rang in my hotel room.

'Is that the world's most abused man?' asked the voice.

My blood ran cold and I answered in the affirmative. 'I'm sorry to tell you that Dan Brazell has died.'

Who was Dan Brazell? He was the man who had once fixed my bike, but I had yet to mention in print. Those three years I had never written about because they seemed too boring, suddenly assumed an unbearable poignancy. I could feel another book welling up inside me.

Everyone picked on me in school because I was in foster care. They could sense the abuse I had suffered and bullied me for it. But within days of my foster parents, the Welshes, moving to Duinsmoore Way, it felt as if a cloud was lifting from my tormented inner self. Here I met Dave Howard and Paul Brazell, the first two boys of my own age not to judge me for my lack of self-esteem.

After a few weeks I decided I could confide in them.

'You have to know,' I whispered, 'that I am the world's most abused person. My mother called me 'It', locked me in the cellar for days on end, set me on fire, made me eat ammonia, bombarded me with sub-atomic particles, ran me over with a steam roller and fed me to a great white shark.'

'Actually, we'd read it all before in your other books,' they yawned, 'and we're bored stiff with hearing about it.'

This was the acceptance I had always craved.

Paul, Dave and I did a lot of crazy things in those years. Occasionally we would break the speed limit and once I narrowly missed hitting someone when I lost control. 'Wow,' said Paul, 'that was close.' 'Cool,' said Dave. I had done something right in someone else's eyes.

I could feel my confidence rising and I once plucked up the courage to ask a girl out on a date. To my surprise I could sense she found me not unattractive and I bent forward to kiss her. Her mother rushed out and ordered me to leave. 'Is it because I is abused?' I asked. 'No,' she replied. 'It's because you're so boring.'

Dave and Paul stayed on at school, but I felt the need to get a job. As a victim of abuse I still needed to prove myself. One day Paul moaned about his dad. I snapped. 'Your dad is great; he once fixed my bike. My dad never told me the three words I longed to hear: "You are famous."'

The three of us went our separate ways. I became a war hero before going on to critical acclaim as a professional victim. They amounted to nothing much.

At Dan's funeral, Paul asked me whether closure could ever be achieved. I checked my bank statement. 'Not for the time being.'

Digested read, digested: The world's most abused man sinks to new lows of literary degradation.

Freakonomics: A Rogue Economist Explores the Hidden Side of Everything
by Steven D Levitt & Stephen J Dubner (2005)

In the summer of 2003 the *New York Times* sent the journalist Stephen J Dubner to interview the heralded maverick economist

Steven D Levitt. What were the chances of two men with extraneous initials being attracted to one another? Higher than you might think. Levitt recognised in Dubner a man with a gift for hagiography, while Dubner knew a meal ticket when he saw it.

Anyone living in the US in 1990 could have been forgiven for being scared out of his skin. Crime was expected to rocket out of control within a decade. What happened? It went down. Why? More police? No. It was because the abortion laws changed. All those who would have grown up to be criminals were never born.

Ever wondered why an estate agent sells her house for more than you? She's better at her job? No. The extra $10,000 you might get is only worth about $150 to her. But when she sells her own house the full $10,000 extra is hers. See. It's simple when you think about it.

Levitt is considered a demi-god, one of the most creative people in economics and maybe in all social science.

If morality is the way we would like the world to work, then economics is how it actually does work. Freakonomics works on a number of premises. 1) Incentives are the cornerstone of modern life. 2) Conventional wisdom is often wrong. 3) Experts use their informational advantage to serve their own agenda. 4) Readers' gullibility should never be underestimated.

Levitt is a noetic butterfly that no one has pinned down, but is claimed by all.

What do schoolteachers and sumo wrestlers have in common? They all cheat. I know this will come as a terrible shock but dreary data proves it is true.

Levitt is one of the most caring men in the universe.

Why do so many drug dealers live with their mom? Amazingly, I can prove that most of them earn far less than you might imagine.

Levitt is genial, low-key and unflappable.

What makes a perfect parent? Research has shown that making a child watch TV in a library is the most effective way of ensuring he gets top grades.

Levitt is about to revolutionise our understanding of black culture. Even for Levitt this is new turf.

Black parents often give their children different names. A boy called Deshawn is less likely to get a job interview than someone called Steven. Maybe Deshawn should change his name.

Digested read, digested: What is the probability that a collection of often trivial and obvious data will be passed off as brilliance? Regrettably high.

The Game
by Neil Strauss (2005)

There were five of us living in the Hollywood mansion. Mystery, Herbal, Papa, Playboy and me, Style. None of us used our real names, only the ones we had given ourselves. Irony was already taken, in case you're wondering. So how did I get here?

I'm not attractive. I'm short and bald. You may have noticed that I haven't mentioned my personality. That's because I don't have one, which is why I had never had a girlfriend.

'Listen,' said my editor, placing a paper bag over my head, 'I've heard about a group of male Pick Up Artists (PUAs) who claim they can get any woman they want just by following a set patter, and I reckoned that if it works for you ...'

A week later I found myself in a master-class being run by Mystery. 'First you approach the three set,' he said. 'You then remove the obstacles and neg the target. Play it right and you can close any woman you like.'

I practised relentlessly and turned out to be a natural. Within months I could sarge any bar and was giving classes myself. But success came at a price; it became tough hearing woman after woman saying, 'You're the best, Style' and I longed for something more meaningful. So when I did make a deeper connection with Caroline, I videoed it to remind myself – and her – how sincere I could be.

My status within the PUA community was now legendary. I once heard someone use my lines to pick-up Paris Hilton and some people even started shaving their heads and sawing off their legs below the knee to look like me. It was all rather sad, really, as no one could have ever come close to matching my prime babe-magnet quality – an overweening sense of self-regard.

I was concerned, though, that my fame might affect my day job as it became tiring listening to so many people negging me by claiming they had never heard of Neil Strauss, the world's best writer. Luckily, the important people weren't put off as Tom Cruise and Courtney Love demanded I should be the journalist to interview them. I like to think neither of them was disappointed on meeting me.

It was the moment for Project Hollywood: five guys, surrounded by an endless stream of perfect 10 babes, living the PUA dream. And yet sometimes, when I was watching myself in the mirror having sex with two porn stars at the same time, I wondered whether there might be life outside my ego.

Please don't get the wrong idea about me. People think that PUAs are predators; but I'm actually an Averagely Frustrated Chump (AFC). I love women – especially women who are a bit stoned or pissed – but I am in fear of them so I have to turn myself into something they want. And if you believe that, you're probably the sort of babe who falls for my patter in bars.

Eventually it all had to come to an end. Project Hollywood fell apart and I met Lisa. She was my one-itis – the woman on whom I had used all my best moves to hypnotise into thinking she had fallen in love with me. This was a relationship we both knew would last for ever.

Digested read, digested: The American wet dream.

The Architecture of Happiness
by Alain de Botton (2006)

1. A grimy terraced house. Not mine, I might add, but one I have driven past. Quickly. Inside, we find peeling wallpaper, stained carpets and Ikea furniture, yet somehow people may have found happiness in such squalor.

2. The Greek philosopher Epictetus is said to have chastised a friend for venerating his surroundings, but attempts to scorn the material world have always been matched by attempts to mould it to graceful ends. Yet buildings fall down and moods change, so how can we define the meaning of architectural beauty? We probably can't, but that is not going to get in the way of my trademark cod-philosophical posturing.

3. There was once a clear idea of what was beautiful. The Classical tradition was revered for many centuries and palaces were built in renaissance Italy that would not have been unfamiliar to Marcus Aurelius. According to Wikipedia, things changed in 1747 when Horace Walpole sparked the gothic revival, and since then the advance of technology has

seen a growing eclecticism of ideas. How lucky you are to have me to point these things out.

4. The Modernist tradition, inspired by Le Corbusier, flirted uneasily with science and functionalism. For instance, you might think that numbering my paragraphs was both scientific and functional: it isn't. It's just pretentious.

5. If engineering cannot tell us what is beautiful, how do we escape the sterile relativism, which suggests that to label one building more aesthetically pleasing is to be undemocratic? By lapsing into an equally sterile relativistic debate about cultural and moral values contingent on architecture.

6. Buildings and objects can convey meaning with a single line or an elaborate flourish. They are the repository of ideas and ideals. I once walked from McDonald's in Victoria to Westminster Cathedral, a journey of only a few yards for ordinary people but a marathon expedition into the soul for someone of my sensitivity and intellect.

7. I seem to be running out of things to say, so let me talk about art for a while. Who cannot admire the sadness in a painting by Pieter de Hooch without coming close to tears? You may feel your eyes welling up as you read; these, though, are tears of boredom.

8. A beautiful building, as Prince Charles once opined, is a transubstantiation of our individual ideals in a material medium. Whatever love is. It is, however, in Friedrich Schiller that we find the clearest elucidation of the ways in which the finest architecture can embody our collective memory and idealised potential.

9. We note, though, that ideals of beauty change over time. This should not stop us making sweeping generalisations. Great architecture has a natural sense of order, one that mirrors the

natural world where I am at the top and you are much further down. I was once recovering from too much thinking in an expensive hotel that was done-up in the neo-renaissance style found in Amsterdam and was perplexed to find myself over-whelmed with anomie. Then I remembered I was in Japan.

10. How can we escape the notion that someone called Derek, Malcolm or Prescott will despoil a green field with box-like structures for the lower orders? By owning your own country estate.

Digested read, digested: The literature of pretention.

Small Dogs Can Save Your Life
by Bel Mooney (2010)

I was sitting in my study, wondering whether I would ever write a book again, when my little dog Bonnie leapt on to my lap and said: 'Oh Bel! / As far as I can tell / You've been through hell.' I ruffled her fur playfully as a solitary tear welled. 'You've been my rock in my painful separation from J, the cleverest man in the universe,' I replied. Bonnie looked me in the eyes. 'Then milk it, you dozy fool. Everyone knows J is Jonathan Dimbleby and at least one publisher must be interested. Even if you do write like a pretentiously overwrought Jilly Cooper.'

Bonnie came unto us one January morning when the pale sun glimmered milkily over the icy Somerset fields. I looked up from Creative Writing for Beginners and noticed a tiny dog tied to a tree. 'You've come to save me, Bonnie,' I said, for I instinctively knew her name. 'Yup,' Bonnie yapped. 'But first I could do with a piss.'

J and I welcomed Bonnie into the warmth of our immensely

successful media lifestyle and she was feted throughout Bath as she strolled through that splendid Georgian town in her Nicole Farhi jacket while reading Jane Austen. The summer of 2002 was the happiest time of my life. J and I had been blissfully married for 35 years and I had never stopped being grateful that this impossibly brilliant man had plucked me from my humble origins and allowed me to blossom into one of the finest writers ever to fill a newspaper column. I was lost in the newness of the Truth.

Then tragedy. J met the soprano Susan Chilcott. It was a *coup de foudre*. He returned to our farmhouse with a first edition of Middlemarch. 'I shall always love you and don't want a divorce and all that, Bel,' he said. 'But Susan and I are in love.' I understood his needs, so Bonnie and I packed our bags for a B&B.

Friends have expressed surprise that I never hated Susan, but who was I – a latter day saint and seer – to deny another woman the love of the world's most charismatic man? And even when she so tragically died a few months later, I could only feel the pain of a great love lost. Besides, I still had Bonnie. 'Let's go shopping to cheer ourselves up,' she would say, as I wrestled with the gravity of Dante and Botox. 'Why don't you buy me that lovely Swarovski crystal collar?'

I was also helped by my immensely successful and influential friends on national papers who offered to send me on expensive holidays to all parts of the world for their travel sections, along with my great friend Robin, a photographer who is somewhat younger than me. We became very close, and though Robin must have understood he will never be as important to me as either J or Bonnie, he asked me to marry him.

My acceptance had nothing to do with the phone call from J the previous day. 'I still love you and all that, Bel,' he had said. 'But I've met this great bird in her 20s and I need a divorce.' How angry I get when people criticise J for having a mid-life! Don't they understand the desires of the Great? Though it was jolly nice to be invited to the wedding of my best friends Prince Charles and Camilla. How wonderful to see a man happy with a woman his own age!

And so my life moved on. How I teetered with indecision when the *Daily Mail* offered me 10 times the money *The Times* was paying for my agony aunt column! Again, Bonnie came to the rescue. 'Take the cash, you moron. I need a pedicure.' So I did and I have never looked back, even when Bonnie had a splinter in her paw and I thought she might die. Fortunately my immense self-knowledge and the words of Kahlil Gibran were a comfort.

Through this time of personal growth I have emerged a stronger person. I know the love J and I have for one another was just too strong for us to stay together, so, as I anxiously await his texts, I happily lie in bed with Bonnie, while Robin curls up in his basket on the floor.

Digested read, digested: Get out while you still can, Bonnie.

I Can Make You Happy
by Paul McKenna (2011)

I am extremely disappointed to find out that after I have made you thin, made you rich, mended your broken heart, changed your life in seven days, given you instant confidence and guaranteed you success in 90 days in my previous books, you are all still as miserable as sin. I only hope you read this book a little more carefully than you have the others. For those who have difficulty reading, I have included a CD; don't worry if you do not have a machine to play it on. Just close your eyes and imagine a CD player in front of you. Now reach down and take it. Easy.

If you have bought this book, you have made a great start to a world of infinite happiness. How do I know this? Because you must be incredibly suggestible to imagine I can make you happy and therefore if I tell you I am making you happy you will probably believe it. If you don't believe this, let's start with me. One of the reasons I am so happy is because you have paid £10.99 for this book. That's right. Each one of you has made me happy, so allow yourself to be happy that you have made me happy. I understand that some of you may be feeling depressed and saying to yourselves, 'Paul is a charlatan'; let me reassure you that scientists have been amazed at how many people I have cured of long-term depression by getting them to press the second and fourth fingers of their left hand against their nose while reciting, 'Paul is Prozac'.

One final thing before we start in earnest. My method works. If you are still feeling unhappy at the end, then I can guarantee you will be feeling less unhappy than if you hadn't read it. And if you really do still feel utterly fed up, then it's because you haven't done everything I suggested, so it's your fault and you deserve every bit of misery coming your way.

OK, let's move on to the practical side. Start by answering this question: on a scale of 1–10, where 1 is suicidal, how low do you feel? If you score between 1 and 3, go straight to the next chapter for five simple steps that will give you an instant pick-me-up. First read some pages with a Zen-like blue tinge round the edges, then stand up straight, stop feeling sorry for yourself, tap your collarbone five times while looking up and down very quickly 13 times and then step forward into an imaginary new you.

There. I can already sense your score has rocketed to 5 or 6, and you are ready to move on to more advanced happiness studies.

Happiness is a habit; it isn't something that comes with new clothes. It's something you have to work at. So start smiling and get out and take some exercise. No one can expect to be happy if they are a bit chubby.

Now imagine some happy dots in front of you and try to join them up. Start giving yourself positive messages. It's hard to be up if you are telling yourself no one likes you; train yourself to say, 'No one likes me but I don't care because I don't like anyone anyway.'

Now we're making progress. Next, you have to learn how to make your happiness permanent. Take time out each day to think of all the things you want to achieve. Now measure up the upsides and the downsides. Suppose there's a girl you would like to date. How would your feelings score if she said no – 3? And if she said yes – 10? So it clearly makes sense to harass as many women as possible until one says yes.

There will still be some negative things in your life that are hard to throw off, but you can diminish their power by turning them from colour to black and white in your mind and then flushing them down the toilet. Trust me. You can always achieve more than you think. A friend of mine was desperate to be an artist, so he dumped his wife and kids and is now really happy living in Paris.

If you sincerely find that none of this is working, it may be that your emotions are blocked. Ordinarily, this might take you many years of intensive therapy to overcome, but I can get you through it in just 20 minutes. See all that anger and guilt? Just let go of them. Whoosh. They've gone. Now you're ready to find the deepest levels of inner happiness and bliss usually known only to Zen masters. Start by looking up my arse.

Digested read, digested: I can make you gullible.

Battle Hymn of the Tiger Mother
by Amy Chua (2011)

A lot of people wonder how Chinese parents raise such stereotypically successful kids. Well, I can tell them, because I've done it. You don't allow them to have any friends, you stop them from playing sport or watching TV and you waterboard them if they get less than an A* in every subject.

Sophia is our first born. At three months old, I left her for days on her own to learn Poincaré's conjecture while I rewrote the US constitution, and by the time she was three she could speak seven languages, play Rachmaninov's Third Piano Concerto and had never so much as smiled. She was the ideal Chinese Tiger Mother's daughter.

My second child, Lulu, was more of a handful. Even though she, too, was far more talented than the second-rate children of decadent American parents, she tried to resist my will at every turn. At the age of two, she refused to do more than 10 hours of maths homework a night and deliberately played wrong notes in the Mendelssohn Violin Concerto. The only thing that worked was to wire electrodes to her hands.

There was a third child, Tiananmen. He was even more wilful and used to get out of his pram and stand defiantly in Times Square. Regrettably, I had to crush him with a tank. His death was not wholly in vain: Sophia and Lulu gave me a lot less trouble after that.

Growing up in the US as the child of Chinese immigrants, I was conscious of how indulgent American parents were. No Chinese parent would dream of praising a child unless he or she got 100% in all subjects, but Americans would congratulate their worthless offspring for getting an A–. I made a vow I would respect my children enough never to show I loved them. Feeble-minded, lazy Americans feel they have a duty of care towards their children. Chinese parents regard their kids as objects to be abused and moulded in their own image and I was determined that neither of my surviving kids should fall short of my own brilliant standards, which I will boast about at length.

I admit I was ruthless and I would fire maths and music teachers at will if they did not keep Sophia and Lulu on course for winning a Nobel prize and playing at the Carnegie Hall. And my husband, Jed, did sometimes question my psychopathic narcissism by suggesting it might help if we were to occasionally tell the children we loved them. I thought about that for a nanosecond and then dismissed it, because I'm always right about everything. 'I am the Chinese Tiger Mother,' I yelled. 'You are just American Pussy Father. Your job is to be useless and defer to me.'

Sophia continued to be the perfect child, winning first prize at everything and playing piano brilliantly. Lulu continued to be more trouble, complaining she was happy to do nine hours' practice a night but not 10. 'You're shaming the whole family,' I screamed at her. 'Go on, give up the violin and make me look like a complete failure. Next you'll be saying you want to have friends.'

Jed interrupted. 'I thought you might like to know my book is now number two in the *New York Times* bestseller chart,' he said. 'Second?' I screamed. 'You pathetic American Pussy Father. You heap greater ignominy on me; even the dog has let me down by coming third at the international dog show.'

These were more difficult times for me as my sister had leukaemia and Chinese Tiger Mothers cannot tolerate such genetic weakness in their families. Luckily she recovered before I had to disown her, and I redoubled my efforts to make sure my children did not show me up. Music lessons were increased to

13 hours a day, all holidays were cancelled and any hint of vulnerability was punished by a week in solitary confinement.

I'm pleased to say it's all paid off magnificently. Everyone says my daughters are the most talented prodigies ever known and that I must be the world's greatest mother, especially as the American Pussy Father is a waste of space. What's more, Sophia and Lulu are two of the happiest kids you could imagine. If you don't believe me, ask them.

'If mummy says we are happy then we are happy,' they say. 'And we're hoping to be penpals with the Fritzls when we're in therapy.'

How sweet.

Digested read, digested: Never has mediocrity seemed more appealing.

How to be a Woman
by Caitlin Moran (2011)

Here I am on my 13th birthday. The Yobs are shouting at me. I'm too fat to run away. The dog is licking her vagina. I don't KNOW what to do!!! I realise I am femin-none. I go home and make a list. 1. USE LOTS OF CAPITAL LETTERS. 2. *Ditto italics.* 3. !!!!!! 4. Never use one bad pun where two will do.

I love Simone de Beauvoir and Germaine Greer yet I didn't have a clue how to be a woman when I hit puberty. I thought it was something I'd discover in the underwear section of a C&A catalogue!!! I mean, WHAT DO YOU DO? How do you stop eating cake, quarrelling with your siblings and LEARN HOW to groom *your pubes* in a feminist kind of way? Much as I enjoyed the *dirty bits*, *The Female Eunuch* just didn't tell a 13-year-old girl how to grow up in Wolverhampton!

OMG! I'm bleeding. I thought it was going to be a lifestyle choice!!! Actually I didn't, it's just HYPERBOLE!!! But tampons and stuff are so confusing when you're fighting with your siblings and *you're trying to have your* first ever wank over Chevy Chase! There, I've said it!! Feminists wank!!! Who would have thought it??? And porn is great as long as the women are loving it and come first. Go, sisters, go.

I've grown some hair!!! Down there!!! When I first see it in my tiny Wolverhampton tin bath, I shave it in disgust, but over the years I've come to take pride in my bush. A *Brazilian* is patriarchal oppression. ENDOV. Though it's fine if you want to give it a neat ironic trim in the shape of a heart like my friend Rachel does on Tris's birthday. I mean, it's the 21st century and women should be relaxed and know how to have a joke about this stuff.

We need to drop the DOGMA about feminism and just get on with having a laugh being women. And there's no laughs in doing the house work, so just chill and get a cleaner and knock back a few bottles of wine and some Es. *This woman business is easier than you think.* Just take charge of your vagina and off you go. Though I like to call mine a FOOF. I've never been sure what to call my breasts though. So I don't call them ANYTHING!!!

I'm going out on a date with Courtney and I'm wearing my Dr Martens that I bought with my first pay cheque from *Melody Maker* when I was nine . . . AND I Don't Know WHAT TO DO. I want to flirt with him, but does he fancy me and, oh my God, I think he thinks I'm fat. Sisters, I was!! *How does a feminist know she's fat*??? When she doesn't look human and when I was out with Courtney I so looked like a row of porta-bogs!!! Which was quite handy, because my CYSTITIS was killing me!!!!

So I've lost weight and I'm in the *Melody Maker* office and I'm doing some flirting and all I'm *getting in return is casual* sexism and a lot of heartache. Man, relationships are a minefield when you'd rather just be getting stoned with your little sister in Wolverhampton!! Love you too, Caz!! Thank God, I met my husband Pete!! He's just about the biggest feminist I know. He never wears thongs – except in bed!!! – he hates high heels and he loves reading all the bitchy bits in Grazia!! *Because you know what*? Being a fifth-wave feminist doesn't mean you can't gossip or wear suspenders.

I literally think I'm dying!!! I'm screaming in pain as my first baby is being born – it feels like I'm shitting a hippo!!! – and Peter is crying and then I'm holding her and it feels like the most feminist thing in the world anyone could ever do. I love my children!!! And suddenly I feel, Woomph, I'm creative, I'm going to write five columns and a book while I'm breast-feeding. Wowzer!! If you want a job done, ask a working mother. They are the most productive people in the UNIVERSE.

And like it's OK if you don't want to have babies too. Because it's a woman's right to choose. Though obviously women who don't have babies are basically lazy!!! Abortions??? If you want one, have one!!! You see, a woman can do anything really in the 21st century. Well, anything as long as I approve!!! If in doubt, just ask yourself, what would Caitlin do????

Katie Price!!! What a solipsistic bitch!! She doesn't ask me a single question when I interview her. What a rubbish role model!!! But Lady Gaga . . . Go girl! Her music is just so brilliant, she takes me to a gay bar in Germany and SHE BUYS ME A DRINK and we get totally trashed and she says she really, really loves my hair before passing out on my lap. Feminism rocks!

Digested read, digested: How to Be Everywhere.

French Children Don't Throw Food
by Pamela Druckerman (2012)

When my daughter is 18 months old my husband and I (he's British, I'm American) decide to take her on holiday. Meals are a disaster. Bean creates havoc. I notice that none of the French children are behaving this badly. I wonder pourquoi. 'C'est par ce que votre fille is called Bean,' a maman confides in me. 'Quel type of ridiculous nom is that? No French parent would call their child Haricot.'

I came to motherhood late and, being a hack and not having much work on, I naturally decided to write a book about it. All I needed was an angle. And then I remembered I was living in France and could pass off some general observations about the few middle-class Parisians I knew as insight.

Americans tend to make a great fuss about the birth; French mothers are more relaxed. 'If it mourir, it mourir,' they shrug. 'We pouvoir always have an autre.' French fathers are equally laissez-faire; few are expected to attend the birth if there is a football match on TV. And this sense of calm seems to be transmitted to their children.

Bean used to scream throughout the night. I thought this was normal until I talked to Martine, who told me: 'Tous French bébés sleeper through the nuit.' 'How do you do it?' I asked incredulously. 'It's facile,' she replied. 'No French maman would reve of breastfeeding as it ruins her tits. So we tipper some cognac into the formula et Bob est votre oncle.' 'But what if they wake anyway?' 'I 'ave les plugs d'oreille.'

One of the first commands a French enfant learns is 'Attendez'. American mothers are taught to respond immediately to their child's demands. 'Why would you vouloir to faire that?' said Agathe. 'It is obvious que all bébés are un morceau d'un fuckwit and haven't un clue what they wanter. That is why all enfants are made to stander for une heure chaque jour with an ashtray strapped to their têtes.' What a refreshing change from the babycentric world of Brooklyn!

My mother was horrified that we were going to put Bean in a crèche, but in France that is routine. 'To be honnête,' dit Marie, 'once le novelty is over, looking after un bébé is pretty ennuyant. En tout cas, it would be impossible to fitter dans my pilates class to tightener my vagina as well as mon cinq-à-sept liaison with Alain without la crèche. Et mon mari aussi needs the time to voir his maîtresse. So it's better all round for tout le monde.'

It's an accepted code of American parenting that the earlier you can get your child to do things, the better. The French don't bother. Rather, they treat their enfants as adults, so they do not encourage them to read before the age of six. 'C'est un waste of temps for kids to lire merde comme Thomas the Tank Engine,' Carla told me. 'So we don't bozzer. We attend till they are vieux enough to read Barthes, Sartre et Lacan.'

French parents don't feel the need to soft-soap their children. When Bean has nightmares, I try to comfort her but a French maman will dire, 'Vie est un bitch, et puis you die' and as a result French children are extremely well-adjusted to existential ennui. Similarly, American parents tend to praise their children for the slightest achievement; French parents laugh at their enfants' drawings. 'Call ça un ferking Picasso?'

Did I tell you I also had twins? No? Well, let me bore on about them for a couple of chapters. Ah, où étais-je? Oh, oui, sex! Simon and I hadn't done it for months. Thérèse was horrified. 'You quoi?' All French femmes need to avoir it off four fois par jour.'

'But what shall I do about Bean?' 'Putter her in her chambre until she is douze. Et then sender her off to her boyfriend.'

'The chose about vous Yanks,' dit Christine, slugging a carafe of vin rouge, 'est que vous turner your kids into a project rather than let them be them-mêmes.' 'I know,' I wailed. 'But what can I do?' 'Stopper écriring about them pour un start.'

Digested read, digested: Bringing up bébé.

Celebrate by Pippa Middleton (2012)

It's a bit startling to achieve global recognition before the age of 30, on account of your sister, your brother-in-law and your bottom. But I am by nature an optimist, so I tend to concentrate on the advantages. Like cashing in while I can. No disrespect, sis, but royal marriages don't have the best track record! So imagine my surprise when Penguin offered me £400,000 and a full editorial team to cobble up a few lame party ideas that would help to promote my family's business, Party Pieces. I hope it takes you as long to read it as it took me to write it!

Halloween
I always think a party gets off to the perfect start with a little poem. So here's mine. *On a misty Halloween / I like to trick or treat the Queen / And if she gets a little glum / I let Prince Harry pat my bum!* Halloween is a scary time of year, so it's a good idea to think of some scary things for people to do. Hollowing out a pumpkin and going 'Boo!' can be quite amusing. It can also be fun to slit a cat's throat and drain off the blood into a wine bottle marked 'cat's blood'. The scariest food I can think of is toad-in-the-hole,

a recipe for which I found in an old copy of the *Daily Express*. If you think sausages in batter are too frightening, you can serve with mashed potato instead. Above all, always plan ahead.

Christmas

I love to decorate the tree / Because everyone stares at my botty / And naughty Harry gets roaring drunk / While all his mates smoke loads of skunk. Christmas tends to come at a time of year when it's quite cold – the baby Jesus must have been a hardy boy – so I always think roast turkey is more appropriate than a barbecue. After someone else has cooked the big meal – go to www.partypieces.co.uk for bookings – I always go upstairs to change into another outfit. Christmas is a very Christmassy time, so it's nice to allow my guests to see me in a variety of figure-hugging dresses. While giving my guests this special treat, I also try not to forget that Christmas is really about children. So if anyone knows any black ones we can use for the photos, please give my publisher a ring as we really are struggling!

Valentine's Day

Now is the time to bump and grind / Against my firm and smooth behind / And Harry sends away his flunkey / Hoping I will spank his monkey. Valentine's Day is the day on which people celebrate their love for one another, so one unusual thing you can try is to give a card to your special one – Me! – with a heart on it. If you can't find any cards like this, you might want to buy me some flowers. A garage will help you out, if you don't find a florist open on your way back from the pub. I also think nothing says 'I love you' more than a raspberry souffle, so I've included another recipe someone found somewhere. And for that final flourish, a box of After Eights is the perfect ending to a romantic evening.

Wedding day

Oh joyous, rapturous day of days / When social climbing pays its way / And Westminster Abbey doth as one all swear / I have the world's best derrière. A wedding is when someone gets married to another person, so the clever party organiser will always remember to bake a cake and order the right amount of chairs for the guests to sit on. On big family occasions like this, it's all too easy to imagine the day is about the bride and groom, and forget that a large, televised wedding is the perfect way to launch your own career. So never be afraid to upstage your sister, and once you have made yourself the centre of attention, you can relax with a glass of wine and a sing-song, knowing you will never have to work again.

Digested read, digested: Cutandpaste.

Antifragile by Nassim Nicholas Taleb (2012)

Wind extinguishes a candle and energises fire. How deep is that? The answer, counter-intuitively, is not quite as deep as me. For I, Nassim Nicholas Taleb alone have discovered the secret of the universe. It is the antifragile.

'What in God's name is that?' Wittgenstein asked me over lunch in a three-starred Michelin restaurant in Paris. Let me explain. You know how some things are quite fragile, and we're really scared of them breaking? Well, my brilliant new idea is that sometimes it's good that things get broken, because that's when important changes like evolution can happen. And because I'm the only person who has ever thought this, I'm going to call it Antifragile.

'I know you are the cleverest man who ever lived,' Einstein told me over cocktails in my private jet, 'but I'm not sure I'm quite getting this.' Think of it like this. In an earlier work of staggering brilliance, I invented the idea of vanishingly rare Black Swan events that skewed our understanding of probability. Well, now I've proved it, as the publishers have assumed that because I got lucky with some bullshit once then I'm bound to do the same again with the next book. The easiest way to understand the concept is this. Think of the fragile as a book for which I've written the antibook. A work of massive consequence for the universe that is so self-important it will go unread by everyone.

Forget everything you ever learned from Harvard drones and Nobel laureates, for in them lies no salvation. They think only in the sort of teleological heuristic iatrogenics that would appeal to a Seneca or a Nero. The world is really composed of Triads: the Fragile, the Robust and the Antifragile. Now abideth these three. And the greatest of these is the Antifragile. Don't just take it from me. Look at this bar chart that shows how everyone else is very stupid, and I am right about everything. Case proved.

A week or so ago, I was bench-pressing 250kg in the luxury gym in the basement of my Manhattan condo, when I was interrupted by Nelson Mandela who wanted to know why I kept repeating the triadic dualistic mantra of fragile and antifragile. 'Dats simpul,' I replied, using the voice of Fat Tony from Brooklyn, a character I created who never fails to make me laugh out loud. Though he may not have the same effect on you. 'Becoz I've nuttin more to say and 400 pages to say it.'

Let me put it another way. When I interrupted the World Economic Forum in Davos to expose the central fallacies of non-optionality in the markets, I was shouted down by everyone except Buddha. But it is now clear to me that I have been proved entirely right on absolutely everything except those things that I may have got wrong. And that uncertainty over which is which goes to the very essence of the antifragile.

But where's your evidence, you might tediously ask? If so, you wouldn't be the first, as I had this out with Plato over a glass of the finest retsina to be found in the Peloponnese. As long as you stay stuck in the mindless pursuit of empirical cause and effect, you will be lost in the darkness. The key to enlightenment is the simple convex transformation that the absence of evidence is not evidence of absence. I will say that again in case you missed it. The absence of evidence is not evidence of absence.

Recall that we once had no word for the colour blue. So we had no word for complete tosser. Until now. The apophatic should always take the via negativa and assume that every doctor is trying to kill you unless you happen to get better. 'How then,' Confucius asked me when I was staying in the Forbidden City, 'am I supposed to be able to tell which changes are antifragile and which are not?' Let go of your doxastic epistemes, grasshopper. The answers lie within.

Digested read, digested: Antimatter.

Manuscript Found in Accra
by Paulo Coelho (2013)

In 1945, two brothers in Egypt found discarded biblical texts. In 1982, Paolo di Canio found a further manuscript in the same area. He gave it to me, Paulo di Coelho, last year. This is what it said.

Today is July 14th, 1089, and the town of Jerusalem, in which both Jews and Muslims live, will tomorrow be attacked by the Christians. All of us are so afraid and have gathered in the square.

Behold! A bald Brazilian man with a neatly cropped beard descends from a cloud.

A man asks him: 'Speak to us about defeat.' And the Brazilian answers: 'Defeat is not so bad, for everything is part of the Divine Energy. Remember the Circle of Life. The gazelle may be eaten by the lion, but the gazelle eats the grass. Such is God's way.'

Another man asks him: 'Speak to us about platitudes.' And the Brazilian answers: 'If I can get away with this drivel, then there is hope for all of us. Even the most useless of you can appreciate the shining of the sun. Unless it is raining. Learn to take pride in all your achievements, however small. If you have stayed at home in bed, delight in the fact you have not driven your car and knocked over a pedestrian.'

Another man asks him: 'Speak to us about fear.' And the Brazilian says: 'None of us can escape the Unwanted Visitor of Death. So learn to chill out. A mountain is not afraid to stay in the same place. A man who has had one leg amputated is not so fearful of having the other one hacked off. You have nothing to lose but your limbs. Difficulty is the name of an ancient tool that was created purely to help us define who we are. Chisel is another.'

Another man asks him: 'Speak to us about beauty.' And the Brazilian says: 'Do not believe those who say it is only Inner Beauty that counts. Otherwise why would God have made me so handsome? Ugliness is a mask worn by hideous people who are too afraid to allow themselves to feel the Divine Energy and be loved. True Love, though, is the Love that Seduces and will never allow itself to be Seduced.'

Another man says: 'That's the biggest load of bollocks I've ever heard. Surely anyone Seduced by True Love cannot Experience True Love?' And the Brazilian gave him a withering look of contempt before replying: 'The rest is silence, Grasshopper.'

A woman asks him: 'Speak to us of sex.' And the Brazilian says: 'It is when two rivers meet to become a more beautiful, more powerful river. And if my meaning is still unclear, email me at holdmylovepump@gmail.com.'

Another man asks him: 'Why are some men poets and some men labourers?' And the Brazilian says: 'One day a man shall come who will write, 'Close your eyes, yet do not sleep/For I will take you to the Deepest Deep.' And that man will be me. Do not chastise yourself for being quite dim. For if you were bright, you would not buy this book and I would not be loaded.'

Another man asks him: 'Tell us what the future holds.' And the Brazilian says: 'The Unwanted Visitor may arrive at any moment. So always have clean underwear and take heed that one man went to mow, went to mow a meadow. Listen to the wind, but do not forget your horse. Or your lawn mower. Think also of a shelf that collapses and breaks an array of painted vases. But do not ask why. Do not fear failure. Each day is a new beginning, so treat it as if it were your last.'

With that the Rabbi, the Imam and the Priest cry 'Good idea' and kill themselves rather than each other, before a final man asks: 'Speak to us of miracles.' And the Brazilian says: 'You've carried on reading till the end.'

Digested read, digested: Manuscript Found in Adustbin.

David and Goliath
by Malcolm Gladwell (2013)

In the heart of ancient Palestine stood a six-foot-nine-inch giant. Against him was a five-foot-nothing midget. No one gave the midget a prayer. The giant's name was Goliath. The midget's name was David. You might have read about their battle in the Old Testament. But the Bible got it wrong. David was not the underdog.

Most people make assumptions about power and jump to ridiculous conclusions. Who does not think the country with the most men and weaponry will automatically win a war? Not counting those of you who lived through Vietnam, Afghanistan and Iraq. Take the American invasion of Grenada. Although Grenada was much the smaller country, it actually held all the aces. Had Grenada played its cards just a little better, the US would have been wiped off the face of the earth.

Vivek Ranadive decided to coach his daughter's basketball team. Vivek realised that most coaches had made the simple error of packing their teams with players who were at least 6ft 7in. His daughter's friends were 5ft 3in. Vivek understood his team could run through the legs of the opposition before climbing on to each other's shoulders to score a slam dunk. They beat the Boston Celtics 89–12. In their dreams.

Can you have too much money? Personally, I don't think you can, or I would have stopped chancing my arm with counterintuitive anecdotes long ago. But research shows you can. Jim was very happy when he didn't have much money. Now he's a top Hollywood producer and not very happy. See what I mean?

Richard is dyslexic. Most people would consider it to be a disadvantage. But Richard worked very hard, got a bit lucky and founded his Virgin empire. Richard could not have done this had he not been dyslexic. Having dyslexia is actually a blessing and anyone who has the condition and has not become a billionaire should be ashamed.

Learning to understand when your disadvantage is an advantage and not a disadvantage can be tricky. Katy was devastated when her entire family was wiped out in an air crash. Then she realised that at least she was alive and would inherit all the money. She went on to become a moderately successful real-estate agent in Florida.

Terry was a large trout in a North American lake. After graduating top of the class from the lake's high school, Terry decided to travel to the ocean to make his fortune. He got gobbled up by Thomas the tuna. Sometimes, it really is better to be a big fish in a little pond, rather a little fish in a big pond.

In 1963, Martin Luther King went to Birmingham, Alabama. Martin Luther King was black. Birmingham, Alabama, was known to be the most racist city in the USA. Therefore, Birmingham, Alabama, was not a safe place for Martin Luther King. But Martin Luther King went anyway. If Martin Luther King had been white, no one would have noticed his presence in Birmingham, Alabama. But because Martin Luther King had the courage to be black and he did go to Birmingham, Alabama, the civil rights movement made significant progress.

Less is sometimes more. And more is sometimes less. It's all a question of perception. Bobby was a career criminal. When California introduced a three strikes and you go to jail policy, Bobby went on a killing spree. The penalties for murder were so severe, they made no difference to him. But when California reduced the maximum sentence from 238 years to 110 years, Bobby decided to go straight. Bobby went to Harvard and became a traffic cop in Iowa.

There was once a boy who looked a bit different. We'll call him Leo Sayer. Because that's his name. Some people laughed at Leo because he had silly hair. Others didn't want to be his friend because he was always telling them that he was right and they were wrong. Leo decided to use his odd hair and off-putting mannerisms to his advantage and changed his name to Malcolm. Malcolm wrote a book telling people how everything they knew was wrong. It became a bestseller. So Malcolm wrote another book just the same. And another. He even rewrote Aesop's Fables. Still no one noticed. Malcolm cultivated a persona of being an outsider while earning huge amounts of money from banks, tobacco and pharmaceutical companies. Malcolm earns more for a one-hour talk than you will earn in a year. So who is laughing now?

Digested read, digested: You make me feel like snoring.

SCIENCE/HISTORY/RELIGION

Empire: How Britain Made the Modern World
by Niall Ferguson (2003)

It has long been fashionable to decry the British empire as a relic of imperial repression, and while it is not my intention to excuse its worst excesses, it is important for a good-looking historian to take a contrary position. So I contend it was also a considerable force for good.

Every iconoclast needs a neologism; mine is Anglobalisation. Other empire builders were little more than pirates, exploiting resources for their own end while seeking to impose their culture and religion on the local inhabitants. Britain, of course, was not entirely exempt in this respect but her interests lay far more in establishing a world free-trade market.

Stroll down the elegant boulevards of old Philadelphia and think of all the things that would not have existed had the world not had the benefit of my, sorry our, munificence. Sydney, Freetown, Bombay, Calcutta: all founded and built by the British. Would they have been created anyway, you might ask? Well, yes, but not nearly so well.

In 1897, the year of her Diamond Jubilee, Queen Victoria reigned supreme over 25% of the world's surface; informally, through her economic activities in Latin America, her imperial reach extended still further. Wondrous times. In a spirit of unflinching altruism Britain exported its peoples and its capital to all corners of the globe, often at significant cost to itself. And where's the gratitude, that's what I want to know.

I have now reached the most solemn point of the story. It was the British Empire that alone stood up to two of the most evil empires in history in 1940 and singlehandedly saved the world from the thousand-year Reich. No greater love hath any empire than it lays down its life for its friends. In an act of Judas-like betrayal, it was the Americans, whose anti-colonial ideals sit uneasily with its own history both within and without its borders, who brought about our collapse. Britain was almost bankrupted saving the world, and America sought to expedite it in the late 1940s to acquire our markets for itself. Blame the Americans for the bloodbath of decolonisation. And what has the US given the world in return? Nothing.

All things considered, both Britain and myself can look ourselves in the mirror and be pretty damned pleased with what we see.

Digested read, digested: Britons never, never, never shall be slaves.

A Briefer History of Time
by Stephen Hawking (2005)

The title of this book differs by only two letters from *A Brief History of Time* that I wrote in 1988. That book stayed on the bestseller list for 237 weeks; a remarkable feat for a book that no one understood. Three years ago, I attempted to simplify my ideas in *The Universe in a Nutshell*, but I now gather that no one understood that, either. So, I'm now giving you a third and final chance. At the very least, you will begin to grasp the concept of circular time.

So pay attention. As Einstein points out, time may be relative, but mine's more valuable than yours. We're searching for a grand unified theory, but haven't got one, because general relativity and quantum mechanics are inconsistent with one another. So let's start with Newton, who gave us the three laws of motion, which describe how bodies react to forces, and the theory of gravity.

Newton refused to accept the lack of absolute space, even though his laws implied it, but he believed wholeheartedly in absolute time. This was a mistake, as everyone has their own four-dimensional spacetime. Einstein's theory of general relativity is based on the revolutionary suggestion that gravity is not a force like other forces, but a consequence of the fact that spacetime is curved. Light rays, too, must follow geodesics in spacetime, as relativity predicts light will be bent by gravitational fields.

Thanks to the Doppler effect, we know that the universe is expanding as the light-shifts of stars veer towards the red end of the spectrum. If you listen carefully, you can also pick up cosmic noise, which is, in fact, the glow of microwave radiation from the early formation of the universe. So how did the universe start? All solutions to Einstein's equations point to the fact that at some time in the past the universe was squashed into a single point with zero size. At this point, which we call big bang, the density of the universe and the curvature of spacetime would have been infinite, so unfortunately all theories of cosmology break down.

Still with me? Probably not. But never mind. I shall carry on regardless. One second after big bang, the universe would have contained mostly photons, electrons and neutrinos, and their anti-particles, together with some protons and neutrons.

Colliding photons might produce an electron and a positron; if they met up they would annihilate each other, but the reverse process is not so easy. Eventually, when the temperature had fallen to allow the strong force to take effect we'd begin to see the nuclei of deuterium. From then on it was downhill through supernovae and black holes to the present day.

But how do we resolve the problem of singularity? Through

supersymmetry? String theory? 10-dimensional space? These are only partial explanations. All we can say for certain is that it is possible to write five sentences that make sense on their own, but when put together in a paragraph are intelligible only to God. And me.

Digested read, digested: Third Time Unlucky.

God is Not Great
by Christopher Hitchens (2007)

If the intended reader of this book should want to go beyond disagreement with its author and try to identify the sins that animated him to write it, he or she will not just be quarrelling with the ineffable creator who made me this way, they will also be defiling the memory of a simple, pious woman called Mrs Jean Watts.

It was Mrs Watts' task, when I was a boy of about nine, to instruct me in lessons of nature and scripture, and there came a day when she said, 'So you see children, how powerful and generous God is. He has made the grass to be green, which is exactly the colour that is most restful to our eyes.'

I was appalled by this. Even though it was to be several months before I was to fully comprehend the subtleties of Darwinian evolution and to unlock the secrets of the genome, I simply knew my teacher had managed to get everything wrong in two sentences. The eyes were adjusted to nature, not the other way round.

I do not believe it is arrogant of me to say that I had uncovered the four irreducible objections to religious faith – its misrepresentations of the origins of man and the cosmos, its combination of servility and solipsism, its dangerous sexual repression and its wishful-thinking – before my boyish voice had broken. Everyone knows I have always been right about everything, even when I have later changed my mind, and there is at least one other person conceited enough to make similar claims. My brother.

Religious friends – I use both words guardedly – often call me a seeker because I have studied the world's sacred texts in greater depth than any scholar. Like almost everything else, this irritates me immensely. I read these books because I am, by nature, tolerant and wish to engage with the idiocies many hold dear. The difference between me and them is that while I would not try to convert others to atheism, they feel obliged to save my soul. This is an important distinction. The purpose of this book is not to prove God does not exist; it is to prove I am cleverer than Richard Dawkins.

Sheltered as my life normally is within the rarefied sanctuary of the Washington intellectual elite, I have always made it my business to give comfort to the world's conflict zones by blessing them with a visit – often accompanied by my dear friend, Salman Rushdie. And I ask you this: if the express purpose of religion is to make you happy, then why is every zealot a psychopathic paedophile?

Yes, more people have died in the name of religion than ... Oh, you've already heard this somewhere before, have you? Well let me tell you something you don't know. The reason that Jews and Muslims don't eat pork has nothing to do with the meat's cleanliness. It comes from their Freudian repression of their lust for pigs.

Religion serves only the self-satisfied and the conceited; it dates back to a period of prehistory when nobody – not even the mighty Democritus – had the faintest clue what was going on and God was needed not just as an explanation but as an instrument of social repression...

But I can see that I am again in danger of losing you in the radicalism and unfamiliarity of my discourse, so let me devote the next 150 pages to a brutal deconstruction of the evils of the Bible and the Qur'an – though they hardly merit the attention of my intellect. I could talk about the weakness of evidence by revelation, but suffice it to say that the Bible is a catalogue of lies compiled by ruthless, amoral, sexually perverted liars and that the Qur'an is a catalogue of lies borrowed from the Bible.

I must also talk about the tawdriness of the miraculous, the priapism of blood sacrifice, the molestation of children and the empty concept of heaven which are endemic in every believer, but I should also like to counter the case against the secularists. Were not Hitler and Stalin the biggest mass-murderers in modern history, say the vicious religious apologists such as Mother Teresa? I say only this. All the Nazis were Catholics and Stalin was a theocrat.

The time for the new Enlightenment has come. Cast aside your false gods and know one thing and one thing only. There is no God but me.

Digested read, digested: Our Christopher, who art in Washington, hallowed be my name.

The Case for God
by Karen Armstrong (2007)

May the words of my mouth and the meditations of my heart make Dawkins and Hitchens burn in Hell, O Lord my Rock and my Redeemer. Amen.

Much of what we say about God these days is facile. The concept of God is meant to be hard. Too often we get lost in what Greeks called logos (reason) rather than interpreting Him through mythoi – those things we know to be eternally true but can't prove. Like Santa Claus. Religion is not about belief or faith; it is a skill. Self-deceit does not always come easily, so we have to work at it. Our ancestors, who were obviously right, would have been surprised by the crude empiricism that reduces faith to fundamentalism or atheism. I have no intention of rubbishing anyone's beliefs, so help me God, but Dawkins's critique of God is unbelievably shallow. God is transcendent, clever clogs. So we obviously can't understand him. Duh!

I'm going to spend the next 250 pages on a quick trawl of comparative religion from the pre-modern to the present day. It won't help make the case for God, but it will make me look clever and keep the publishers happy, so let's hope no one notices!

The desire to explain the unknowable has always been with us, and the most cursory glance at the cave paintings at Lascaux makes it clear these early Frenchies didn't intend us to take their drawings literally. Their representations of God are symbolic; their religion a therapy, a sublimation of the self. Something that fat bastard Hitchens should think about.

Much the same is true of the Bible. Astonishingly, the Eden story is not a historical account, nor is everything else in the Bible true. The Deuteronomists were quick to shift the goalposts of the meaning of the Divine when problems of interpretation and meaning were revealed. So should we be. Rationalism is not antagonistic to religion. Baby Jesus didn't want us to believe in his divinity. That is a misrepresentation of the Greek pistis. He wanted everyone to give God their best shot and have a singalong Kumbaya.

We'll pass over Augustine and Original Sin, because that was a bit of a Christian own goal, and move on to Thomas Aquinas, in whom we can see that God's best hope is apophatic silence. We can't say God either exists or doesn't exist, because he transcends existence. This not knowing is proof of his existence. QED. A leap of faith is in fact a leap of rationality. Obviously.

Skipping through the Kabbalah, introduced by the Madonna of Lourdes and Mercy (1459–), through Erasmus and Copernicus, we come to the Age of Reason. It was unfortunate that the church rejected Galileo, but that was more of a post-Tridentine Catholic spat than a serious error and it didn't help that a dim French theologian, Mersenne, conflated the complexities of science with intelligent design, but we'll skip over that.

Things came right with Darwin. Many assume he was an atheist; in reality he was an agnostic who, despite being a lot cleverer than Dawkins, could not refute the possibility of a God. Therefore God must exist, or we drift into the terrible nihilism of Sartre where we realise everything is pointless. Especially this book.

The modern drift to atheism has been balanced by an equally lamentable rise in fundamentalism. Both beliefs are compromised and misconceived. The only logical position is apophatic relativism, as stated in the Jeff Beck (1887–) lyric, 'You're everywhere and nowhere, Baby. That's where you're at.'

I haven't had time to deal with the tricky issues of the after-life that some who believe in God seem to think are fairly important.

But silence is often the best policy – geddit, Hitchens? And the lesson of my historical overview is that the only tenable religious belief is one where you have the humility to constantly change your mind in the face of overwhelming evidence to the contrary.

God is the desire beyond this desire, who exists because I say so, and the negation of whose existence confirms his transcendence. Or something like that.

And if you believe this, you'll believe anything.

Digested read, digested: The case dismissed.

Religion for Atheists
by Alain de Botton (2012)

The most boring question one can ask of any religion is whether or not it is true. Manifestly, none are. Yet this should not stop us cherry-picking the bits we like and repackaging them as self-help aphorisms for a liberal middle-class who consider themselves too clever for Paulo Coelho. I was brought up a committed atheist, but even I had a crisis of faithlessness that originated in listening to Bach's cantatas, was developed by exposure to Zen architecture and became overwhelming on reading my own prose.

Why then should secular society lose out on the benefits a religion can offer merely because it rejects certain of its catch-phrases? Is there not a middle way where Karen Armstrong and Richard Dawkins can join hands and teach the world to sing in perfect harmony? My strategy, then, is to take various religious principles completely out of context and apply them as feelgood, quasi-spiritual soundbites to areas such as education, literature and architecture. And if mention is made here of only three of the world's largest religions – Christianity, Judaism and Buddhism – it is no sign of anxiety that I might get a fatwa if I also rope in Islam.

One of the losses modern society feels most keenly is that of a sense of community. Religions may have evolved out of a need to enforce social cohesion, but one cannot deny the sense of belonging that going to church confers on the participants. In our atavistic, rationalist world we have lost these connections. While we may surrender up to half our income in taxation, we have no sense of how that money is being spent. How much better it would be if the less fortunate members of the polity were able to congregate in one place to say thank you to me in person while the Monteverdi Choir sings Mozart's Mass in C Minor.

A squalid new-build university in north London. Not at all like the university I went to, but one to which the little people can reasonably aspire. Yet what are they being taught? Land reform in 18th-century France? What is the purpose of that? Literature and history are superficial categories. How much greater benefit would there be to student and society alike if universities were to have a Richard and Judy Department for Relationships or a Deepak Chopra Centre for Personal Growth? Imagine also the power of hearing Montaigne's essays rewritten as versicles and responses with a 100-strong student chorus after every sentence.

Religion may offer empty promises of a happier afterlife, but we should not overlook its power in helping people to cope with the fact that they are never going to be as rich or as clever as me. Face it, some people are born losers and some aren't – and the losers need whatever consolation they can find. The orthodoxy of modern science is that we will eventually be able to explain every-thing in material terms, yet what science ought to be doing is helping us celebrate those things we will never master. Thus we would do well to prostrate ourselves in front of an image of Brian Cox and meditate on the 9.5 trillion kilometres that comprise a single light year.

One of the great miseries imposed on atheists is the renunci-ation of ecclesiastical art. Yet what person has not been enriched by the altarpiece by Matthias Grunewald for the Monastery of St Colin in Beckenham? The stations of the cross help the religious in their suffering, yet what is to stop us imposing our own spiritual needs on modern art? What was Christ's crucifixion but an existential dilemma? Viewed through this perspective, the secular can once more reclaim the Sistine Chapel as a symbol of a male midlife crisis. So let's do away with the grubby architecture of northern British towns and rebuild a new Jerusalem in north London, a temple to myself and Auguste Comte.

Digested read, digested: Yet more De Bottonanism.

Wonders of Life
by Brian Cox (2013)

Here's a photo of me standing on a rock looking wistful. Here's another photo of me sitting on a bench looking soulful. Here's yet another photo ... Cut them out. Put them on your wall. Make a calendar. B xxx

I confess that when we began thinking about *Wonders of Life*, my first thought was 'Why me?' as I gave up biology as an academic subject in 1984. But then I looked in the mirror and I thought: 'Yeah. That's amaaazin.' Evolution, DNA and butterflies. They're amaaazin, too. I mean, look at this blade of grass. It's basically made of the same shit as you and me. That's like, mind-blowin. More so for me than for you. I am he as you are he as you are me and we are all together.

Water. It's magnificent. Every time a new star is born, a chain of events is set in place, catapulting hydrogen and oxygen atoms on an interstellar journey of billions of miles that ends up in my bath. I find it so hard to get my head around that. Did you know there are two species perfectly adapted for walking on water? One are insects known as *gerridae*; the other is me.

Then there's sunshine. Virtually every living thing on the planet is ultimately powered by sunshine, which is why I started writing this sentence lying down in a field near the South Downs and finished it on a train in Mexico. See my tan? That's what happens when UV photons travel millions of miles to react with the melanin in my skin. Beautiful, isn't it? It's OK if you linger on this page. I don't mind.

Colours. They are amaaazin and all. Who'd want to do all those drugs when you can just go out into nature and see all these reds and blues and yellows and greens. Wow! And then there's my eyes. Have you ever seen such a hypnotic brown? Pigment of the gods.

Now take a look at this picture. Do you notice anything unusual about it? Yes, that's right. I'm not in it. It's just a boring shot of cyanobacteria under the microscope. So let's move on. Air. Weird how something so light can be so heavy to explain. Like when did it first support life? I mean, what is life anyway? Not even Schrödinger knew for sure. So here I am on the Taal volcano in the Phillipines to purr on about the first law of thermo-dynamics. Are you getting sweaty? I know I am. Try hard and you can measure your desire.

Now let's think about photosynthesis and entropy. On second thoughts, let's not. Let's just look at some more amaaazin pictures of animals and birds and fish and insects and all sorts. Some of them are really, really big and some of them are really, really small and the totally amaaazin thing is that it's not a coincidence. We're all one big family made out of the same molecular compounds. Though some of us are arranged rather more photogenically. And the most amaaazin thing of all is that we are all still evolving, so it's possible that there will one day be a scientist even lovelier than me.

There's so much left to say about carbon and quasars and mitochondria but what really does my head in is that there are over half a trillion galaxies in the observable universe; the idea that there are no other planets out there with webs of life at least as complex as our own seems to me an absurd proposition. Which means that somewhere in a parallel space-time continuum, there is another drop-dead gorgeous rock legend standing on a Pacific atoll as David Attenborough whispers from on high: 'Verily it is written that you are the chosen one.'

Digested read, digested: The Life of Brian.

THRILLERS

Liberation Day
by Andy McNab (2002)

The sub surfaced just off the Algerian coast. 'Ready?' I barked to Hubba-Hubba and Lofti. They slung their waterproof bags over their shoulders and nodded. We dived in and headed for the shore. A three-mile swim in icy waters was nothing compared to my training in the Regiment. It was then just a 20km sprint to Zeralda's compound.

Lofti lobbed a stun grenade, and Hubba-Hubba and I ran in. 'It's a fuck-up,' shouted Hubba-Hubba. Instead of just Zeralda, there was another man, Greaseball, and a gang of frightened boys. 'Leave these pervs,' I yelled. 'It's Zeralda we want.' I tapped him twice in the forehead and sliced his head off.

'I swear I've given up all my dirty op work,' I said to Carrie, back in Boston.

'I know, I love you.'

'That's funny,' countered George, Carrie's father. 'I could have sworn you had been working for me in Algeria.'

'You bastard, Nick,' Carrie shouted at me. 'I'm never talking to you again.'

'You bastard, George,' I said.

'No hard feelings, Nick, but we need you. Your Algerian job has put the wind up al-Qaida. You took out one of their main hawallada, their money man, and now they are panicking. They're sending two men to France to collect cash from their three other hawallada. Your job is to kill them and prevent world terrorism.'

'Jesus fuck, Greaseball is our contact,' I said. 'But we've got a job to do, so let's do it.'

Hubba-Hubba, Lofti and I recceed the marina. 'I've spotted the

Romeos.' Lofti replied with two clicks. 'Preparation is everything,' I told them. 'We must leave no traces.' I sliced off my fingertips, burnt them and drank the ashes with a glass of my urine.

I slid on to the boat, set the charge, and followed the Romeos to the first meet. I dosed the mark with ketamine, and dumped him into the back of the Megane. One down.

'Fuck, it's a trap.' Hubba-Hubba and Lofti bled to death as the lead flew.

'Don't worry,' said George. 'Greaseball has double-crossed al-Qaida and stolen their money. So let him go.'

I thought of Hubba-Hubba and Lofti and of that pervert making off with the dosh. It wasn't enough to have prevented dozens of major terrorist incidents around the globe. I wanted revenge. I dialled the code into my phone and Greaseball's boat turned into a fireball.

Digested read, digested: Nick Stone saves the world again and still nobody can be bothered to thank him.

Resurrection Men
by Ian Rankin (2002)

DI Rebus pulled deeply on his cigarette and eyed up his new colleagues. The Wild Bunch – McCullough, Gray and Ward. All of them known for pushing the law to the limit – too far at times – and who, like him, now found themselves on punishment block at Tulliallan police college for retraining.

'We'll start with team building,' said DCI Tennant. 'Look at the Lomax case. See if there's anything that got missed.'

Could this be a coincidence? Did they know that Rebus had

been more involved in this case than he had ever admitted? Maybe it was him being set up, rather than the Wild Bunch.

'I'm not happy about this,' said Rebus. 'I got myself thrown off the Marber case to help you out here, and I feel like I'm making no progress.'

'Just keep at it,' soothed the chief constable. 'We know they took the Bernie Johns money, we just can't prove it. Go and have a drink.'

Rebus poured himself a large whisky, put Led Zeppelin on the turntable and settled back into his chair. Somehow he felt that the Weasel, the Diamond Dog and Big Ger would soon be making an appearance. He picked up his phone.

'How's the Marber case?' he asked.

'Well. Laura the prostitute's been killed by Donny Dow, one of Big Ger's boys and...' DS Siobhan Clarke's voice tailed off. She'd been well trained by Rebus. She had a well-stocked record collection and she was learning not to tell anyone anything. With any luck, she would soon be a fully fledged maverick with a book of her own, rather than playing sidekick to Rebus.

'I hear the Diamond Dog turned up dead,' McCullough taunted Rebus. 'Bit convenient for you and Big Ger, eh?'

'There's a warehouse full of drugs being guarded by the police,' he said to the three of them over several drinks. Do you fancy a piece of the action?'

'Yeah, all right,' they replied.

'Well, you can't. It's far too dangerous,' Rebus responded nervously. Damn, his plan had gone completely wrong.

'I've got the feeling that McCullough, Gray and Ward are involved in the Marber case, but I need some help proving it,' Rebus whispered to Clarke.

'Jesus, sir, you look half dead,' she said a little while later.

'You should see the others,' he laughed.

'Well you've solved both the Marber and the Lomax cases. How do you do it?'

'Do you think I'd tell you?'

Digested read, digested: The bodies pile up as fast as the drinks, as Edinburgh's finest makes his annual appearance.

Avenger by Frederick Forsyth (2003)

Freddy put down his copy of the *Daily Telegraph* and sighed. The stock market hadn't been kind to the Master Storyteller. He pressed the secret panel of his large oak desk. It was time to bring his trusty Montblanc fountain pen out of retirement.

* * *

Anyone watching the 51-year-old wheeze along the New Jersey streets could have been forgiven for not realising they were in the presence of the fittest, cleverest, noblest and most dangerous man in the world.

Calvin Dexter had been brought up the hard way. He fought in Vietnam and he and his senior officer became the most feared Tunnel Rats in the US army. Their nicknames were Mole and Badger.

When the war ended Cal put himself through law school and became a brilliant public defender. After his wife and child tragically died he left the law to disappear into anonymity. Only those who really needed his services would know where to find him.

* * *

It had been many years since Ricky Colenso had disappeared in the former Yugoslavia. At last, his grandfather, the Canadian billionaire Steve Edmond, had a lead. A body had been discovered in a slurry pit and the man suspected of the atrocity was Serbian warlord Zoran Zilic.

'I don't care how much it costs, I want him brought to justice,' said Edmond.

It was June 2001.

* * *

Cal checked the small ads. He had a job. His superb tracking skills quickly picked up the trail. His aircraft had been spotted in the emirate of al-Fujairah, and from that it was relatively simple to deduce that Zilic was now living in a heavily protected fortress in Surinam.

It was July 2001.

* * *

CIA chief Paul Deveraux leant forward and spoke to his deputy, Kevin McBride. 'We can't let anything happen to Zilic,' he said. 'We know al-Qaida is about to launch a major attack on the west and Zilic has promised to lead us to Osama bin Laden.'

It was August 2001.

* * *

'So,' thought Cal, 'the Americans are on to me. Shouldn't make much difference.'

Armed only with a penknife, Cal skipped through the inhospitable terrain, waltzed past the private militia, swam through the piranha-infested stream, pirouetted through the dogs and the minefields and boarded Zilic's private jet.

'You are coming with me to face justice in the land of the brave and the home of the free,' he snarled.

It was September 9 2001.

* * *

'Project Peregrine is dead in the water,' said Deveraux. 'Ten more days and Bin Laden would have been ours. But just who did tip off Avenger?'

McBride smiled to himself, the outline of a badger tattoo just visible through his shirt.

It was September 10, 2001.

Digested read, digested: This year's winner of the Jeffrey Archer prize for creative writing.

The Da Vinci Code
by Dan Brown (2003)

Renowned curator Jacques Sauniere shuddered. The first page of a Dan Brown potboiler was no place for any character. 'Count yourself lucky,' growled Silas the monk, as he chastised himself with his chalice. 'I've got to hang around for another 400 pages of this grabage.'

The phone rand in Robert Langdon's hotel room. After his previous adventure with the Pope, nothing should have surprised him. But he was surprised. 'I am surprised to be summoned to the Louvre in the dead of night,' he said to himself.

Inspector Bezu Fache was a sangry as his name suggested. 'I don't like it when the renowned curator of the Louvre is found dead in the gallery at the dead of night in suspicious circumstances,' he muttered. 'So Monsieur Langdon. What do you make of Paris?'

'It is a very beautiful city, steeped in art and religion,' replied Langdon earnestly. 'And if I'm not very much mistaken, the pose monsieur Sauniere has adopted in death is highly symbolic.'

'Not so fast,' said a young woman, who identified herself as Sophie Neveu, an agent of the French cryptology department. 'You have a phone call'. She took him aside to the toilets. 'Inspector

Fache suspects you of the nurders,' she whispered. 'You must run away with me, for I am Jacques Sauniere's grand-daughter.'

'Not before I have solved the riddle your grandfather left.'

13-3-2-21-1-1-8-5

O Draconian devil!

Oh, Lame saint!

'Hmm, the numbers are the Fibonacci sequence,' squeaked Sophie. 'And the words are an anagram of Leonardo da Vinci and A Load of Hokum'.

They rushed to the world famous painting, known as the Mona Lisa. There they found another clue.

'It's another anagram,' yelled Langdon. 'Madonna of the Rocks'. They rushed to the world famous painting, known as the Madonna of the Rocks. There they found a key, only narrowly evading the combined forces of the Parisien gendarmeries.

'That was close,' squealed Sophie.

'Thank goodness we have a 20 page car ride to our next destination so I can indulge in some more bogus art history.'

Sophie struggled to stay awake as Langson droned on about Leonardo, the Feminine and the Priory of Sion.

'Wasn't all this bollocks in *The Holy Blood and the Holy Grail*?' she asked.

'Yes, but the Yanks will have forgotten all about it,' Langdon replied.

'They arrived outside the private Swiss Bbank, 'You will need a combination as well as a key.'

'It must be the Fibonacci sequence,' Sophie shouted, as they collected the keystone to the Grail while barrowly evading the combined forced of the Parisien gendarmerie.

'We must take a long car journey to the home of Sir Leigh Teabing, the eccentric crippled Grail expert who lives in France,' said Langdon, 'as this will allow me to fill you in on some more bogus art history. Did you know Jesus married Mary Magdalene and your grandfather was the Grand Master of the priory of Sion and you are a direct descendant of Jesus?'

'And you sentence construction is pitiful,' she laughed.

'Aha!' said Sir Leigh, heaving his crippled leg across the room. 'We have no time to lose if we are to unlock the riddle of the keystone. We must fly to England.'

The private jet arrived at Biggin Hill, narrowly evading the combined forces of the Parisien gendarmerie. Langdon used the atbash cipher and turned the keystone to S-O-F-I-A. It unlocked to reveal yet another riddle.

In London lies a knight a pope interred

They rushed to the Temple church. 'This is a dead end,' said Langdon as Silas and Sir Leigh's manservant appeared. 'Help! He's been taken hostage,' cried Sophie.

Langdon fretted over the riddle. He was in the wrong place. He rushed to Sir Isaac newton's tomb in Westminster Abbey. There was Sir Leigh.

'I was the baddy all along,' sneered Sir Leigh. 'The Priory of Sion weren't going to release the secrets of the Grail so I persuaded Opus dei to kill Sauniere. Now I've killed Silas and the manservant and I want the cryptex.'

Bezu fache burst in and arrested Sir Leigh. 'I aplogise,' he said to langdon. 'You weren't the killer after all.'

Langdon and Sophie took the train to Rosslyn in Scotland, near England. 'Will we find the grail here?' asked Sophie.

'No,' said an old woman who happened to be Sophie's granny.

Langdon shivered as he kissed the direct descendant of Jesus for the first time. Sophie smiled. Maybe she would see him again. Langdon headed to Paris to start digging in the vaults under the Louvre. There he knelt before the bones of Mary Magdalene. 'You took your time,' Mary smiled, before ascending into heaven.

Digested read, digested: Millions of readers can be wrong.

State of Fear
by Michael Crichton (2004)

A scientist dies in Paris after having sex with a mysterious stranger. A supplier of mining equipment is also killed in Canada. Nobody – least of all the reader – pays any attention. Except Kenner, the MIT-educated, special-forces-trained lone wolf.

'Hmm,' he smiled grimly to himself. 'The environmental activists are on the move.'

Back in California, Nick Drake, head of the National Environmental Resource Fund (Nerf), was sharing his thoughts with George Morton, his tycoon backer.

'It's really heavy,' said Drake. 'The water level of the Pacific has risen so much that these islands are going to be swept away. We need money to sue the multi-nationals for global warming.'

'You got it,' replied Morton. 'I love this planet.'

Peter Evans, Morton's attorney, and Sarah, Morton's impossibly beautiful PA, nodded in agreement. 'We love this planet.'

Two weeks later, Morton appeared drunk when he got up to speak at a Nerf gala. 'Global warming's a load of rubbish,' he shouted, before driving off in his Ferrari.

Peter and Sarah tried to follow him, but found only his wrecked car. There was no sign of his body. 'Guess he must have been thrown into the ocean,' they sobbed.

'Give me Morton's money,' yelled Drake.

'I can't,' replied Peter. 'His estate is in probate.'

Drake stormed out.

'What are we going to do now?' asked Sarah.

'Not so fast,' said Kenner, abseiling in through the window. 'You two are coming with me.'

On the way to Antarctica, Kenner delivered a long lecture on how global warming wasn't really happening, and that many scientists had allowed themselves to be lured into a state of fear by environmental pressure groups.

'Nerf is funding terrorists to create environmental catastrophes to reinforce their message,' warned Kenner. 'We have to stop them.'

A day later, Sarah and Peter crawled out of a crevasse. They were bruised and bloodied, but at least they had prevented a huge piece of the ice-shelf from being calved off into the ocean.

Two days after that, Sarah and Peter crawled out of a mudslide in Arizona. They were bruised and bloodied, but at least they had prevented another disaster.

'Just the Solomon Islands to go,' yelled Drake.

Sarah and Peter looked at each other. They were about to die trying to save the world from a tsunami and they hadn't declared their love for one another.

'I'm alive,' shouted Morton, as he rescued them. 'The world is saved, and I'm going to start a new environmental organisation based on truth.'

Author's note: I'm very, very clever and have read a lot and you're all stupid wishy-washy liberals.

Digested read, digested: In the beginning was the Word, and the Word was with Crichton, and the Word was Crichton.

Hannibal Rising
by Thomas Harris (2006)

Imagine opening the door on Dr Hannibal Lecter's memory palace. Let us journey portentously into its deepest recesses in a laboured bid to milk a prequel out of America's cleverest serial killer.

The eight-year-old Hannibal sat beside the castle moat with his younger sister, Mischa. A black swan begged for food. 'Yes,' he thought. 'This is indeed a credibly gothic start to my story.'

'Hurry children,' their father cried. 'We must escape the Nazis.'

It was the second day of Operation Barbarossa. Grutas, Kolnas, Milko and Grentz committed indescribable acts of cruelty that were described in great detail. For that's what Nazi collaborators always did.

The Lecter family survived in the woods for more than a year, with young Hannibal wiling away his days memorising Euclid, until they were captured by the Nazi collaborators. Only Hannibal was found alive by the Soviets, a chain still attached to his neck.

'The poor boy has been left mute,' wept Hannibal's uncle Robert, a noted painter.

'Indeed,' replied his wife, the impossibly beautiful and exotic Lady Murasaki. 'He has suffered unimaginable horrors that readers can all too easily guess. We must take him back to our French chateau.'

The fall, as the French don't call autumn, was late that year as Lady Murasaki nursed Hannibal back to speech. First, a farting flubber sound; then fully formed words.

See how Hannibal looks at Lady Murasaki. Hear how he cries out, 'Mischa' in his nightmares. Notice how the text switches to italics and the present tense. Recognise the hand of a master story-teller with no editor.

'Oi, Japonnaise,' yelled the coarse butcher, who was well known in the village as a Nazi sympathiser. 'Does your pussy go crossways?'

Robert dropped dead from a heart attack, as Hannibal entered Lady Murasaki's boudoir and removed her samurai sword. Later that day the dismembered body of the butcher was found next to the post-box.

'I want to run a polygraph test on you, young Hannibal,' said Inspector Popil. 'Be my guest,' replied the 13-year-old evenly.

Not a flicker. 'My, but you're a poisson froid,' Popil countered. 'I know you did it but I can't prove it.'

Hannibal and Lady Murasaki moved to Paris, where the young man became the most remarkable boy in the capital by memorising every textbook within minutes and becoming the youngest ever medical student. Lady Murasaki feels an intense longing for Hannibal. Yet she knows she cannot reach him. She can also sense that Popil has feelings for her.

'We have reached that random point in the plot where I need to introduce some looted art treasures,' said Popil. 'So I need your help tracking down your family's long-lost Leonardos and Titians.'

'Ah, good,' laughed Hannibal. 'I expect the looters are the same people who killed my family. That will give me an excuse to go to Lithuania and kill a few of them in graphic detail.'

'I know you executed those people and ate some of their flesh,' Popil snarled, 'but I can't prove it.'

'Oh Noh, Hannibal,' sobbed Lady Murasaki, undoing her gown and exposing her nakedness. 'You can take me if you renounce your course of violence.'

'I can't,' Hannibal said. 'For they ate Mischa.'

See how the reader struggles to feign surprise.

'You must hand these Nazis over to me,' Popil implored.

'But did you not yourself collaborate with the Nazis?'

'I did, but only a little bit once. We are all imperfect.'

Hannibal returned to the dissection table and opened the brain of a recently guillotined man. Over the next few days Milko and Kolnas were found hideously mutilated, their wounds lovingly documented over many pages.

Only the showdown remained.

'You ate Mischa, too,' Grutas laughed.

See how the reader struggles to feign surprise.

A bloodbath ensued.

Hannibal smiled. He had got away with his greatest crime to date. A bestselling thriller with no thrills at all.

Digested read, digested: À la recherche de corps perdus.

Beneath the Bleeding
by Val McDermid (2007)

Dr Tony Hill was working late at Bradfield Moor secure hospital. He heard a noise outside his office and went to investigate. The last thing he saw before he lost consciousness was an axe hacking into his knee, splintering bone and pumping jets of blood across the corridor.

'You're awake then,' DCI Carol Jordan observed as she visited Tony in the ICU.

'What are you doing here?'

'Oh, I dunno. Just creating a little sexual frisson between us before the main action kicks off.'

'My leg is agony,' he gasped.

'Tough,' DCI Jordan laughed, pressing on his open wound. 'If you couldn't stand a little pain and gore, you should have stayed in an Ian Rankin book.'

In another part of Bradfield, Yousef began to carefully prepare the explosives. 'Only a few days to go,' he muttered to himself.

Robbie Bishop lay dying of ricin poisoning, his bloated body as unrecognisable as that of Bradfield Victoria's star midfielder.

DCI Jordan called in her team.

'I'm a lesbian,' announced Chris. 'And I'm proud to be out.'

'Me, too,' chipped in Paula.

'Great,' said Carol. 'Now we've established that two-thirds of the women in my squad are gay, have you got anything for me?

'Bishop and his celebrity DJ girlfriend had a stalker,' they replied.

Tony shook his head. 'It's not him. He doesn't fit the profile.'

'I don't care,' said Carol. 'There's always one pointless wild goose chase in detective fiction so I'm going to waste 50 pages going after him anyway.'

Tony entered the mortuary. If he was going to get anywhere with the case he had to deal with some unresolved issues concerning his mother; and for that he needed to be alone with Bishop.

'So my mum is a bit of a nightmare,' he whispered in Bishop's putrid ear. Suddenly he felt his mind clearing. 'The person who did this to you has killed before.' He limped to his computer and began a search. 'Got you,' he smiled, as he came across a lottery winner who had been poisoned with belladonna.

'Bishop and the lottery winner went to the same school,' Tony said. 'Our man will be a classmate who is jealous of their success.'

'That's the most ridiculous piece of psychobabble I've ever heard,' said Carol.

Yousef checked his watch. It was time. He drove the van to Bradfield Victoria's ground. In a couple of hours, everyone in Britain would have heard of him. So be it. He would be thousands of miles away.

Tony settled down with Carol in front of the TV to watch

Bradfield play Spurs. Midway through the first half, a massive explosion tore through the stands. Limbs and torsos were scattered everywhere.

'OK,' said Carol to her team, 'We've got a major incident here.'

The door cracked open and two stubble-faced men barged in. 'We're from the counter-terrorism squad,' they snarled. 'This has all the hallmarks of al-Qaida. We're going to shake down every Mozzer in town.'

'You're wrong,' Tony muttered. 'This doesn't look like terrorism to me. What we've got here is a Jewish woman who tricked her Muslim lover into blowing himself and her husband up.'

'That's absurd,' said Carol. 'Why would anyone blow up 35 people just to get rid of a husband and lover?'

'Look,' Tony snarled, 'as we're in a thriller written by a woman, you've got to expect an abnormally high body count. And as you caught the poisoner who went to school with Bishop, I think you owe me an apology.'

'You're right,' Carol concurred. 'Again.'

'It's nothing,' Tony replied tenderly, taking her hand. 'It's all in a book's work.'

Digested read, digested: DCI Jordan is not quite yet over the Hill.

The Troubled Man
by Henning Mankell (2011)

The rain hammered against the window. Kurt Wallander sank lower into his armchair, his thoughts returning to the futility of his existence. What had he to show for his career? A failed marriage, a lonely old age and still Ystad was teeming with paedophiles and political corruption. His phone rang. He picked it up wearily.

'How are you, Dad?' It was his daughter Linda. 'Cold, depressed and I think I'm getting Alzheimer's.' 'Then at least you'll have forgotten what a bad parent you were. But that's not why I'm calling. Hans and I have just had a baby.' 'What's its name?' 'It doesn't have one yet. Hans's parents are having a party next week so you can see it then.' 'Do I have to go?'

The sleet stung Wallander's face as he walked up the Von Enkes' path. 'It's good to finally meet the other grandfather,' said Håkan and Louise. 'Is it?' Against his better judgment, Wallander had begun to enjoy himself when Håkan invited him into his study after dinner. 'I'm a worried man,' Håkan said. 'I was a submarine commander during the cold war and I believe there were spies in the Swedish navy who have never been unmasked.' 'Whom do you suspect?' Wallander asked. 'I cannot say right now because that would spoil the story.' Wallander remained silent. He had the feeling Håkan had been trying to tell him something. But what?

Hail reduced visibility to near zero. Wallander felt a tightness across his chest. He was having a heart attack. What a sad way to die, he thought, not even knowing his granddaughter's name. He undid his shirt button and the pressure eased. Maybe he just needed a new shirt. His phone rang. He picked it up wearily. 'We're calling our daughter Klara,' Linda said. 'And Håkan's disappeared.'

Louise said nothing as Wallander searched Håkan's study. After an hour he found what he was looking for. An address book. He called Håkan's two oldest friends: Sten in Stockholm and Steve in San Diego. 'Do you think Håkan was a Russian spy?' he asked them. 'Certainly not,' they replied. 'He was a true patriot.' 'I've discovered he and Louise had a profoundly disabled daughter that they've never told anyone about, who has been in an institution for the past 40 years.'

'How does this affect the story?'

'It doesn't, but it makes it gloomy and Swedish.'

Wallander felt there was so much he didn't understand as he went on one pointless journey after another. How come Steve had suddenly appeared on his doorstep and then had phoned him from America without seeming to remember he had been in Sweden? Was it him or Henning who was losing his memory? The phone rang. He picked it up wearily. 'It's Louise,' said Linda. 'She's been found dead. By the way, Mum is in alcohol rehab.'

The wind howled and flurries of snow caught in his throat. He phoned one of his old contacts in Copenhagen. Too late. He had died five years earlier. Suddenly Wallander knew where Håkan was. He rowed out to an island on the archipelago. 'I've been in hiding,' said Håkan. 'I'd always suspected Louise of being a Russian spy. But I didn't kill her.'

Wallander arrived home to find Baiba outside. She had been the love of his life and he hadn't seen her for over 10 years since she had rejected him. 'Why are you here?' he asked. 'Because I'm dying of cancer and I wanted to say goodbye.' Wallander said nothing, as she drove away into the fog. There was a loud crash. She had hit a wall and killed herself.

Now Wallander knew he had to go to Berlin to meet Talboth. The drive was pleasingly bleak and he had disappointing, anonymous sex with a stranger in a hotel. His penis stung when he urinated. Great, he thought, I've got chlamydia.

'There were a lot of spies in the 70s and 80s,' Talboth said, enigmatically. Suddenly everything made sense. He called Sten and together they rowed through a blizzard to see Håkan.

'It's true,' said Håkan. 'I am a CIA spy. But I never killed Olof

Palme. You'll never take me alive.' 'How could you?' said Sten, shooting his best friend through the head before turning the gun on himself.

Wallander went home. Others could find the bodies and sort out the loose ends. Who cared how Louise had died, who had killed her or what secrets Håkan had given away or how? Luckily his memory now had as many holes in it as the plot. At least the rain was still falling horizontally.

Digested read, digested: Not with a bang but a whimper.

Carte Blanche
by Jeffery Deaver (2011)

The train piled high with radioactive cargo raced through the Serbian night. Bond checked his iPhone. No updates. All he knew was that an Irishman called Niall Dunne was planning to send the plutonium to the bottom of the Danube. A sixth sense told Dunne he was being watched and he slid out of sight. A seventh sense told Bond the Irishman had moved out of position. Bond reacted in an instant. A large explosion tore the track in two and Bond looked on as the train came to a halt short of the river. The world was saved. But the Irishman had escaped.

'Good work, Bond,' said the Admiral on his return to London. 'But you've still only got four days to save the world from another disaster the Irishman is planning. The only lead we've got is his business partner: Severan Hydt, the garbage and recycling magnate.'

On his way out of M's office, Bond noticed an attractive young agent chatting to Moneypenny. Ding-dong! Stockings or tights? 'The name is Bond, James Bond,' he said. 'Ophelia Maidenstone,' she replied. 'I've split up with my fiancée. Would you like to take me out to dinner?' Bond smiled to himself. He might have been 30 for the past 50 years but he hadn't lost his edge. Yet an eighth sense told him that however much she might enjoy spending the night with him, he ought to save her from himself. 'I've got to go home to my Chelsea flat to put out the recycling.' he said. 'But have a bottle of Chablis on me.'

Severan Hydt had been enjoying looking at photographs of decomposing bodies when he was interrupted by the Irishman. 'A ninth sense tells me we are being watched,' Dunne said. 'If Project Gehenna is to work and we are to destroy the world on Friday we must leave via the back door.' Bond smiled to himself as he followed at a safe distance in his Bentley. A 10th sense had told him that the Irishman was expecting to be watched and he had organised a decoy surveillance. He tailed them to an underground dump; an 11th sense told him someone was going to die there and he would have to go to Dubai.

The heat was stifling in the Emirate as Bond met up with his old CIA contact, Felix Leiter. 'You're being followed, Bond,' Leiter said. 'I know,' Bond had replied evenly, checking the time on his Rolex. 'It's better to keep your enemies where you can see them.' Hydt and Dunne were relieved a 12th sense had told them they were being followed and had doubled back on themselves. Bond was ahead of them. A 13th sense had told him Hydt and the Irishman would double back on themselves. Now he knew he had to go to South Africa.

'Welcome to South Africa, Mr Bond,' said Bheka Jordaan, the head of Cape Town counterintelligence. 'With a name like that you are obviously not going to try to have sex with me, much as you are obviously gagging for it.' 'Correct, Mr Bond,' Bheka replied longingly. 'Now, how can I help?' 'You can create me an identity as Mr Theron.'

'We can do business, Mr Theron,' said Hydt. 'But first we must go to a charity auction.' Hydt left early to look at some decaying flesh, leaving Bond with the head of the food programme. 'I'm Felicity Shagwell,' she said. 'Something tells me we are going to end up in bed,' Bond smirked.

A 14th sense told Bond he was being followed. 'Who are you?' he asked, trapping him in a corner. 'I'm not sure. I think I've got into the story by mistake.' Bond tied him up and mused on whether his parents had been Russian spies. It was good to have some pathos in the backstory. He checked his Rolex. Time to break into Hydt's plant and foil Gehennna. He called M on his iPhone: 'They are planning to blow up York University.' A shot rang out. Hydt fell dead.

'Congratulations, Bond,' said Bheka, 'case over.' 'Not quite,' said Felicity Shagwell triumphantly, as she put a gun to Bond's head. 'Dunne is working for me and Hydt was a decoy. The world is about to be destroyed.' 'That's what you think,' Bond laughed, evading her aim. 'A 15th sense told me you were a baddy and I had to pretend to let you capture me to find out.' 'It could have been so different, James,' Felicity cried, as Bheka handcuffed her.

'Indeed it could,' said Bheka. 'If you had stayed a bit longer you could have slept with me too.' 'Another time, maybe,' Bond replied. 'M needs me in London. Someone else is trying to destroy the world.'

Digested read, digested: Carte him off.

Phantom by Jo Nesbø (2012)

Captain Tord Schultz sighed as he landed the plane. As the opening character in a thriller, he knew his only purpose was to die a slow, agonising death. Within 70 pages a brick studded with nails had ripped off half his face.

I'm a thief and a junkie. God help me, I've also prostituted my foster-sister, Irene. It was all going so well. Oleg and I were selling for Ibsen and Dubai, and then we got greedy and started doing the violin ourselves. Now they are coming for me.

Harry Hole ran his titanium finger along the scar that ran from his mouth to his ear. It had been three years since he'd been in Oslo, three years since he'd been kicked out of the police, three years since he'd been on the booze. Three years since he'd watched Spurs on TV. Every inch of his body ached with the excruciating pain of the maverick. He'd cornered The Leopard. Survived The Snowman. But this was worse. Much worse. This was personal. It was a Gooner. Flooding Oslo with a new opiate, violin, that was six times more powerful than heroin and being sold by dealers wearing Arsenal Fly Emirates shirts.

Then there was Rakel. The love of his life. The woman who would be better off without him. But he couldn't not come back for this. Oleg, her son, the boy he'd almost come to think of as his son, was in prison charged with murdering his dope-dealing associate, Gusto. 'He didn't do it,' Rakel had said. 'You're the only one who can help him.'

As the new head of Kripos, Mikael Bellman didn't mind if the readers were unsure he was a bent cop. It added to the tension and as the most handsome man in Norway, he was used to people mistrusting him. Besides, he had a date with Isabelle Skøyen, the femme fatale of the council, who had helped clean up the city's drug problem. Truls Bernsten was really ugly, so there were no doubts he was a burner, the cop who tidied away Dubai's inconvenient evidence. Still, accidentally putting a drill through a dealer's skull had been a little much, even for him.

I should have kept my mouth shut. But writing in a different font and from the past is a great way of filling in the back story. I was doing OK just selling smack for Dubai. Then Ibsen came along with the violin. He grassed all the other dealers to his contact in the council. Oslo was ours.

Sergei had never been convinced he had what it took to be Dubai's hitman. And as Harry withdrew the corkscrew from his oesophagus and he took his last three breaths he was certain of it. Harry gasped. He recognised it was some achievement to be the undisputed top dog of Scanda-crime noir, but it was taking it out of him. Sure, he had stopped a prisoner killing Oleg, had got the boy released, had closed down Oslo's power supply, had dug up Gusto's grave, killed a small army of Dubai's goons, unmasked the true identities of Ibsen and Dubai, rescued Irene, almost drowned in a Nazi escape tunnel, fallen off a horse into a ravine and turned down a shag with Isabelle even after she had flashed her shaven pussy (nice detail), but it had taken half a bottle of Jim Beam to do it all.

'I love you, Harry,' said Rakel. 'And I will marry you even though you are clearly deranged.'

Harry switched off his stolen phone. He had waited years to hear those words. But he had to do what was right. And what was right would mean she would have to marry her dull solicitor. He drove to the final showdown. 'It was you all along,' he said. Two bullets ripped into him and Harry could feel the rats gnawing at the open wounds. 'Is this it?' he wondered. He checked Nesbø's contract and smiled. Almost certainly not.

Digested read, digested: Harry's Black Hole.

A Delicate Truth
by John le Carré (2013)

In a characterless hotel in Gibraltar, a pleasant if not remarkable man in his late 50s is in his room. What was his assumed name, he asked himself. Anderson. Paul Anderson. That was it! He is as jumpy as the tenses. However had he got himself into the situation.

'We've got a situation,' said Fergus Quinn. Junior foreign minister. Dynamic and bulky. Cell phone pressed to an ear. Close-cropped ginger hair, greedy eyes and a pout of privileged discontent. Paul knows from the outset that any man who gets three damning sentences of description is a baddy, but as a civil servant he has a duty. 'I want you to supervise a mission. You'll be working with private contractors, Ethical Outcomes.'

Paul senses the irony is being rather trowelled on, but it's now too late. Elliott, a South African – you can never trust a South African – calls him to say the operation is on. 'We'll be picking up Punter when he meets Aladdin. You wait at the top of the Rock with the Brit special forces. The Americans will go in when you give the all-clear.'

Jeb, the leader of the British squad, is as unhappy as Paul. 'We're basically just mercenaries,' he says. Paul said there was no sighting of Punter but Elliott sent the Americans in anyway. 'All clear,' says Elliott. 'Another jihadi in the bag.'

In Whitehall, Toby Bell, newly appointed private secretary to Fergus Quinn, is feeling jumpy. He too has read the three-sentence description of his new boss and can tell he is a baddy. He called his old mentor, Giles Oakley, for assistance and was alarmed to find he also was given a contemptuous three-sentence description.

Toby is disappointed. He has been told by George Smiley that one of the most enjoyable qualities of starring in a le Carré novel is that nothing is ever black and white, but now it seems his anger at New Labour and the privatisation of the intelligence services has got the better of him. 'Ah well!' he thinks. At least he knows where he stands. It does still seem curious to Toby that Quinn should have got away with similar practices while at

Defence – not even Peter Mandelson could have hoped for a reprieve after getting caught out like that – and it also feels unbelievable that Quinn should now be having private meetings without the knowledge of his staff. He breaks the habit of a lifetime and secretly records the meetings between Quinn, 'Paul' and another man with three dripping-with-hatred sentences from Ethical Outcomes.

'Oooh ahh, oooh ahh.' Three years have passed and to show we are in Cornwall, the locals are talking in dialect. Sir Christopher Probyn is enjoying his retirement from the civil service, though he did sometimes wonder if his last unmerited posting to the Caribbean, and the knighthood that came with it, might have had something to do with Gibraltar and his secondment as 'Paul'. A decrepit man appears at the Bumpkins Annual Fayre. Christopher looked at Jeb in amazement.

'The Gibraltar operation,' Jeb spits. 'It was a cover-up. The intelligence was wrong. There was no jihadi. The Americans killed a Muslim woman and her child.'

'Good God!' Christopher replies, his conscience and his knighthood gnawing away at him. 'We must do something. But what?'

Toby always knew he'd be dragged in again. His suspicions had been proved right when Quinn had been moved sideways again and Giles had underlined his corruption by taking a job in a merchant bank. It was just that he rather missed the old cold war days where nothing was ever quite as it seemed, where every sentence had a double, if not treble, negative, and espionage was coated in layers of repressed homoeroticism. Now he was just in a straightforward thriller. Anyone could now see that Jeb's life was in danger and that Christopher was too dim to sort things out. It was down to him. He retrieves the memory stick from its hiding place. If he plays his hand right, there is still time to see this one out to a suitably downbeat and inconclusive ending.

Digested read, digested: Tinker, tailor, soldier, sledgehammer.

The Cuckoo's Calling
by Robert Galbraith (2013)

The buzz in the street was like the humming of flies. Snow fell steadily as a large group of paparazzi stamped their feet on the pavement that was as icy as frozen water, hoping to snap the body of the young supermodel Lula Landry, who had just jumped to her death from the balcony of her Mayfair apartment.

Cormoran Strike's eyes were as chilly as the world outside. His prosthetic leg ached in the chilly chill; he had just split up with his wealthy girlfriend and he was down to his last three shillings. He sucked deeply on a cigarette, pondering a future that looked as empty as a room with no furniture. Just then, the office doorbell rang.

'Hello,' said a young woman who, to Cormoran's trained eye, looked as if she might be engaged to an accountant named Matthew. 'I'm your new PA.'

'I can't really afford to pay you, but what the hell?' he said as rashly as someone with a bad case of shingles. He extended his hand like one of those ladders that came apart to make a longer one. 'Cormoran Strike.'

'That's an unusual name,' she said.

'Every fictional PI has a silly name. Mine just happens to be an anagram of JK Rowling. Not many people know that.' Cormoran smiled like a person who had just heard something funny. 'What's yours, by the way?'

'Robin. It's an anagram of borin'.'

'My father is the ageing pop star Jonny Rokeby, and my mother was a supergroupie who died of a heroin overdose. But I don't want to talk about that, as the memories are still as painful as the leg of mine that was blown off in Afghanistan.'

'I will never mention that again,' said Robin as sincerely as one of the most sincere people you can imagine. 'What would you like me to do now?'

'Nothing much. I haven't had any work for at least six months.'

Just then, a stranger blustered his way into the office like a spring squall on a blustery day. 'I'm John Bristow,' he said eventually. 'My adopted sister was Lula Landry. The police are calling her death suicide, but I think it was murder. I want you to investigate.'

'Why me?' Cormoran asked as existentially as Jean-Paul Sartre.

'Because, though you may not remember, 30 years ago you were friends with my adopted brother who died by riding his bike over a cliff when he was 10.'

'That all makes perfect sense,' Cormoran said, as grimly as one of the Brothers Grimm.

'This is so exciting,' cried Robin. 'Where do we start?'

'There are two types of detective fiction,' Cormoran explained. 'In one, the writer keeps the action flowing and the pages turning. In the other, the detective just wanders around aimlessly talking to every character in the book before announcing who the killer is.'

'Great, shall I get my gun?'

'We're the second type actually, Robin. Now could you arrange for me to talk to Lula's junkie boyfriend, a black rapper, a film producer, members of her family, a dress designer called Guy whose name is pronounced Ghee, a homeless depressive named Rochelle, and a mysterious African who may be the victim's real father?'

The days passed slowly but slowly, as Cormoran's extensive

knowledge of the London transport system allowed him to navigate his way across the city in search of his quarry.

'I can't 'elp you wiv nuffink,' said Rochelle, the homeless depressive. 'I think you'll find you just have,' Cormoran said, as knowingly as the Dalai Lama.

Then, on page 320, something finally happened. 'Something has finally happened!' Robin exclaimed.

'There's a maniac on the loose!' said Cormoran.

'It doesn't feel like it.'

'London is in the same amount of danger that would result from the traffic lights at the Old Street roundabout failing for five minutes!'

'Hooray!' yelled Robin. 'You've solved the murder. Isn't it odd that the killer is always the one you suspect the least? There's just one thing I don't get. Isn't it a coincidence that JK Rowling's cover was blown before the book went into paperback, meaning the publisher could maximise hardback sales when people were going on holiday?'

'Some things must remain a mystery,' said Cormoran mysteriously.

Digested read, digested: The golden goose's calling.

COOKING AND GARDENING

A Cook's Tour
by Anthony Bourdain (2001)

Yo, motherfuckers. I'm sitting in the bush with Charlie, deep in the Mekong Delta, drinking hooch. My hosts, VC war heroes, pass me the duck. I chomp through its bill, before cracking open the skull and scooping the brains out...

When you've just had a big score with an obnoxious and over-testosteroned account of your life, your publishers tend to fall for any dumbass plan. So when I told them I wanted to go round the world eating all sorts of scary food in a search for the perfect meal, they just said, 'Where do we sign?'

Y'know, most of us in the west have lost contact with the food we eat. It comes merchandised and homogenised. The same goes for chefs. Cooking isn't about knocking up a few wussy monkfish terrines out of fillets that have been delivered to the kitchen door; it's about badass guys going deep into their souls and looking their ingredients in the eye.

Which is why I am in Portugal, outside the barn while Jose and Francisco restrain several hundredweight of screaming pig. I unsheathe my knife, bury it deep into the neck and draw it firmly towards me. The pig looks at me in surprise and fury. I lick the blood from my arms, make another incision and rip out the guts. The women pan-fry the spleen. It's indescribably good.

I take my brother to France to look for the oysters and foie gras of my youth. I only find memories of my dead father. That's not what being a chef is all about. Cut to Mexico. The restaurant owner's 10-year-old pet iguana hoves into view. Big mistake. Its meat is tough and the claws are inedible; this is more like it.

I'm a sucker for sushi, but my main reason for being in Japan was to eat fugu, the puffer fish whose deadly nerve toxins in the liver kill scores of devotees a year. I watched Mr Yoshida prepare the fish. He was too clean, too careful. Not even the hint of a psychotropic high. Fuck that.

So off to Nam for fried birds' heads and monkey steaks. But even this wasn't really hard. I needed to be in Cambodia, driving along the heavily-mined highway to Pailin, Kalashnikov on my knee and with skulls the only road signs. The restaurant owner brought in a live cobra and slit its throat in front of me. He wrenched out the heart and placed it, still beating, on my plate. 'Make you strong,' he said. I do feel strong. I have my machete. I'm in the bamboo plantation. And there's the giant panda.

Digested read, digested: Colonel Kurtz Bourdain goes deep into the heart of darkness and returns the sole survivor of the culinary bloodbath.

Gordon Ramsay Makes it Easy
by Gordon Ramsay (2005)

My name is Gordon Ramsay and I'm here to help. Simplicity has always been at the heart of my cooking and I'm going to show you how you too can become a star in the kitchen by learning how to boil an egg properly... Oi, sonny, who the fuck are you? Get out of here. Who? You're my son? Fuck. I didn't recognise you.

Look Gordon, we've got your kids in for the shoot to give you a cosier image, so do try to make it look like you spend time with your family.

There's nothing quite like a proper breakfast to start the day. I'm never at home myself, but I encourage the family to vary their breakfasts and make the most of seasonal fruit. So here's some easy-to-make recipes involving scallops, new potatoes and fresh cherry compote.

Fantastic Gordon. OK, let's move on to the next chapter. Gordon, do you have to wear that pin-striped jacket? It really doesn't...

Do you want to make something of it, you fuckwit?

No, No. You look absolutely splendid as you are.

Eating together as a family is important to me... Fuck this. We're doing this fucking bollocks about how I love to eat Sunday roast with the family and they've all bleeding well fucked off.

It's OK, Gordon. I've given them a break, but we can get some lovely photos of you looking moody with some fish at the market.

Jesus. Right. Here's some fucking fillet of red mullet and here's some fucking roasted pork belly. Satisfied?

Er, perhaps you could try it with just a little more charm...

When I'm relaxing at home in the summer, I invariably fire up the barbecue. Who writes this shit? Do you really think I've got the fucking time to sit around at home and fire up a fucking barbie when I've got restaurants to run, Michelin stars to protect and telly projects on the go?

I know, Gordon, but we're selling a lifestyle here. The punters need to think you're basically just like them.

Are you fucking mad? Do you really think I've worked my fucking guts out so I can have a fucking Corsa?

Please, Gordon.

OK. Let's just get this thing done. Right. Here's some seared tiger prawns and here's a lemon tart. Let's move on to party food. When Tana and I throw a party we never quite know how many we are catering for – not something you lot have to deal with, I know, but fucking get over it – so finger food and champagne cocktails are an easy option. What else? You want something posh? I'll fucking give you posh. The secret of a good halibut bourguignon is mastering the cuisson. Romance as well? We should all make time in our lives for romance. But I don't. Will that do?

Wonderful Gordon. Lights to fade and closing credits.

Alright lads let's hear it. Delia's going down, she's going down, Delia's going...

Digested read, digested: Gordo sells his sole.

Jamie's Italy
by Jamie Oliver (2005)

Italy is that long thin country dangling in the Mediterranean and ever since I was a kid I've been obsessed with it. So when I was feeling completely burnt out this year after giving school dinners a makeover, I thought what better way to relax than to go there on my own with a camper van and a film crew to make a TV series and write a book.

I feel at home the moment I arrive in Italy because I love the sense of humour. It's great to arrive in a town and hear the old men stand around and joke, 'Who is this Oliver James?' But most of all I love the food. It's so localised, it's villagional. So without any more ado, let's get cooking.

Antipasti are the first course and vary considerably. It's good to get a mix of flavours. You can try bruschetta and my own favourite, fritto di salvia e alici. All you need is a tin of anchovies and you're away. How simple is that?

I'm really excited about this chapter on street food because most cookbooks steer clear of them. Perhaps it's because the writers don't know the Italian for Westler's. I have to be honest. Some street food is well dodgy and you'll notice that I haven't washed my hands for the pictures in order to give you the true Neapolitan flavour. You can try something poncey like polenta fritta croccante con rosmarino e sale, but for my money nothing beats a pizza di Dominos.

What on earth can I say about pasta that hasn't already been said? Not much, really, but I'll say it anyway. Always use real egg dough rather than Heinz spaghetti hoops and you won't go far wrong. And I just know you're going to love this chapter on risottos because I haven't bothered with any authentic Italian recipes and have invented my own. Chopped parsley in a white risotto with roasted mushrooms: yum. Sod the Italians if they don't like it.

Italian salads can be a bit ropey, to be honest, so I'll mention the insalata tipica delle sagre before moving on to fish. If I've learnt anything from the Italians about fish – which I'm not sure I have – it's that less is more. You don't need variety; just something simple and fresh. Like turbot. Or – at a push – octopus.

Italy is a land of hunters and they never forget that meat comes from animals. Even rabbit. That's why I'm showing you a picture of a dead sheep. You can cook it how you want, but it's nice on a kebab. Italian farmers have a very special relationship with pigs. They bring them up as if they were their own children and then kill them. There's a lesson there for all of us, so think twice before buying some factory-reared meat from wankers back home.

I don't normally bother with dolci unless it's for a special occasion, but everyone who's been to Pizza Express loves a good tiramisu. All you need is some sponge fingers, mascarpone, vin santo and some chocolate and Roberto is your zio.

And that's it. Thanks to Jools and my beautiful girls and the million other lovely people I spent time on my own with. Big love.

Digested read, digested: The digested feed.

Breakfast at The Wolseley
by AA Gill (2008)

Breakfast is a meal apart. It isn't like the other organised consumptions of food in which I partake. It is a meal for which I am sometimes obliged to pay with my own money. Today, the blonde is lying abed and there is no one on hand to serve me at home, so I head to The Wolseley – conveniently close to my Savile Row tailor – to break my fast.

Piccadilly is chilly and dark as my chauffeur pulls up outside. I step over the human detritus of the night before, and allow the doorman to take my cashmere coat as I am welcomed into the timeless grandeur of the seemingly fin-de-siècle dining hall. The jolly Nigerian cleaner bows courteously.

At the front desk the maître d'hotel is going through his reservation list. The names come with a code, abbreviations to note 'regular', 'very regular' or 'smug twat'. He shows me to my regular table, shielding me from the glare of the arrivistes who are seated nearest to the entrance.

Hidden away in the kitchen, the tourier, a Malian, or possibly Bangladeshi immigrant, has been turning the dough for the croissants for 12 hours or more. It's a thankless task, but Viennoiserie is all about attitude. I take a bite out of my croissant and let its texture dissolve on my tongue, before leaving the rest unfinished on my plate; it will be a welcome morsel for the Brazilian plongeur

There are few things quite as xenophobic as breakfast. Apart from me. So the Wolseley must cater for all tastes. Even Americans. I peruse the menu and order Eggs Benedict, the Marilyn Monroe of brunch. Hollandaise sauce is considered tricky to make, but it's actually a simple mixture of physics and thermodynamics that even an Italian chef can make.

The perfectly fried egg
- Crack one Duchy free-range egg into frying pan with knob of butter.
- Have a tantrum and send it back if not completely satisfied.

Nothing, though, can compare to the glory of the Full English. Foreigners may look askance as the waiters bring a cacophony of piggy-ness to my table, as few of them have the stamina or resolve for bacon, sausage and black pudding at this early hour. And it is true that, once the Full English has been consumed, you can be often overtaken by the need to go back to bed again. This is not a problem that unduly concerns me as I seldom have anything to do before lunch anyway.

There are 13 varieties of coffee at the Wolseley. This abundance of choice may be more than sufficient to satisfy the palates of City artisans and denizens of the media demi-monde, yet I still insist on summoning the Jamaican barista to check that the Blue Mountain beans have been harvested from the eastern flank of his private estate.

The perfect cup of coffee

- Ask for unlisted Arabica blend, but remember that the Indonesian, Kopi Luwak bean is considered distinctly nouveau riche.
- Shout loudly at South African waiter to check water was heated to between 97–98°C before being poured on to ground coffee.

Cereals were invented in America to promote colonic health and, as I reluctantly swallow a mouthful of muesli, I feel the onset of a bowel movement. I walk to the loo, casually noticing the checkmate in 17 moves for the person playing black as I pass the idiosyncratically placed chessboard. The lavatory attendant unfastens my trousers and polishes the bowl as I enter the stall. A self-satisfying movement follows and I look down at my perfectly formed excrement. And wonder just who on earth will buy it?

Digested read, digested: Completely pointless. Just like the author.

Nigella's Christmas
by Nigella Lawson (2008)

I'll be honest. I never thought I'd write a Christmas book. But then my publisher called to gossip about the credit crunch. 'What's that got to do with me?' I yawned, stretching out on my chaise longue.

'Nothing, sweetie,' she said. 'It's us here at Chatto I'm worried about. We're desperate for a Christmas bestseller to help us make budget and we wondered if you could help us out.'

What is Christmas, I thought, if not an opportunity to help out one's friends? And it would take care of that extension to the extension Charles and I had been promising ourselves. So maybe the Domestic Goddess would do a quick turn as the Domestic Druidess after all!

'OK, darling, you've twisted my arm,' I cooed. 'But there are a few ground rules. My Christmas isn't some kind of austerity family hold-back affair. I want to be able to forget the sad, grey little faces of all my neighbours who have lost their jobs at Lehman Brothers and luxuriate in guilt-free greed and over-indulgence.'

'That's perfect, Gelly Baby,' she laughed. 'Just the kind of pointless consumerism Christmas publishing is all about. Getting people to buy expensive crap that never gets read.'

So where to start? How about with a feeble pun about how we always call Prosecco 'Prozacco' at casa mia? Bubbles on their own can be crashingly dull, so how about livening them up with a bottle of Grand Marnier and some pomegranate? And now we've got into the party mood and the camera filter has been set to the softest of focuses, let's get cooking!

I'm far too clumsy to be the canapé queen. But if you nip down to your nearest over-priced deli – I recommend the gorgeous Marco in Holland Park – you're sure to find something you can pass off as your own. To make it look festive, try decorating it with a Christmas theme. Any small objets de tat will do; Charles tells me that Chinese is in this year and you're welcome to call him if you've got a spare mill for a plastic giant panda.

You might be wondering what the 'welcome table' is. It's a term I made up for the table in the hall that's laden with whole pigs and cold swans for all those guests who arrive feeling a little peckish and aren't sure if they can make it to the dining-room without dying of starvation. Anything can go here, provided it's got enough kick to give you a heart attack.

I haven't given a proper dinner party for years, but at Christmas the Baudelairian yearning for home is at its strongest and we like to have 60 of our closest friends round for sups in the nursery. Catering is a challenge but I always find it best to recycle some of my recipes from previous books and hope no one notices.

For the main event you need to get your staff cooking several days in advance to prepare the stuffings and marinades for the turkey. All cooking instructions are based on the assumption you have a double oven. If you don't, be prepared to have a shitty meal at 10pm! Be generous with quantities; allow at least 27 chipolatas per child.

At 5pm, everyone will be desperate for tea and you don't want to be caught looking like some kind of Scrooge. This is when you should push the boat out. Here's my recipe for my all-time favourite, The Angel of the North cake:

1. Commission Antony Gormley to make you a special cake tin.
2. Take three tonnes of flour, two tonnes of sugar and 11,765 eggs and cook at gas mark 5 for 35 minutes.
3. Get your husband to buy it for his gallery.

And that's about it. Oh, they want me to write a little more. How about something on how I once made 96 Christmas cupcakes for the school PTA just to show off. No? Then how about making your own food to give as presents? Just buy some Sharwood's mango chutney, put it in a different jar, sprinkle with gold dust and holly and you're done. But don't try that on me, babes! You know where Tiffany is!

Digested read, digested: Nigella's Christmas turkey.

Noma: Time and Place in Nordic Cuisine
by René Redzepi (2010)

A plateful of milk skin with grass, flowers and herbs. Something most of you would go a long way to avoid. Especially at £27.50. But this was not any milk skin, it was René Redzepi milk skin. Redzepi is the genius who has wrested Nordic cuisine away from the Mediterranean influences of El Bulli and Pizza Express to reclaim the soul of Kierkegaard. He understands that a potato cannot be separated from the soil in which it is grown; that is why at Noma the chips are covered in dirt and served in a jus de earthworm.

The reviews were polite but not much more when Noma first opened for business in Copenhagen in 2003 and Redzepi realised he had to rethink his gastronomic concept. The only way to return to the purest essence of boiled cabbage was by going on a Nordic tour to source some of the most inedible foods imaginable. Within a matter of years Noma had been voted the best restaurant in the world. Here are some excerpts from René's diary of that momentous journey.

Mandag Kristan greets us at Torshaven airport in the Faroe Islands with some sea-buckthorn berries. Wow! They are utterly disgusting. We must use them. They will go well with raw puffin and turnips.

Lordag Edda takes us to Iceland's lava landscape to steam vegetables in the hot springs. The sulphurous smell is overpowering, but I think I will be able to replicate it in the Noma kitchens.

Tirsdag Vigdis serves fresh whale. The meat has a strong taste of iron, but I can reduce that by taking out the harpoon.

Onsdag Sverrir takes us out among the Greenland ice floes. The scallops caught at 35 metres are not good. I suggest we try somewhere deeper. We send a diver down to the seabed at 1,200 metres. He dies of the bends on the way up, but it is worth it. The flavour is exquisite. I place an order for several tonnes a year; Sverrir places an order for several hundred divers.

Bouillon of Steamed Birchwood, Chanterelles and Fresh Hazelnut Chop down one 12 metre birch tree and soak in an ice bath to lock in the flavours. Then boil for seven days until it is soggy. Macerate the remaining branches and boil for a further 10 days. Force the pulp through a fine sieve, then reduce the liquid until just 50ml remain. Add some chanterelles and garnish with a hazelnut.

Reindeer with Celeriac and Wild Herb Gel Shoot reindeer in back yard. Slice 200g of meat from the shoulder and the loin and preserve the hide. Vacuum-pack the shoulder and cook for three hours at 84°C. Poke it and cook for a further three hours at 87°C. Blend the loin with celeriac very quickly (no longer than 3.7 seconds) then put in thermomixer and add to the shoulder and poach for 14 minutes at 68°C. Boil up the reindeer hooves and wild herbs into a glue and stick the hide back on.

Sea Urchins and Frozen Milk, Cucumber and Dill Remove sea urchins from hyperbaric chamber and get junior member of staff to cut off spines so you don't spike yourself. Poach the spines for seven hours in a water bath at 37°C then throw away. Rinse the orange urchin tongues before adding seven grains of Norwegian sand. Incinerate the cucumber until carbonised then crush into a powder. Separate the cream from the milk for 11 minutes before mixing them back together and freezing with liquid nitrogen. Mix everything together and blow-torch.

Snails and Moss Feed 32 snails on beetroot until they turn red. Boil them alive, making sure none escape. Scrape some moss from the side of a fjord and blanch until colourless. Then reform snails and moss into the Danish flag.

Blueberries surrounded by their Natural Environment Remove several large blueberry bushes from the garden, taking care to preserve as much of the root ball as possible. Reattach any blueberries that fell off while you were moving the plant with maltodextrin and xanthum gum. Bring Arctic foxes into kitchen and palpate their bladders until they have urinated on the blueberries. Repot the bushes in Greenland tundra and serve with vanilla Häagen-Dazs ice-cream.

Digested read, digested: Nochance.

Notes From My Kitchen Table
by Gwyneth Paltrow (2011)

This book is dedicated to the Wigmore-Reynolds, the Van Nices, the Turly-Burnses, the McCartney-Willises, the Nadal-Saxe-Coburgs, the Cameron-Cleggs and all the other little people with whom I have shared so many wonderful meals. But the biggest thank you goes to the trees who gave me their permission to be pulped.

I literally could not have written this book without the literal assistance of Julia Turshen who literally did all the cooking and writing while I literally did yoga classes and literally had my hair done for the photo-shoot.

'Why,' you may ask, 'would the world's greatest actress wish to share her kitchen secrets?' It is because I have the secret of eternal life. When my beloved father, who taught me so much about cooking, was diagnosed with cancer in 1998, I became convinced I could cure him with a macrobiotic diet. Sadly he died, but only because he had eaten too much steak and chips when he was young. But with these recipes my children and possibly your children, if they have double-barrelled surnames, can live for ever, and if you think I'm going to mention my idiot husband Chris and his rubbish band then you've got another think coming – he's never supported my ambition to be hailed as the new lifestyle goddess of those with too much time on their hands.

How to use this book Get a member of your staff to read it out loud while you are having a pedicure. If a recipe sounds tasty, ask him to cook it. If some ingredients are unavailable, call my favourite gourmet organic deli in Bel Air and have them flown over.

Vegetarian chilli When my daughter, Apple, was six months old she informed me she was a vegetarian. This is a recipe she has come to love. It's really very easy. Feel the pain of the carrots as you dice them and fry gently. Add some beans until you have a sludge. Serve with rice. (NB: I only use wholegrain rice grown near the Tibet border. This takes four hours to cook, which is why I like to involve my children in the kitchen experience. Apple likes nothing more than staring at a saucepan while I nip out to phone Sting and Trudie.)

Bitter leaf salad Few things are as good for your liver as bitter greens – they support its detoxification. When it's cold and you feel like a hearty meal, there's nothing better than a puntarelle or escarole head. Go easy on the anchovy vinaigrette, or you could bloat.

Stick insect pancakes After meditating with some of LA's most profound mystics, I have come to realise that you are what you eat. If you eat pork, you will look like a pig. If you eat stick insects . . . just look at me. Place stick insects in cold water, then bring to boil while praying for their immortal souls. Add to pancake mix. Do not, under any circumstances, serve with sugar.

Asian portobello burgers I've come to realise that meals are a very special time when families come together. Ours is no exception, so my people have created a special app so that I can talk to Apple and Moses if I am in the gym when they are having lunch. As an American I have burgers in my DNA and there's nothing quite like the thrill of telling kids you are cooking them burgers, then seeing the disappointment on their little faces when you serve them up a mushroom!

Duck ragu One year Jamie Oliver came round to cook me lunch on my birthday. I expect he does that for you, too. He cooked this amazing duck pasta and I have literally spent the last 250 years trying to perfect it. Get a surgeon to give another duck at the Malibu Center for Desperately Sick Mallards a chance of life by transplanting the heart of the duck you are going to eat. Roast duck for two hours, then discard all fat. Not that I have any. Serve with spaghetti.

Apple crumble Slice one Apple into quarters and sprinkle with a light crumble. Put in oven. (NB: Not suitable for vegetarians).

Digested read, digested: Thank you, thank you for . . . indulging me.

Gardening at Longmeadow: Monty Don (2012)

I first saw this garden on a dank autumnal day in 1991. It was piled high with rubble and weeds, and there was nothing to suggest that one day it would be filled with lustily growing plants, or that two million women from the shires would tune in to *Gardeners' World* each Friday to swoon at me running my fingers, scored with decades of Herefordshire loam, through my tangled, wayward curls.

Every year, I have an almost tangible sense of renewal in January. I can feel the light seeping back into the Jewel Garden as the snowdrops emerge and the days stretch out, longer minute by minute. But generally speaking, there's sod all going on, so I'll fill up the chapter with some stuff about cavolo nero and leeks.

February is my favourite month of the year and, if I listen carefully when I wake, I can hear the faint chattering of birds that heralds the first sounds of spring. On some days, I even like to sit outside and lean against a tree moodily while my photograph is taken. But beware! February can still be very cold, and it's vital to keep your tenderest plants well-wrapped in their fleeces. Otherwise, there's still next to nothing going on, but I can do a bit of digging if I'm bored.

As I get older, March has become my favourite month as there is a real sense of vibrant growth in the air. The stigmata on the trees are beginning to heal from their annual pruning – a necessary task that causes me far more pain than them – and I can start planting my cheerful bedding in the greenhouse. It's also the time of year when my favourite flower of all appears: the gentle primrose, a plant as common and as humble as myself.

On reflection, April is my favourite month. It is a time of intense activity, and I feel possessed by the garden. The longer evenings, warmed by the first genuine heat of the sun, are an ideal time to get my Jewel Garden, Coppice, Courtyard, Soft Fruit Garden, Walled Garden, Vegetable Garden and Writing Garden in order. Not to mention give the cricket pitch its first mow of the year. I guess some of you won't be quite so busy.

There can be no more jubilant time in the calendar than May. Everything is bursting with life. Alliums, aquilegias ... I could go on through the plant alphabet. So I will. June and July are also months of intense joy, months that answer the questions that the rest of the year poses. Not least: 'What shall I do with all the creepy-crawlies that are eating all my plants?' I cannot condone killing aphids. They have as much right to life as any of us. Much better to join them in group therapy and work out a way we can share all the bounties nature has to offer.

I have come to appreciate August and September for their subtlety. Many gardeners think there is not much going on at these times, but a closer relationship with your lawn and a chance to smell the wild comfrey can be far more rewarding than a fortnight in your villa in Tuscany. Which is why I haven't taken a summer holiday for years.

October, November and December used to fill me with dread. I could physically feel the closing-in of winter, a sense of impending horticultural anti-matter, but since I've been on *Gardeners' World*, I've realised that things aren't so bleak and that it's never quite as dark outside as you think it is if you get the garden lighting right. And there's lots to do, like picking the rotten apples off the ground and sweeping up leaves. Best of all, it's a time to think ahead, to plan what I'm going to do with all the cash I've made from people buying this book as a Christmas present.

Digested read, digested: Quietly flows the Don.

Bread by Paul Hollywood (2013)

It's time to take Paul Hollywood off the side-plate and put him back where he belongs: in the centre of the table. My book has two aims. First of all, I want to teach you how to groom the perfect 'Lady Pleaser' beard. It's no coincidence I'm called 'Hollywood'. Or 'LA' for short to my 'Brazilian' friends, if you get my drift. Feel free to lick the breadcrumbs from my Fifty Shades of Grey tache as I knead your shoulders …

And then I want to teach you that Mary Berry is just so over. For far too long, I've had to work in her simpering, smiling shadow, looking on as she reassures some useless Middle Englander that their lemon meringue pie is acceptable. Well, let me tell you right now: there's nothing safe or cosy about baking. Baking is dangerous. Baking is sexy. And it doesn't come any more dangerous or sexy than when you're baking bread with me.

OK. So we're ready. We'll start with something gentle. The bloomer. Take 500g of strong – and I mean strong – white flour. Add 10g of salt, 40ml of olive oil, 240ml water and then thrust your hands deeply into the mix. Manipulate till firm (you, not me) and the dough begins to ooze between my strong, manly fingers. Nice. Then leave to prove – baby, I can prove it all night – before taking a sharp knife and slashing some cuts into the top. Put in the oven for a bit and you have a loaf fit for Greggs.

Let's move on to something a little harder. Rye, ale and oat bread. I first made this during a weekend voyage of discovery at the Totnes Bread and Fairy Cake Summer Solstice Festival. It went down well. As do I. The look of this loaf is important, so make sure you are wearing something appropriately artisan. A T-shirt made of organic cotton and some faded denim should do it. Then do much the same as you did for the bloomer, only add some rye, ale and oats.

Nothing oozes pheromones quite like a continental loaf. I know it's hard not to associate a ciabatta with the spindly fingers of a metrosexual Italian. But, take it from me, in the right hands – mine – it is a bread that can be both powerfully manly and erotic. Just stretch out the dough to a magnificent 12 inches and then lie back on your banneton and close your eyes as I whisper 'fougasse' into your ear. Play your cards right and I might even add a raspberry before I focaccia. Mmm.

And that's about it. There really doesn't seem to be a lot more to say about baking bread, because it's all pretty much the same. Flour, water, yeast, salt and anything else you care to throw in to spice it up. Have I mentioned spelt flour? I love the word 'spelt'. It's so sensuously exotic. It reminds me of intense orgasms on a lazy Sunday morning in bed.

Um ... I've been told we haven't got quite enough material for a book, so I've been asked to pad it out a bit. So let me remind you that bread need not be the 'missionary position' of food. It can also be a French toast. Used creatively, bread can be used in countless other recipes. Here are a few of my favourites. The Ploughman's: take a lump of cheddar, a pickled onion, some Branston pickle and a freshly baked sourdough loaf and you have a meal for a stud.

Then, for when you're right out there on the sexual wire, there's the Doner Kebab. Cut yourself a thick slice of mechanically recovered meat, wrap in a bit of pitta bread, and let the horse juices drip down your chin. Always be inventive. Dangerously inventive. Let your imagination go wild. Make a jelly. Wobbly, but not too wobbly. Place a cherry on top. And when your desire is irresistible and your senses are at near overload, cut yourself a slice of Mother's Pride.

Digested read, digested: Feel the knead in me.

TRAVEL

Down Under
by Bill Bryson (2000)

Gee. Australia is a very, very big country and no one knows much about it. Especially Americans. Which makes it the ideal spot for another of my homey little travelogues.

So what else can I tell you by way of background? Well, it's very, very big, there are loads of deadly creepy crawlies (yuck!!), it was colonised by convicts (imagine!!) and the present inhabitants can be fairly chippy. But let me say, right here, right now, that I love Australians.

So where shall I start my trip? A colour magazine is paying me to turn around a quick piece on the Sydney-to-Perth Express so that seems as good a place as any. The train stops at Broken Hill. Pause, while I read up the history books and repeat some amusing anecdotes. We go for a day's driving out in the bush and when I get back I look at the map and see we've hardly moved out of Broken Hill.

Gee, it's a big country. The next leg of the train ride goes smoothly. I go in the cab for a bit and then I slum it in third class for a couple of hours. Scar-ry. And this is Perth, but I can't stick around as I've got another job to do in the Middle East.

Hi. I'm back. But not for long as I've only got a month and I'm hoping to cover the whole of the south-east corner, so we'd better get going.

Hey, look, there's a pet food shop that sells porno out the back. That's really neat. And, wow, the cricket on the car radio really cracks me up. 'I wonder if he'll chance an offside drop scone here or go for the quick legover.' Crazy. Why can't all these guys play exactly the same games as the rest of us? Such as American football.

Here's Adelaide (pause for some historical anecdotes) and

there's the fascinating museum. Unfortunately it's closed for the day and my schedule's too tight to hang on.

Oh, and that might have been Melbourne and, wow, I must be back in Sydney and I'm outta here.

Right, I'm back for a few days so we're going up north. Ah, it's the rainy season. I hadn't thought of that. So Cairns is as far as I get. Let's take the plane to Darwin (not very nice) and drive to Alice Springs. Now, I'll just nip to Ayers Rock for a couple of hours as I've forgotten to book a hotel, then it's over to Perth for a suntan and Bob's your uncle. My cheque's in the bank.

Digested read, digested: Bill goes walkabout and sees everything and nothing.

Stephen Fry in America
by Stephen Fry (2008)

I was so nearly an American. I was that close. In the 1950s my father went on holiday to the USA and had quite a nice time. If he had stayed, and if my mother had been stupid enough to join him, I might have been christened Steve, not Stephen. So who better than me to have a six-month holiday at the BBC's expense?

'Don't worry,' I told the producers. 'It won't be yet another documentary series presented by some clever clogs that tells us next to nothing we didn't already know about the USA through a series of choreographed set pieces.' 'Oh yes it will,' they said, 'but we don't care because you're a national treasure.' Mirabile dictu.

So it was with a light heart that I began my journey in Maine to travel through all 50 states in a London taxi and went in search of my first spontaneously pre-arranged encounter. Ouch! I've been bitten by a lobster. What a silly arse I am! This fishing business is hard work and I'm completely won over by the uncomplaining heroism of the men who risk their lives on the sea.

I drive through the eastern states meeting the ordinary people who have shaped the character of this great country; people like presidential hopeful Mitt Romney and Oatsie Charles, grande dame of Rhode Island society. Eventually, I make my way to upstate New York to go hunting deer.

'This hat is rather a sudden orange,' I complain.

'Hunting orange, they call it,' says Tom. 'Other huntsmen know not to shoot you.'

'Please take it off then,' the film crew beg me.

New Jersey is very working-class, so that won't detain me long and I drive to Pennsylvania for a cup of Twinings and to listen to my own recording of the Gettysburg Address that never fails to move me to tears. In Tennessee and Kentucky, I meet more fascinating rich people with horses before I find my first black person in South Carolina. What a pleasure for her.

Florida restored a sense of bien-être as I blew the budget swimming with dolphins and taking an airboat on the Everglades. But then I had to take a short break in Amazonia to allow me to earn a few quid making another documentary and the team to organise some more adventures on my behalf and, silly billy that I am, I broke my arm, so I entered Louisiana in a sling.

Apparently you have to look as though you care about Hurricane Katrina when you get to New Orleans, but after a few sensitive pieces to camera, I'm soon on my way again and chatting to Morgan Freeman in Mississippi. It really is amazing all the different people you meet on your travels.

The middle of America is really very dull but I stay awake for the sake of appearances and eventually I find my way up north in

Illinois where, to my great surprise, I found myself doing live improv on stage in Chicago. As you do. Many of these northern states are very cold and I couldn't understand some of the local accents as they sounded Danish, but I did fit in some down time in Montana with Ted Turner and Jane Fonda.

I pose briefly in a cowboy hat in somewhere called Nebraska and chunter merrily on my way through Oklahoma and Texas, before heading north again to ride on a speedboat in Utah and thence to San Francisco to dine with Jony Ive, the inventor of the iPod, and stock up with 30 of all the latest models to help me pass the time on the pointless, but comedically necessary, sasquatch hunt in Orgeon. There's just time for a quick tour of Alaska, where I fail to bump into my old friend Michael Palin, and to hum the theme tune to Hawaii Five-0 on Waikiki beach and then I'm done.

So what have I learned? That Americans have very rum pronunciations and that they are all different but are quite nice if you say you are Stephen Fry and are making a television show. But someone's got to do it – and it did give me some respite from Alan Davies crawling up my botty on QI.

Digested read, digested: Stephen in Fryland.

The Last Supper
by Rachel Cusk (2009)

At night I would be woken by unearthly groans from outside my window, inchoate monologues imperceptible to less sensitive souls. We were living in Bristol at the time and I was increasingly feeling the pain of the city's history of slavery, a subject on which

I would frequently digress to my Bulgarian cleaner. I needed to escape the disenchantment.

I was also stuck for anything to write about, so a prolonged summer holiday in Italy seemed an ideal prescription.

Our friends are sorry to see us go, for their lives will be so much less fulfilled without us, but I have a higher duty to my restless mind. The children are aghast to find there is no organic muesli on board the ferry, but I wave their concerns aside as I wonder at the pastel shades of the leatherette banquettes that would not have been out of place in a Tintoretto masterpiece.

We motor slowly through France at a steady 8mph, yet still I feel as if the world is escaping me as I seek to write down every inconsequential detail while the children draw Old Masters in the back. We stop for the night at a decaying chateau and the Monsieur asks whether the children would like to eat pizza. For a while I am annoyed, but then decide, after much agonising reflection, that he is right. Now is not the moment to induct minors into the specialités du terroir.

I throw the Italian phrase book to the floor in disgust. Some of the words are not as I imagined they would be and it feels as if my sensibilities have been brutally desecrated, but I manage to compose myself by the time we arrive at our palazzo near Arezzo. At last I feel alone in the process of liberation.

There is a knock and a Scottish man called Jim announces himself. I am perturbed to find I am not the only foreigner in Tuscany but contain my ire and wave him in. He invites us to dinner and I do not want to go for I fear the other guests will not be worthy of me. Yet the children point out he has a face like a Giotto painting so I reluctantly acquiesce.

In one of the more adumbrated recesses of the palazzo, I find a book about Piero della Francesca that tells me little I do not already know. That night I have a dream and I am impelled to seek out Constantine's Dream. What does it mean to dream? I do not know but in an instant I realise that Piero and I are as one in our quest for a truth beyond human concerns.

As April gives way to May, I manage to contain my disappointment that Vasari had not been able to comprehend the violation of spatial perception and our days are immersed in existential games of tennis with Jim, and I take delight in seeing that my children, whom I have barely noticed for weeks, have become spiritually resolved at some deep level through their PlayStations of the Cross.

In Florence, I gasp at Raphael's sublimation of the self. How quite unlike myself! Yet I sense a longing in his paintings, as if the question Raphael is constantly asking is 'Who am I?' How sad he should have to wait more than 500 years for me to tell him.

My book is almost complete. Jim sends me a love letter, unable to bear the pain of my departure, yet we must go briefly south. Naples is a broken place, somewhere only Raphael could mend, and we hasten north once more to the Vatican, where Catholicism's empty promises fail to cure my blisters. A phone call informs me the South Koreans have paid far too much for the rights to one of my books – not a mistake they will make with this one – yet even so we are running out of money.

The signpost points towards Paris, but I hate being given directions so we turn off to spend our last night abroad in a pension among the yellow-white fields of the Charente. The children are disturbed by Madame's Salle de Jeux. I, too, shudder at the lifeless froideur of the mannequins Madame has created and imagine an artist immersed in an empty, onanistic self-congratulation. Madame catches my eye and we give each other a smile of mutual recognition.

Digested read, digested: The Last Straw.

PHENOMENON

Harry Potter and the Deathly Hallows
by JK Rowling (2007)

Harry Potter took off his Invisibility Cloak as he entered the Dursleys' house in Privet Drive. He was back where it had all started six books previously. It had seemed much more fun in the beginning. No Muggles queuing up at midnight; no Winnebagos on the film set; just him, Ron and Hermione and a box of magic tricks. Now, he felt a little jaded. Still, he thought, if I can keep it together for another 600 pages, I'll be off the hook. Free to pursue a different acting career.

His reverie was interrupted by the arrival of Arthur Weasley, Ron, Hermione and 10 other familiar characters. 'We've got to get you out of here,' said Arthur. 'The protective charm runs out when you are 17, and You Know Who and the Death Eaters will be after you. Six of us are going to take some Polyjuice potion to create some decoy Harrys.'

Harry knew he was up against it this time. A favourite character from an earlier book had been killed off within the first 80 pages. That Rowling woman meant business. 'OK,' said Harry, grimly, as Ron and Hermione embraced. 'There might have been time for that kind of adolescent awakening in books five and six. Now, it's time to get serious.'

Hermione recovered her customary poise. 'You're right, Harry,' she replied. 'The Ministry has been taken over by Voldemort, and the Order of the Phoenix is compromised. Nowhere is safe. You must continue your quest for You Know Who's Horcruxes.'

The scar on Harry's forehead burned, but an intense migraine was a small price to pay for giving the reader a chance to find out what Voldemort was doing and catch up with more back story.

It was the morning of Fleur's wedding to Bill Weasley and Harry, Ron and Hermione were examining the strange bequests they had been left in Dumbledore's will.

'Why have we been given this effing rubbish?' Ron laughed. 'I've told you before that book seven is not the place for jokes and swearing,' Harry answered sternly. Just then he saw Ginny passing. He didn't know why – though he suspected it was something to do with letting the reader know that although he was a goody-goody on the outside, he was a rampant horny hetty on the inside - but he kissed her passionately. 'Stay safe for me,' he whispered knowingly.

'I've found a strange mark in this book,' exclaimed Hermione. 'What do you think it means?' Harry frowned. 'I've no idea,' he murmured, 'but my scar will start hurting again soon and we'll find out.' Sure enough, the tingling sensation soon returned.

As he came out of his dream, which revealed yet more back story about Dumbledore, Harry intoned solemnly: 'It's the sign of the Deathly Hallows. We must find them and the Horcruxes.'

Harry, Ron and Hermione had criss-crossed the country getting out of ever-tighter scrapes with wizard spells, but still Harry felt no nearer to knowing what to do. Yet he had the strange feeling everything was becoming clearer.

'I'm leaving you two,' Ron declared one day. 'I need to create some narrative tension.' Harry was lost again but a Patronus spell led him to the Sword of Gryffindor. He had to step naked into an icy pool to retrieve it. 'I knew getting the lead part in the school production of Equus would come in handy,' he thought.

'I'm back,' said Ron, as Harry's scar continued to reveal yet more of the seemingly endless back story. Sometimes Harry didn't know if he was awake or asleep, alive or dead, as so many old characters flashed through his mind. 'Don't worry,' said the figure of Dumbledore. 'This time, no one knows what's going on either.'

So Harry made his way back to Hogwarts to face Voldemort. It would end as he had always known it would. With everyone wondering what JK would do next.

Digested read, digested: Harry Potter and the End of the Gravy Train.

Acknowledgements

The Digested Read has always been a collaborative effort. So thank you to all the editors and sub-editors over the years who have guided, supported and saved me from hideous errors. Both of judgment and fact. Thank you to all the literary festivals in Britain and around the world who have invited me to go off message. Thank you to all the publishers and authors who have treated me with far more generosity than I have treated them. Thank you also both to the column's fans from Britain and around the world and to its critics. You have all made me think hard about what I am doing and kept me honest.

Names must be mentioned, though. At the *Guardian*, in order of appearance: Felicity Lawrence, Michael Hann, Toby Manhire, Ian Katz, Kath Viner, Lisa Darnell, Claire Armitstead, Paul Laity, Justine Jordan, Clare Margetson, Emily Wilson, Malik Meer, Tim Lusher, Robert Hahn, Melissa Denes, Andrew Gilchrist and Liese Spencer. My illustrators: Neal Fox, Matt Blease and Nicola

Jennings. At Constable & Robinson: Andreas Campomar and Charlotte Macdonald. My agent: Matthew Hamilton. My family: Jill Coleman, Anna Crace and Robbie Crace. The biggest thanks must go to Professor John Sutherland, the friend who taught me how to read properly. This book is dedicated to him.

Index